Other Books by Richard Hofstadter:

American Violence: A Documentary History 1970
(edited, with Michael Wallace)

The Idea of a Party System 1969

The Progressive Historians 1968

The Paranoid Style in American Politics and Other Essays 1965

Anti-intellectualism in American Life 1963

American Higher Education: A Documentary History 1961
(with Wilson Smith)

The American Republic 1959
(with Daniel Aaron and William Miller)

Great Issues in American History 1958

The United States 1957
(with Daniel Aaron and William Miller)

The Age of Reform 1955

The Development of Academic Freedom in the United States 1955
(with Walter P. Metzger)

*The Development and Scope of Higher Education
in the United States* 1952
(with C. DeWitt Hardy)

The American Political Tradition 1948

Social Darwinism in American Thought 1944

America at 1750

America
at
1750

A SOCIAL PORTRAIT

BY

Richard Hofstadter

ALFRED A. KNOPF   NEW YORK

1971

CONTENTS

PREFACE

America at 1750 is the first section of what the author intended to be a three-volume history of American political culture from 1750 to the recent past. The eight chapters published here are complete, but the book as it now stands presents certain problems of omission and scale. How it was originally planned can best be gathered from the following proposal written for the publisher in May 1969:

> *"Over the next 18 years I propose to write a history in three volumes of the United States centered mainly on politics, from mid-18th century to the recent past. Each volume will run to about 500,000 words and will cover the span of about 75 years.*
>
> *"What I have in mind is a political history of the American people, but one that is not narrowly construed, since I propose to include whatever is necessary in the way of economic, cultural, and biographical background.*
>
> *"During the past 20 years and more there has been an extraordinary proliferation of first-rate historical monographs, and several areas of American history, notably the Revolutionary and Federal periods, Jacksonian Democracy, Civil War and Reconstruction, and the Progressive Era have been intensively recon-*

sidered. Much important work has also been done in various areas of institutional history relevant to the development of American political culture—notably in economic history, social history, and the development of party systems, the recruitment of leadership, and the like. Thus far, however, no one has attempted a general interpretive synthesis of the findings of the past generation of professional historians that would be accessible not only to students of history at various levels but to the general educated public that reads and makes intellectual use of sophisticated history.

"What I hope to accomplish is a large-scale history that will deviate from the conventional general histories of the past to the extent that a primarily interpretive focus will govern the inclusion of narrative material. Narration will be included not for its own sake but in order to provide background, to pose the essential problems, and to illustrate through the exploration of decisive episodes the meaning of historical events. Special attention will be given to such matters as the role of elites and of leadership, the development of our political practices in a comparative setting, the effect of urbanization on politics, the role of social mobility in American political culture, slavery and the history of the Negro, ethnicity and status in their relationship to political behavior, the history of political ideas and of focal institutions like the political party, and, in the final volume, the development of America as a world power and the emergence of a mass society. I propose to draw upon the central original sources of our history and to supplement this reading with an extensive effort to cull out that which is sound and translatable into

broad public terms from the extraordinary mass of significant historical research that has been produced in our time."

This is an ambitious scheme for any one man to undertake, no matter what his health. Our daughter once called it "Hofstadter's Monumental History"; my husband laughed and replied, "No, Hofstadter's Monumental Folly."

The material in this book was meant primarily to set the scene for what was to follow. Some themes were fully explored in these opening chapters, but others were merely touched on, to be developed in later chapters as they became central to the history of the country.

The model for the kind of historical description which the author had in mind was the first volume of Halevy's *History of the English People* in the nineteenth century, *England in 1815.* He began work, as was his habit, not with the material he planned to cover in the first chapters, but with a subject already familiar to him, in this case religion and the Great Awakening. He wrote chapters VI, VII, and VIII first, and considered them finished. He then went on to what he judged to be the most crucial of the problems of colonial America, white servitude and black slavery. The material on these subjects, which appears here as chapters II, III, and IV, went through several drafts, and for the most part satisfied their author. Chapter V, on the middle class, is in the same substantially complete form.

Chapter I, on population and immigration, was written last, and in some haste. My husband wanted to get on with the chapter he planned on colonial elites, thinking he would return to chapter I.

In August 1970, he stopped work on the colonial elites
and began an introduction to all he had written thus far.
As the reader will see, this introduction breaks off
abruptly; this is the only section which is incomplete, but
what there is seemed to me to merit publication. Further,
it was my husband's way of saying that he hoped that
if he did not live to write more, what he had written
would be published, although what he had written on
elites was too fragmentary for publication, and two important sections which he had planned, one on colonial
politics, the other on imperial wars, had not even been
started.

What follows, then, is for the most part complete in its
own terms, though it comprises only a small portion of
the entire project as it was first conceived.

Beatrice Kevitt Hofstadter

NOTE: *The spelling of quoted
passages has been modernized.*

INTRODUCTION

IT is hard now to imagine, but it is a matter of record that a mid-eighteenth-century mariner approaching the American strand could detect the fragrance of the pine trees about 60 leagues, or 180 nautical miles, from land. Before landfall he might thus be reminded, even after more than a century of white settlement, of the essential newness of the New World. On landing he could hardly escape fresh remembrances: he could see the trees themselves, arrayed in such formidable ranks that they were attacked and felled in careless numbers by settlers eager to get at the untilled soil beneath; he could see beaver pelts and deerskins brought to market, tokens of a teeming animal life in the interior; he might hear about the fish, spawning in such numbers and growing to such size in the rivers and offshore waters that the ease of catching them had become a legend and a joke. There were also conspicuous absences: there were few imposing buildings, public or domestic, and many roads were still mud hollows. Travelers and writers have said it often since: there were no monuments and no ruins; it was the scenes of nature, not edifices put up by man, that stood out to be admired by those who were not already too busy to admire them. In his own country an Englishman need not have gone far to be aware of Roman survivals, of ruined castles, and of tumbled monasteries and smashed faces of

church idols, relics of religious furies that had now sub-
sided. In Europe, in England, one could see all too easily
the physical evidences of the decay of human institutions,
the evanescence of human creeds and arrangements.
America seemed to hum to the sound of some new beginning, free of the weight of the past, and impeded
mainly by a great thicket of nature.

Perhaps it was a bit deceptive, for the new beginning
that was so evident in America was itself an importation,
a version only, of the new beginning upon which Europe
had long since been launched. The English colonies of
the North American mainland, the rude provinces that
would in time form the nucleus of the United States,
were the elements of the first post-feudal nation, the first
nation in the world to be formed and to grow from its
earliest days under the influence of Protestantism, nationalism, and modern capitalist enterprise. This was the
transcendently important reality about this new country:
its wholly post-Protestant, post-nationalist, post-capitalist
history. In the modernization that was re-creating all
Europe, England was rapidly taking the lead, and America, the offspring of the avant-garde nation, was a kind of
distillation of certain aspects of the new European world.

To gain some perspective on this newness of old Europe,
it will be useful for a moment to jump backward from the
mid-eighteenth century, which is our focus of inquiry, to
the year 1650, simply to mark out how much of the trans-
formation of Europe had already taken place at a time
when English settlements in North America were still
very young. So many volumes have been written on the
very earliest settlements that their bulk tends to conceal
the important fact that the population in these settlements was negligible in number. These studies are neces-

sary because there is much to tell: so many of the institutional foundations of the colonies had already been laid by 1650—the transit of parliamentary order, as shown in the town meeting and the House of Burgesses, the establishment of New England Congregationalism, the emergence of the tobacco plantation, of indentured servitude, and even, in most of its aspects, of slavery. But this institutional framework embraced a population consisting in 1650 of about 50,000 souls, most of them huddled in Massachusetts and Virginia, a population then not more significant than that of the tiny island of Barbados, or, to put it another way, than that of Bozeman, Montana, today. America was peopled almost entirely after that date; the great changes that swept the European and English world from the Reformation to the time of the Civil War in England and the Thirty Years' War in Germany had all taken place before English settlers occupied anything more than a trifling bridgehead on the shaggy continent that confronted them.

Between the time of the Reformation and 1650, the effects of the Protestant upheaval had been naturalized in European politics and the place of Protestantism had been fought out and worked out. The national state system had emerged, and nationalism had elbowed religion aside as the controlling civic passion of Western man. The Commercial Revolution had broken down most of the remaining vestiges of localism in economic life, had moved the center of European trade from the Mediterranean to the Atlantic world, and had confirmed the global character of that trade. Mercantilism had put policies of state at the center of consideration, and had introduced the idea of a national economy and a national labor force, conceptions as new and important as the conception of

gross national product has been in our time. Monetary
inflation arising from the Spanish treasure of the New
World had stimulated the European economy and had
transformed the class structure of the Western nations. In
Spanish America and the Caribbean extensive slave empires had been established, to which millions of blacks
were being transported from Africa. In England the Civil
War had already taken place, Charles I had been beheaded, and Cromwell was governing under the Commonwealth. But more to the point, despite the Crom-
wellian interregnum, England was rapidly accumulating
and absorbing those experiences which would soon enable
her to make large changes in parliamentary and mon-
archical government; and in the course of the Civil War
certain ideas about popular rights had been aired with
striking force and clarity, laying the foundation for modern Anglo-American democratic thought.

It has often been said that Protestantism enthroned the
individual conscience. The prevalence of this idea suggests, if it suggests nothing else, that a good many Protestants have written histories. Of course, in the long run,
anything that cracked the unified facade of Christendom
and ended monopoly in the marketplace of creeds must
have done something to ease and to advance the position
of private conscience. But in the shorter run, which was
long enough, one must be impressed by the numbers of
persons who suffered grievously or died over questions of
faith between 1517 and 1648. It had not been the intention
of very many Protestants to unleash the individual conscience. What Protestantism did was to free kings and
princes who had broken with Catholicism to enforce
their own regal consciences on their subjects. This was
the principle recognized and sanctified in the Peace of

Augsburg which ended the religious wars of the sixteenth century: *cuius regio, eius religio.*

One of the most impressive things, in fact, about Protestantism is not what it did to foster the religious conscience of the common man but what it did to promote a secular mentality in heads of state. For a time Protestant loyalties were used, by such figures as William the Silent, Henry VIII, Elizabeth, and some of the German princes, to stir up the national militancy of their subjects and followers. But within a century Europe had passed from a condition in which religion had been a primary motive power in foreign wars and domestic upheavals to one in which religion was a marginal and occasional force. The Peace of Westphalia, closing the Thirty Years' War in 1648, marked the end of wars fought in the name or for the interests of a creed. The essentially secular modern state system was gradually dispensing with religious convictions as a *raison d'état,* although it might from time to time make cynical efforts to mobilize them. The dream of a single realm and a single faith for Christendom had long since died with Philip II of Spain; what mattered now to monarchs and ministers was not the propagation of a faith but the manipulation of the balance of power. It is too little realized how important the half-secularized mentality of men of state in early modern Europe was for American development. With our eyes too firmly fixed on the Puritans, we fail to see that hundreds of thousands of immigrants were rounded up and persuaded to come to America by men moved by secular motives of empire and profit; and that so many of them came without firm religious attachments (or at least without seeking to reproduce them here) that the American colonies at the end of the eighteenth century were perhaps the most unchurched regions in all Christendom. Religious tolerance, and after it religious liberty, were the creations of a jumble of faiths too complex to force into any mold, and of a rising secularism too urbane to care to try. Puritanism, after all, was not America's gift to the world but England's; what America brought was the separation of church and state.

In these changes England was usually the leading agent, and from them she emerged as the foremost power. At an earlier date than the other nations, under the Tudors, she had reached a high degree of internal civic unity. Her monarchs had defied the authority of the Pope and had punctured the inflated dreams of Philip II. The price inflation set off by Spain's American treasure in the sixteenth century, ruinous to some nations and troublesome to others, seems to have advanced considerably the state of England's industry. The general crisis of the European economy in the seventeenth century, which strengthened absolutism in many countries, created in England a freer political order congenial to the growth of commercial and industrial capital, as Eric Hobsbawn has suggested.[1] By mid-seventeenth century, having reckoned with the Spanish, the English were ready to begin taking commercial European supremacy away from the Dutch. But before that, in the 1640's, England had made her boldest leap forward into the modern world, with the Puritan Revolution, the army debates over the rights of the common man, and the ultimate taming of monarchy within the framework of a parliamentary system.

1. "The Crisis of the 17th Century," Part I: *Past and Present* 5 (May 1954), 33–53; Part II: *Past and Present* 6 (Nov. 1954), 44–65.

America at
1750

CHAPTER I

✣

Population
and
Immigration

1

IT was growth—growth consistently sustained and eagerly welcomed, growth as a source of grand imperial hopes and calculating private speculation—which was the outstandingly visible fact of mid-eighteenth-century life in the American colonies. Populations surged upward everywhere in the Atlantic world, brightened as it was by improvements in agriculture, feeding, and sanitation, but nowhere was there a century-long growth comparable to that of the North Atlantic colonies. The population of England and Wales grew healthily by about 23 per cent from 1700 to 1760. In the same years the population of the American mainland colonies, flourishing on open lands, attracting strong spurts of immigration, and pro-generating at a goodly rate, multiplied six times. In 1700 the colonies were small outposts of Western civilization, an advance guard on the fringe of the raw continent numbering about 250,000 souls. By 1750 there were 1,170,000, and before the end of the century the United States was a thriving nation that numbered more than 5,000,000.[1]

In 1751 Benjamin Franklin wrote a little tract on the growth of the colonies to which, when it was printed four years later, he gave the title *Observations Concerning the Increase of Mankind, Peopling of Countries, etc.* His purpose was to oppose a recent act of Parliament which threatened to inhibit Pennsylvania industry by putting restrictions on iron manufacture in the colonies. His intellectual strategy was to project an American future in which the high cost of labor would prevent any considerable industrial production, by portraying a vast agricultural population that would long continue to serve England as a source of food supplies and as a great market for industrial goods. America, he argued, was not like the "settled old countries" of Europe: it had no crowded cities where men must delay marrying until they could bear the cost of a family. In settled countries laborers were abundant and wages low. But in America land was plentiful, "and so cheap as that a labouring man that understands husbandry, can in a short time save enough money to purchase a piece of new land whereon he may subsist a family." Under these conditions more of the people married, they married earlier, and the population grew rapidly, but since "no man continues long a labourer for others," labor would never be cheap. In Pennsylvania now, despite the immigration of many thousands, labor was no cheaper than it had been thirty years before.

1. I have used the estimates in *Historical Statistics of the United States* (edn. 1960), which will someday be superseded. The best brief account of colonial population is that of J. Potter, "The Growth of Population in America, 1700–1860," in D. V. Glass and D. E. C. Eversley, *Population in History* (1965), 636 ff.

Reckoning four births to a marriage in Europe and (here somewhat on the generous side) eight in America,[2] and assuming that half the children grew to maturity and married at twenty, Franklin concluded: "Our people must at least be doubled every twenty years." With this increase, an immense demand would arise for British manufactures, and the unnecessary effort to restrain manufacturing would only weaken "the whole family" of the empire and benefit foreign powers. How much better it would be to develop the internal balance of the empire, Franklin added, since even if the colonials were expected to double in number only every twenty-five years, they would "in another century be more than the people of England, and the greatest number of Englishmen will be on this side of the water." The two sides together would then comprise a vast, secure, and prosperous empire.

In asserting that the population doubled every twenty years, Franklin was astonishingly close to the mark, miscalculating only slightly on the side of generosity. (Malthus later said it had doubled every twenty-five years, but he may have underestimated the rate of growth.)[3] During the years from 1730 to 1750, the colonial population had grown from 629,000 to 1,170,000, and in the next twenty years would grow to 2,148,000. His own province, Pennsylvania, showed by far the most impressive growth of all the colonies: it had leaped from 51,000 in 1730 when Franklin was still establishing himself as a young printer to 119,000 the year he wrote this pamphlet, and in another twenty years would rise to 240,000. Franklin, mildly

2. For family size, see Potter; and the projections of A. J. Lotka, "The Size of American Families in the Eighteenth Century," *Journal of the American Statistical Association*, 22 (1927), 154–70.

3. *Cf.* Potter.

avowing a prejudice for his own color, closed his pamphlet by pleading briefly for the exclusion of blacks. In the colonies as a whole, the black population, spurred by the slave trade, was outstripping the growth rate of the whites. Negroes, almost all of them slaves, were a good deal more than doubling their numbers every twenty years. In 1750 there were about 236,000 in the colonies, and the number had trebled since 1730. The number of blacks too would almost double again by 1770. In the economy of the South and in the mind of the white man the Negro already loomed large.

It suited Franklin at the moment, since he was not only against the importation of blacks but cherished an English prejudice against German immigrants which he later came to regret, to play down the effects of immigration and to stress the natural increase. Still, the natural increase was remarkable—Malthus spoke of it in 1798 as "a rapidity of increase probably without parallel in history"[4]— and the general rate of population growth in America was perhaps twice that of England. Franklin's idea that early marriage was a major factor, an idea sometimes repeated by historians of the American family, is doubtful, at least in the North, where marriage was often delayed for economic reasons. In New England men commonly married in their middle twenties and women at about twenty. There were regions and classes in American society where delayed marriage was the usual practice: in New England villages, for example, especially those that had been settled for three or four generations, and everywhere among poor immigrants and indentured servants, colonial marriages were contracted at an age comparable to though perhaps

4. *Essay on the Principle of Population,* ed. Michael P. Fogarty (Everyman's edn., 1958), I, 305–6.

slightly lower than European.[5] But modern demographic studies show other grounds for rapid population growth: despite what has been written about heavy infant mortality in the eighteenth century, an unusually large proportion of American children for that epoch survived to maturity, and the longevity of the comfortable classes in the American colonies was surprising. The average number of births per fertile marriage may well have been as high as seven. In an agricultural society the work of children might easily be worth more than their keep as early as the age of eight or nine. Children were thus at a premium, family life was a material as well as a social and spiritual asset, and widows and widowers remarried as soon as they could. From New England to Georgia the average family size was buoyed up by some remarkably prolific families, and forty-year-old grandmothers were not uncommon. Near the end of the seventeenth century Governor Thomas Dongan of New York credited the story of an old Dutchwoman, still alive, who claimed "upwards of 360 living descendants." An extraordinary Rhode Island woman lived to a hundred and counted 500 descendants, 205 of whom were living at the time of her death. William Penn said of the Swedes along the Delaware: "They have fine children, and almost every house full: rare to find one of them without three or four boys and as many girls; some six, seven, and eight sons." Henry Melchior Muhlenberg, the patriarch of American Lutheranism, had eleven children; seven survived to maturity and gave him twenty-nine grandchildren to exult

---

5. For regional information on demographic questions, see Philip Greven, *Four Generations; Population, Land, and Family in Colonial Andover, Massachusetts* (1970); Kenneth Lockridge, *A New England Town: The First Hundred Years* (1970); and John Demos, *A Little Commonwealth: Family Life in Plymouth Colony* (1970).

in. In Virginia large planter families were common, and a few were astonishing: Patrick Henry, born in 1736, was one of nineteen children; John Marshall, born in 1755, was the eldest of fifteen. Governor Arthur Dobbs reported from North Carolina that among the thirty to forty families on his lands whom he had visited there were, with two exceptions, "not less than from five or six to ten children in the family, each going barefooted in their shifts in the warm weather." [6]

Franklin, rudimentary demographer though he was, included the superior birthrate of the country people in his calculations. Although with the exception of static Boston the five substantial towns on the eastern seaboard were growing at a respectable pace, and Philadelphia, soon to pass 20,000, was on its way to becoming one of the largest cities in the British Empire, the proportion of the whole population living in the major towns was actually falling.[7] The largest concentration of population in 1750 lay in the two tobacco colonies, Virginia and Maryland, which together had more people—372,000—than any other region. Second to them were the four colonies of New England with 359,000. (The fourth New England colony, the frontier province of New Hampshire, was already nearly as populous as Rhode Island, and would overtake it well before the Revolution.) The four Middle Colonies numbered 294,000, Pennsylvania of course vastly overshadowing the others. New York, hampered by its vast patents and ungenerous land policies, grew slowly, and ranked in 1750 as a small or medium-sized colony

6. A. W. Calhoun, *A Social History of the American Family*, I (1917), 170, 203, 286–7; *cf.* P. A. W. Wallace, *The Muhlenbergs of Pennsylvania* (1950), 268. For the Rhode Island woman, see Potter, 647n.

7. Carl Bridenbaugh, *Cities in the Wilderness* (1955), 303; *Cities in Revolt* (1955), 216–17.

little larger in population than New Jersey. Most of the
142,000 people of the three colonies of the deeper South
were divided, more or less evenly, between North and
South Carolina. The small buffer state of Georgia, still
struggling after eighteen years to establish itself, had
only about 5,000 colonists.

"So vast is the territory of North America," Franklin
proclaimed, "that it will require many ages to settle it
fully." After nearly a century and a half of settlement, the
English provinces were still confined east of the Appalachian Mountains, the irregular line of settlement reaching
its deepest point of penetration in the valley of Virginia,
which was less than two hundred miles inland. Shorter
fingers of settlement pointed into the continent along a
dozen major rivers from the Merrimack to the Savannah,
and here and there in the interior were distant and isolated enclaves of farmers. But east of the fall line there
were enormous tracts of unsettled lands, and the half-
known upland country west of it still belonged to scouts,
trappers and traders, soldiers and Indians. The West, with
its hundreds and hundreds of miles of wild forest and
rugged mountains, prodded the energies of explorers and
filled the dreams of land speculators, but in it also lurked
dangers and uncertainties, French forts in the North,
Spanish garrisons in the South, and everywhere potentially hostile Indians.

2

Pivotal to Franklin's vision of the American future was
the assumption that since land was plentiful and cheap,
labor would be dear. The vacant land seemed like an
enormous sponge endlessly capable of soaking up the

labor that could be brought to it. Land was an enticing
outlet for investment, a magnificent means of converting
political influence into profit. Yet raw, idle land could be
made profitable only when settlers were brought in to
work, rent, or buy it. "Lands, though excellent, without
hands proportionable," wrote Sir Josiah Child in 1690,
"will not enrich any kingdom." [8]

The process by which, from the early seventeenth to
the late eighteenth century, the American land was
carved up into real estate is breathtaking in its careless
rapture. In North America the Crown and the colonial
proprietors, with broad, grandiose strokes appropriate to
the Restoration kings and their favorites and to the oli-
garchs of the eighteenth century, were disposing of an
area several times the size of England, Ireland, and Wales.
Moreover, they were wrestling with the laws of wilderness economics. To make profits, or to strengthen the
dangerous borders of their contested New World empire,
Crown and proprietors alike had to find settlers. A Fairfax
might receive five million acres in Virginia, but the grant
would be fruitless until it was sold or tenanted. Privileged
speculators, receiving titles to hundreds of thousands of
acres, might skim off a handsome profit when they sold
these lands, but they could sell them only when the
price was brought within reach of men who could occupy,
manage, and dig in it.

At mid-century, only the older colonies of New England
had outgrown the passion to entice labor into their boundaries. Their problem by then was to parcel out a limited
supply of land to meet the needs of a growing population.
Under the town system, the New England legislatures

8. *A New Discourse of Trade* (1741), 134.

allotted new lands collectively to church congregations or groups of new settlers. The partition of new lands was not equal—being rated according to the means of the new settlers and the amount of land it was thought that they could make good use of—but neither was it grossly unequal, as in New York and in the South. For example, when Wallingford, Connecticut, was founded in 1670, its proprietors were divided into three ranks. Members of the highest rank received 476 acres each, the middle 357, and the lowest 238.[9] In its land system New England thus laid the foundation for a rural society of only modest landed inequalities.

Landholding in the Middle Colonies was more diverse. Here, unlike New England, grants were made to individuals, not groups. In New York, where the example of the Dutch patroon system was followed and huge grants preempted vast acreages, settlement was slow, and tenant disturbances climaxed a long and unhappy history of choked development. In New Jersey, where land distribution was generally more evenhanded, some portions followed the New York pattern, and there land riots also occurred. These two colonies became a kind of test case which proved the impracticability of transferring feudal notions of land distribution to American soil. Pennsylvania newcomers could buy land from the proprietary government's land offices for prices ranging from £5 to £15 per 100 acres—that is, from one to three shillings an acre at a time when carpenters were earning about three shillings a day. Even so, German and Scotch-Irish immigrants who either had no cash or were stubbornly determined to realize overnight the promises they had heard in Europe

9. Jackson Turner Main, *The Social Structure of Revolutionary America* (1965), 8.

about the New World often took up lands as squatters,
and at one time perhaps two-thirds of the acres occupied
were held without legal rights. But squatters who made
improvements upon their land were in the end able to
convert their precarious tenures into full titles.[1]

In the Southern colonies the standard way of bringing
labor to the land in the seventeenth century was the
headright system, under which a newcomer was granted
50 acres free of charge in return for transporting himself,
unencumbered, to the colony. This practice was soon
transmuted into free grants for bringing others—indentured servants, for example. At first intended to bring
about compact, small settlements, the headright system
in fact made large holdings as possible as small; like almost everything else bearing upon colonial lands, headright requirements were open to fraud and evasion. Newcomers made numbers of claims by repeated entries,
planters entered claims for two sets of headrights for
bringing in one person, and bald forgeries created imaginary entries. Headright claims became negotiable instruments: sea captains could acquire a right for each servant
or slave they imported, and sell the rights to a planter;
indentured servants, achieving freedom, sometimes sold
their rights for cash instead of taking the land to which
they were entitled. In Maryland the headright system was
abandoned in 1683 for a policy of land sales, and in Virginia the practice ceased to be of central importance
early in the eighteenth century. But the pattern of a
rather steeply differentiated system of land tenure had
already been built up. At the beginning of the eighteenth
century in Maryland it was possible to get 100 acres for

1. Percy Wells Bidwell and John I. Falconer, *History of Agriculture in
the Northern United States 1620–1860* (1925), 72–3.

£5 sterling, in Virginia for about ten shillings, and land was still cheaper farther south, notably in North Carolina. Grapevine communication about land values was astonishingly efficient, and the great mid-century flow of population southward was a hunt for land bargains. Outside New England, then, where communal and collective settlement was still effective, and except for a few troubled areas of miscalculation, the attempt to transmit feudal and manorial systems to the New World had substantially broken down, and a commercial market for land had replaced all other mechanisms. Successful speculators made good profits. But as speculator competed with speculator and colony with colony, and as settlers flocked toward low-price areas, the cost of land remained low.

The difficulties of sustaining feudal relations in a vigorous land market and among an obdurate citizenry are manifest in the history of quitrents. The quitrent was a feudal relic emblematic of an inferior or impaired title to ownership of land. In medieval theory all land had an overlord, ultimately the king, to whom the tenant owed both personal fealty and a fixed rent. Quitrents originated when feudal services began to be commuted into money; their payment made a tenant quit—that is, free—of personal service or other obligations to his lord. Quitrents were intended to become in America, as they had been in England, a considerable source of income, and they were an important motive for the efforts nobles made to get American land grants. Some quitrents, exacted from large grantees, were only ceremonial affirmations of the inferiority of their titles to that of the king; they were fulfilled by the stipulated annual presentation of a rose, a beaver skin, an ear of corn, a peppercorn, an Indian arrow. Quitrents exacted of ordinary settlers, however,

were in cash. They were not an economic rent: the same
tenant in Virginia, for example, might pay a customary
rent to his landlord and a quitrent to the Crown. In the
wilds of the colonies quitrents were roughly half of what
they were on the more cultivated acres of England—
usually about two or four shillings a year for a hundred
acres. Except when payment in silver was stipulated they
were not usually a serious burden to those colonials from
whom they could be collected at all. Proprietors and
Crown officials assumed that a few shillings collected annually over acreage increasing by hundreds and thousands would in time yield goodly sums to the accounts of
the proprietors or for the administrative expenses of the
realm. Their arithmetic was accurate, but they reckoned
without the resistance of the colonials and the costs of
collection in a country where settlers were dispersed over
a wide territory and where collectors were few in number and unsupported by sufficient authority. In time the
quitrents fell into arrears before the sustained sabotage,
sometimes tumultuous, usually slow and quiet, of thousands of settlers; and though quitrents were still being
collected in several colonies on the eve of the Revolution
they sometimes yielded more discontent than revenue.

Only in Pennsylvania, Maryland, and Virginia were the
quitrents an institution of consequence. The Puritans held
to a theory of free tenure of land in which no overlord
was recognized as legitimate. Quitrents were never collected in Massachusetts, Rhode Island, or Connecticut,
and brief efforts to institute them in New Hampshire and
the Maine district faltered in the face of the competition
of Massachusetts lands still available as freeholds and
against the resistance of settlers who would take up lands
on no other terms. In New York and New Jersey large and

powerful speculators as well as small settlers opposed quitrents with substantial success, in New Jersey riotously for a time. In Pennsylvania, where the Penns had expected a large yield, both the trials of collection and of political resistance were enormous, and the quitrent issue became important in the politics of the province. Collections were only a little more than one-third of what was due and by 1779 total arrears, excluding interest, came to £118,569.[2] In Maryland and Virginia, where a large number of land-holders were within easy reach and where administrative plans for collection were relatively efficient, the quit-rent system was successful, yielding worthwhile annual revenues to the Calverts in Maryland and to the Crown in Virginia. South of Virginia, where royal officials took over chaotic systems from the proprietary regimes of the Carolinas and Georgia, quitrents were never a substantial source of revenue. Yet it is ironic that where quitrents were efficiently collected, they probably acted as a mar-ginal brake on large-scale, long-term land speculation, because it was so expensive to engross thousands of un-tenanted acres for any length of time if they were annually liable for four shillings a hundred acres.[3] Feudal monop-oly and capitalist monopoly, as they moved into the wil-derness, thus impeded and tripped over each other.

3

Strong as the lure of cheap land might be, it was never so strong as to lure enough hands across the ocean. Those who had possessions were reluctant to risk them; those

2. Beverly W. Bond, Jr., *The Quitrent System in the American Colo-nies* (1919), 161.
3. Ibid., 446; see C. P. Gould, *Land System in Maryland* (1913).

who had nothing were often wretched and demoralized. The multiple uncertainties of the New World would be prefaced by the grim certainty of a long and hazardous ocean voyage, which many would not survive. Men would not come unless they were gulled into great expectations, stirred by some searing resentment or compelling ideal, or traduced or forced. There was never an adequate supply of voluntary immigrants having enough capital or skill to establish themselves on a firm basis upon arrival. Hence two other solutions were resorted to: the importation of increasing numbers of Africans; and the immigration—advertised, subsidized, suborned, lured, forced, even on occasion kidnapped—of persons without capital, indentured servants or redemptioners, who would, if fortunate, work their way to freedom and independence. The great immigrations of the eighteenth century were a motley compound of the white and the black, the free, the semi-free, and the enslaved.

When one counts the various peoples—the Scots, Welsh, and Irish, the Dutch, Swedes, and Finns, the French, Germans, Swiss, and Jews—the pluralism of white America even at the end of the seventeenth century seems impressive. But if one counts people rather than varieties and gives due weight to numbers, the basically English character of the colonies as they entered upon the eighteenth century emerges. Except for the Dutch in New York, who made the only sizable dent in the English culture of the colonies, and a mixed area around Philadelphia, the homogeneous Englishness of the white colonials stands out. From the Northern seaboard to the Southern the English had been able to maintain or to impose their basic institutions on all the competing cultures. England until then had provided the bulk of the immigrants, and almost everywhere it was English that was spoken. New England was strikingly homogeneous, and so were the two great tobacco colonies. And of the non-English only the Huguenots, with their imported capital, their distinguished men, and their entrepreneurial morale, ever joined the elite leadership of the colonies.

During the eighteenth century, however, the ethnic homogeneity was rudely and finally shattered, as Germans, Swiss, Scotch-Irish, Africans, and peoples of other stocks migrated or were imported in such substantial numbers that by the time of the Revolution half the population south of New England was non-English.[4] Emigration from Europe to America was always in episodic waves, as men responded to some outburst of persecution or some sudden visitation of economic disaster. Such a wave had come, for example, in the great Puritan migration of 1630–40, when the persecutions of Archbishop Laud gave the first great spur to the settlement of New England. Other waves would bring in masses of Germans and Scotch-Irish between 1710 and 1740, and new recruits of Scotch-Irish and Scots from the 1760's to the outbreak of the Revolution.

For more than thirty years after 1683 Europe was almost continuously at war. The war years were not propitious for emigration, but after the wars spread to the American theater and empire became a war aim, Englishmen on both sides of the Atlantic began to think of immigration as a pawn in the strategy of imperial security. Immigrants, to be sure, were often greeted with a mixture of welcome and misgiving by older settlers, mistrusted as

4. "Report of the Commission on Linguistic and National Stocks in the Population of the United States," American Historical Association *Proceedings* (1931), I, 103–408.

strangers and competitors, and at the same time accepted as bulwarks to colonial strength and security. Acceptance was readier if they could be lured or attracted into zones where they might constitute a protective screen between the old settlements and the French, Spaniards, and Indians on the frontiers.

After the Peace of Utrecht in 1713, and the series of subsequent treaties that settled the remaining issues, Europe entered upon a long and on the whole well-guarded period of peace lasting more than three decades. It was then that the great streams of non-English emigrants embarked for the American colonies from Europe and the foundation of a large and heterogeneous white American population was laid. The two major streams were the Scotch-Irish and the Germans. Together the immigrants from Ulster and from Germany brought something decisively different into the political and religious culture of the colonies, especially on the frontier. The new immigrants were Protestants but not Anglicans. They were recruited from the middle and lower classes. The Scotch-Irish brought not only an outlook quite different from that of English settlers but a distinctive tone of hardihood and combativeness that expanded in frontier conditions. The Germans were important not as a force in war and politics but as the carriers of a tradition of skilled and loving husbandry that far surpassed the farming practices of most Anglo-American settlers.

There had always been a few scattered Germans in the colonies, settled alongside the Dutch and the Swedes. William Penn, the first promoter to see the possibilities of large-scale German settlement, was chiefly interested in recruiting minority sectarians who were suffering the sort of persecution his Quaker brethren had long endured.

Through his pietistic acquaintances he was able to mobilize a number of interested sectarians, who formed the
Frankfort Company to aid and finance settlement. Led by
a young lawyer, Francis Daniel Pastorius, who was
charmed at the prospect of taking a community to lead "a
quiet, godly, and honest life in a howling wilderness," in
1683 a pioneer group settled in what was to be called
Germantown, not far from Philadelphia, which became a
center where German immigrants collected before moving out into the neighboring counties of Pennsylvania.
Pastorius's pioneers were followed by a smaller group led
by Johann Kelpius, a hymnographer and mystic of ingrati-
ating saintliness and eccentricity, one of the first of a long
line of visionaries to be drawn to America. One of Kelpius's associates, a distinguished astronomer who died en
route, had projected that the millennium would come in
1694, and hoped to greet the end of the world in America.
Kelpius himself, who was given to withdrawing to a cave
for prayer and contemplation, hoped to achieve a kind of
immortality, but confessed himself mistaken on the eve
of his death in 1708. For some, America has always been
a land of disappointment.

About 1708 the number of German immigrants began
to increase significantly; during the first three-quarters of
the eighteenth century at least 100,000 Germans arrived
in the colonies. In 1775 the population of Pennsylvania
was estimated by several contemporaries to be one-third
German. They came for a variety of reasons. In the wars
before the Peace of Utrecht French armies repeatedly
devastated German Palatine towns along the Rhine, laid
waste the fields, and left great numbers in destitution.
With English encouragement, great numbers of Palatine
Germans settled in England in 1708 and 1709, and the

Lords of Trade were hard put to know what to do with these refugees. Under the leadership of a Lutheran minister, Joshua von Kocherthal, one group went not to England but to New York and established Neuberg (Newburgh) on the Hudson. Kocherthal returned and took larger numbers in 1710. In the same year the new governor of New York, Robert Hunter, conceived the idea of employing the Palatines to manufacture tar and naval stores, and arranged the transportation of a group of 3,000 under the leadership of Johann Conrad Weiser to settle in the Hudson Valley. The naval stores were never produced, and the new settlers fell into a prolonged conflict with the governor and the Dutch land speculators of Albany. Eventually these immigrants moved southward along the Susquehanna and Juniata rivers, some to settle in New Jersey but most in Pennsylvania, where the warmth of their reception and the generosity of provincial land policies encouraged them to send home favorable reports. Philadelphia now became the primary port of entry, where German and Swiss immigrants began to arrive in substantial numbers, both as self-sufficing settlers and as indentured servants.

Throughout the rest of the colonial period minority sectarians continued to flock to Pennsylvania. A colony of Swiss Mennonites came in 1710, and many of their brethren followed. The first Dunkers (or Tunkers—the name derived from their method of baptism by dipping, *eintunken* in German) came in 1719 and then encouraged others. The Schwenkfelders, a group of Silesian sectarians who had been much persecuted, emigrated in 1733-4. In the 1740's, as the number of Germans grew, the religious complexity of German Protestantism came to be more completely represented. Lutherans and German

Reformed churchmen began to outnumber the denominations, although the Moravians, the third largest German
church, were a substantial group. Many of the German
sectarians were quietistic and relatively apolitical: for
them, coming to the New World represented withdrawal
rather than assertion. Their nonresistant principles made
trouble for them—indeed the Moravians first came to
Georgia, but left the farms they had cleared there for
Pennsylvania in 1738 and 1739 rather than bear arms
against the Spaniards. The Lutheran and Reformed Germans differed with their Mennonite and Moravian com-
patriots over the principle of nonresistance, and opposed
the Quakers as well.

The cumulative arrivals brought Germans in Pennsylvania as far west as the Susquehanna River; from there
the immigrants moved southward along the Appalachian
frontier. Before the era of the Revolution there were
German colonists in the valley of Virginia, parts of western Maryland, especially Frederick County and the region
around Hagerstown, and as far south as western North
Carolina. Before mid-century German immigrants began
arriving at the ports of Charles Town and Savannah and
settling in South Carolina and Georgia. In 1732 a group of
Swiss under the leadership of John Peter Pury of Neu-
châtel formed the first German-speaking colony in Beau-
fort County, South Carolina, thirty miles inland on the
east bank of the Savannah River. Promised a liberal
bounty for every able-bodied man he could bring from
Switzerland by the South Carolina government, Pury
recruited about four hundred colonists. Later, Germans
and Swiss began to settle in the Orangeburg district along
the Edisto and Congaree rivers and westward through
nearby counties. By 1750, a German population had

become a prominent element in the central and south-western part of South Carolina. In Georgia, a community of Salzburgers settled in 1734 at New Ebenezer, not far above Savannah.[5]

Since there was, as well, a small settlement of Germans founded in 1740 as far north as the coast of Maine, it could be said that the Germans straddled the continent from North to South before mid-century. The path of eighteenth-century German settlement can still be traced by a set of place-names along a wide arc which begins in Waldoboro, Maine, sweeps westward and southward through Herkimer, Mannheim, Newburgh, and New Berlin in New York, moves down through a series of Pennsylvania towns—Germantown, Bethlehem, Emmaus, Ephrata, Nazareth, Gettysburg, and Hanover—touches base in Hagerstown and Frederick, Maryland, and Fredericksburg, Virginia, and then moves closer to the coast, to New Bern, Ebenezer, and Orangeburg, South Carolina.

So great an influx of immigrants from a single national background could hardly help but stir a nativist reaction, especially in Pennsylvania, where they were concentrated. Franklin feared, he wrote a friend in 1753, that "through their indiscretion, or ours, or both, great disorders may one day arise among us." He thought the German arrivals "the most stupid of their nation," and was worried that their suspicions could not be set right because English-speaking colonials could not communicate with them. "Their clergy have very little influence on the people, who seem to take pleasure in abusing and discharging the minister on every trivial occasion. Not being used to liberty, they know not how to make modest use of

5. See Albert Bernhardt Faust, *The German Element in the United States* (1909).

it." German culture, he thought, was so self-perpetuating that he anticipated the day when it would be necessary to have interpreters in the Assembly. "In short, unless the stream of importation could be turned from this to other colonies, . . . they will soon outnumber us, that all the advantages we have, will in my opinion, be not able to preserve our language, and even our government will become precarious." [6] But in time these anxieties were substantially calmed.

4

Although the eighteenth-century German migrations eventually brought thousands of poor who entered as indentured servants, one is impressed by the caution and the solidity of the first arrivals. The early German immigrants came in groups under leaders of some considerable rank and quality, sons of magistrates, clergymen, burgomasters, and leading guildsmen, who had been educated in the universities, and who were themselves clergymen or, as in the case of Pastorius, other professionals. Other groups were already unified by kinship or place of origin or by religious conviction, and some came with enough capital, their own or that of philanthropists, to give them a start. They had a nose for good land, which they lovingly cared for, and as they moved inland away from settled areas they were able to buy much of it at reasonable prices. They established their own internal empire of

6. Franklin to Peter Collinson, May 9, 1753, quoted by F. R. Diffenderfer, *German Immigration into Pennsylvania* (1900), 110–12. Franklin's fears were shared even by earlier German immigrants, such as the Reverend Henry Melchior Muhlenberg, who wrote in 1751: "So many rotten people are coming . . . and acting so wickedly that the name [of Palatine] has begun to stink." Quoted in Bridenbaugh, *Cities in Revolt*, 87.

Gemütlichkeit. A lyrical traveler of the 1760's, after seeing the German communities in the Shenandoah Valley, grew eloquent over the happy, healthy, pastoral life they enjoyed there, amid a scene of uncommon natural beauty: "They know no wants and are acquainted with but few vices. Their inexperience of the elegancies of life precludes any regret that they have not the means of enjoying them; but they possess what many princes would give half their dominions for—health, contentment, and tranquility of mind." [7]

A less cautious but even more powerful strain was infused into colonial America by the Scotch-Irish, the largest single non-English ethnic group to come before the Revolution. During the Walpole era, a period of material progress and substantial toleration in England, English immigration slowed to a trickle of indentured servants and transported convicts. The great bulk of eighteenth-century emigrants from the United Kingdom came from Scotland and Ireland, and of these by far the most were neither Scots nor Irish Catholics but Ulstermen from Northern Ireland, the Scotch-Irish, who were, to their disgust, frequently and inaccurately characterized by the colonials simply as "the Irish." Along with a considerable body of Englishmen, many Scotsmen had moved to Ulster in Ireland in the early seventeenth century during the protracted persecution of Irish Catholics, and confiscations of their lands, which displaced a great many Irishmen from their own soil. By the middle of the seventeenth century about 100,000 Scots, mainly from the Lowlands, and about a fifth as many English had settled in

7. Henry Howe, *Historical Collections of Virginia* (1849), 468, as quoted in Diffenderfer, 132.

the Ulster lands opened to them first by the Crown and then by Cromwell. These Scottish and English aliens were hardened and disciplined by the fierce hatreds and savage reprisals that swept Ireland during the era of the Civil Wars, and not surprisingly the Scotch-Irish became noted for their political truculence as well as for the dogmatic Presbyterianism of their religious leaders.

A Parliamentary Act of 1704, which was enacted in turn by the obedient Irish Parliament, touched off a new period of intense religious controversy between Anglicans and Presbyterians in Ulster. Presbyterians were excluded from all civil and military Crown offices. Presbyterian magistrates and postmasters were removed from their jobs. Some Presbyterians were excommunicated for the crime of being married by their own ministers, and Presbyterians were compelled to pay tithes for Anglican rectors. At the same time, British commercial policy was discriminating against the woolen and stock-raising industries in Ireland; the linen industry, for a while the surviving economic mainstay, was similarly injured not long afterward. Before long, substantial numbers of Ulster Scots, sometimes the larger part of whole communities, began to leave for the West Indies and the mainland American colonies.

Many of the early Scotch-Irish emigrants thought of going to New England, and at first their leaders were greeted with some cordiality by prominent Puritan ministers. Costly Indian wars were still vivid in the memories of the older inhabitants, and it occurred to some New England leaders (as it would continue to occur to others elsewhere in the colonies) that the tough Scotch-Irish would make excellent settlers on the frontier fringes of New England, as a buffer between the Indians and older settlers. In 1713, when Worcester, close though it is to Boston, was still regarded as part of the frontier, a group of Scotch-Irish had been permitted or encouraged to settle there, and within the next half-dozen years other modest settlements were made along the western shore of the Connecticut River in what was to become Vermont, along the Kennebec River and on Casco Bay, Maine, and in southern New Hampshire—places for the most part well removed from Puritan settlements. But while Puritan leaders were receptive, most New Englanders were cold and forbidding. The Calvinism of the newcomers made no difference; they insisted on regarding the newcomers simply as Irishmen, and they talked a lot about the cost of relief for strangers who were poor. (The colonial view of poor relief was tribal; responsibility was readily accepted for "one's own" poor, but strangers and vagabonds were unwelcome outsiders.) Boston was already familiar with the costly business of caring for poor war refugees from the interior; after 1717, at the very time when provisions and stores were rapidly rising in price, the Scotch-Irish began to arrive in substantial numbers. Bostonians began to worry, as one of them put it, that "these confounded Irish will eat us all up." When one ship arrived in 1719, its forty-nine passengers were warned to get out of town immediately, and in the next two decades over five-hundred strangers were similarly warned off. In 1723, all who had come from Ireland were compelled henceforth to register with the town clerk. In 1729, after unusually large arrivals from Belfast and Londonderry, an immigrant ship was greeted by a mob who took it upon themselves to prevent immigrants from landing and corn from being exported. Throughout the period, the costs of poor relief were rising, and Bostonians were finding it increasingly expensive to care for their own poor, without accepting strangers.[8]

By the 1740's the testing time for the Scotch-Irish was about over. One incident in Worcester added force to the inhospitality of Boston. In 1736–7, the Presbyterians of Worcester were turned down when they petitioned to be relieved of the necessity of supporting the Puritan minister of the town as well as their own. The next year they organized a company to buy a new township about thirty miles west of Worcester and planned to settle it on their own church principles. Some stayed behind in Worcester and began building their own church. When this structure was well begun, the Puritan inhabitants of Worcester gathered in the dark of night, leveled the structure to the ground, and burned or carried off the building materials. Thereafter Worcester Presbyterians scattered to more remote parts. The point seems to have been established that New England Puritans and Scotch-Irish Presbyterians would not willingly or peaceably live side by side. At the cost of much exertion in Boston and a little violence in Worcester, New England succeeded in preserving its essential homogeneity. Henceforth, the Scotch-Irish looked southward, and, as with the Germans, Pennsylvania became the first and largest beneficiary of their immigration.

Landing in Philadelphia or New York, the Scotch-Irish pushed inland along the valleys and streams, notably the Delaware and the Susquehanna, and formed large settlements in places as far west as the vicinity of what later became Pittsburgh. In time they occupied an entire region in western Pennsylvania, which came to have great weight in the politics of the province. Rugged, fearless, com-

8. Henry Jones Ford, *The Scotch Irish in America* (1915), 225; Bridenbaugh, *Cities in the Wilderness*, 231, 250–1, 391–3.

bative, and self-regarding, the Scotch-Irish immigrants
were not tender about the interests of Indians or land-
holders. The reports of them given to John Penn by James
Logan, once William Penn's secretary and now an important provincial official, reveal a strong undercurrent of
anxiety about their ways, although Logan must have been
aware, along with many Pennsylvanians, that they were
rapidly forming a protective cordon around the pacifist
Quakers and the relatively passive Germans of the colony.
As a land speculator, Logan was understandably disturbed
by the Scotch-Irish attitude toward titles. These "bold
and indigent strangers," he told Penn, gave as answer
when titles were challenged "that we had solicited for
colonists and they had come accordingly." Both Palatines
and Ulstermen, he reported in 1727, were arriving in great
numbers yearly. "Both these sets frequently sit down on
any spot of vacant land they can find, without asking
question." Only the previous week a Scotch-Irish leader
had "applied to me in the name of four hundred, as he
said, who depended all on me for directions where they
should settle. They say the Proprietor invited people to
come and settle his country; they came for that end and
must live. Both they and the Palatines pretend that they
will buy, but not one in twenty has anything to pay with.
The Irish settle generally toward the Maryland line, where
no lands can honestly be sold until the dispute with Lord
Baltimore is decided." Two years later he wrote: "It looks
as if Ireland is to send all its inhabitants hither. . . . The
common fear is that if they thus continue to come they
will make themselves proprietors of the Province. It is
strange that they thus crowd in where they are not
wanted. . . . The Indians themselves are alarmed at the
swarms of strangers, and we are afraid of a breach between them—for the Irish are very rough to them."

The following year, generalizing his trials in the land office, Logan remarked that "the settlement of five families from Ireland gives me more trouble than fifty of any other people. Before we were broke in upon, ancient Friends and first settlers lived happily; but now the case is quite altered." Not long after he reported that the Scotch-Irish had in an "audacious and disorderly manner" taken up the fifteen-thousand-acre tract of Conestoga Manor that the Penns had reserved for themselves, arguing simply that "it was against the laws of God and nature that so much land should be idle when so many Christians wanted it to labor on and to raise their bread." [9]

During the 1730's the Scotch-Irish began to stream southward into the Shenandoah Valley and the back-country of Virginia, where the speculators in new lands and patents and Governor William Gooch, who was alert to the need for buffer settlements, encouraged them. Worried about their religious condition under Virginia's Anglican establishment, they petitioned Gooch in 1738 for freedom to follow Presbyterian worship. The governor granted what they asked, saying that he had "always been inclined to favour the people who have lately removed from other provinces to settle on the western side of our great mountains." [1] The tide of Scotch-Irish immigration moved on southward through Virginia into the Carolinas and upper Georgia, where it met and mingled with other Ulstermen who had entered at Charles Town, South Carolina.

Few colonial contemporaries confused the Scotch-Irish with proper Scots who came in far smaller but still substantial numbers directly from Scotland. They had been migrating both to Ulster and to the Americas, first to

9. Quoted in Charles A. Hanna, *The Scotch-Irish* (1902), II, 62–3.
1. Ibid., II, 48.

Barbados and then to the mainland, in the seventeenth century, but it was not until the mid-eighteenth century that large numbers came. A constant grinding poverty was the chief cause of this Scottish emigration. Scotland, a country of meager agriculture and almost no manufactures, was one of the poorest areas of Europe, and the pressure of its population on the limited subsistence it afforded was not yet much diminished by the trading enterprises which strengthened the economy as time went on. But even when conditions improved, the pump had been primed, and steep rent rises kept pushing Scots out. In the 1760's emigration began to flow in a steady stream, especially from the Highlands. In the twelve years before the Revolution perhaps 25,000 came to the colonies.[2] There were Scots at both ends of the social spectrum, prosperous mercantile agents who were part of the colonial elite, and indigent Highlanders who spoke only Gaelic. Except in New York, Scots rarely went to the frontiers, and for the most part they mingled very little with the Scotch-Irish. Whereas the Scotch-Irish readily resented England and were enthusiastic revolutionaries, the Scots, many of them lately arrived, stayed preponderantly loyal to the Crown. Scots long had a rather poor reputation in America, in part because of resentment against the conspicuous Scottish merchants and in part against their lack of Revolutionary fervor.

5

One can hardly overestimate the importance of the eighteenth-century migrations for the American colonies.

2. I. C. C. Graham, *Colonists from Scotland* (1956), 188–9.

By the time of the Revolution the total white immigration was probably as large as or larger than the entire colonial population of 1700, and the English homogeneity of the colonies had been decisively broken. The migrations considerably increased the numbers of colonials who were indifferent or hostile to Anglicanism, and in the case of the Scotch-Irish they brought a large infusion of persons who had already suffered from acts of Parliament and had little piety about English rule. The military position of the colonies vis-à-vis the French, Spaniards, and Indians was greatly strengthened, and the colonials were beginning to push into decisive areas of conflict, posing at once a challenge to French strategists and a problem in policy to the rulers of empire in London.

Arthur Young, the agricultural writer, who saw much of the Scotch-Irish emigration in process, once remarked on its quality: "Men who emigrate are, from the nature of the circumstances, the most active, hardy, daring, bold and resolute spirits, and probably the most mischievous also." [3] "The most mischievous also"—one should not neglect this. The psychological and temperamental selectivity of migration is a matter that probably defies the historian's usual resources for proof, but Young may well have been right. Men left Europe to get away from something—because they had suffered from economic miseries or from religious oppression, or, as in the case of the Scotch-Irish and many of the Palatines, from both. Yet for every poverty-stricken or religiously oppressed emigrant who risked the hazardous and frequently fatal Atlantic crossing and the uncertainties of the strange wilds of America, there were many more, enduring precisely the

3. Ford, 208.

same hardships, who preferred to stay at home. Young was suggesting that the most venturesome or visionary, the most impatient and restive under authority, the most easily alienated, the most desperate and cranky, were the most ready to leave, giving at least the initial population of the American colonies a strong bias toward dislike of authority. This one cannot know, though it is easier in more objective and measurable respects to see how emigration worked as a selective process. The eighteenth-century settlers of America were men and women who had seen with their own eyes in Ireland and on the Continent the ravages of war and social conflict, and whether they came as freemen with some capital, as indentured servants, or as transported convicts, they were the off-scourings and the victims of the wars and economic dislocations, the exploitation and residual religious persecution, that racked Europe at the end of the seventeenth and the beginning of the eighteenth century. What permanent effects, if any, these experiences had upon their ways of thought is a matter of conjecture, but it is not conjecture that the migrations brought a skewed sample of the European populations. "The rich," said Crèvecoeur, "stay in Europe, it is only the middling and the poor that emigrate." [4] The nobles, the wealthy, the established and the contented, stayed at home; it was the aggrieved middle classes and the impoverished who found themselves, voluntarily or involuntarily, becoming Americans.

4. Hector St. John de Crèvecoeur: *Letters from an American Farmer* (Everyman's edn., 1912), 58.

CHAPTER II

White
Servitude

1

THE transportation to the English colonies of human labor, a very profitable but also a very perishable form of merchandise, was one of the big businesses of the eighteenth century. Most of this labor was unfree. There was, of course, a sizable corps of free hired laborers in the colonies, often enjoying wages two or three times those prevalent in the mother country. But never at any time in the colonial period was there a sufficient supply of voluntary labor, paying its own transportation and arriving masterless and free of debt, to meet the insatiable demands of the colonial economy. The solution, found long before the massive influx of black slaves, was a combined force of merchants, ship captains, immigrant brokers, and a variety of hard-boiled recruiting agents who joined in bringing substantial cargoes of whites who voluntarily or involuntarily paid for their passage by undergoing a terminable period of bondage. This quest for labor, touched off early in the seventeenth century by the circulars of the London Company of Virginia, continued by William Penn in the 1680's and after, and climaxed by the blandishments of various English and continental recruiting agents of the eighteenth century, marked one of the first con-

certed and sustained advertising campaigns in the history
of the modern world.

If we leave out of account the substantial Puritan migration of 1630–40, not less than half, and perhaps considerably more, of all the white immigrants to the colonies
were indentured servants, redemptioners, or convicts.
Certainly a good many more than half of all persons who
went to the colonies south of New England were servants
in bondage to planters, farmers, speculators, and proprietors.[1] The tobacco economy of Virginia and Maryland was
founded upon the labor of gangs of indentured servants,
who were substantially replaced by slaves only during the
course of the eighteenth century. "The planters' fortunes
here," wrote the governor of Maryland in 1755, "consist in
the number of their servants (who are purchased at high
rates) much as the estates of an English farmer do in the
multitude of cattle." Everywhere indentured servants
were used, and almost everywhere outside New England
they were vital to the economy. The labor of the colonies,
said Benjamin Franklin in 1759, "is performed chiefly by
indentured servants brought from Great Britain, Ireland,
and Germany, because the high price it bears cannot be
performed in any other way." [2]

Indentured servitude had its roots in the widespread
poverty and human dislocation of seventeenth-century
England. Still a largely backward economy with a great
part of its population permanently unemployed, England
was moving toward more modern methods in industry and
agriculture; yet in the short run some of the improvements

1. Abbott E. Smith, *Colonists in Bondage* (1947), 3–4; Richard B.
Morris, *Government and Labor in Colonial America* (1946), 315–16.
2. Smith, 27; M. W. Jernegan, *Laboring and Dependent Classes in
Colonial America* (1931), 55; see also K. F. Geiser, *Redemptioners and
Indentured Servants in . . . Pennsylvania* (1901), 24–5.

greatly added to the unemployed. Drifting men and women gathered in the cities, notably London, where they constituted a large mass of casual workers, lumpen-proletarians, and criminals. The mass of the poverty-stricken was so large that Gregory King, the pioneer statistician, estimated in 1696 that more than half the population—cottagers and paupers, laborers and out-servants—were earning less than they spent. They diminished the wealth of the realm, he argued, since their annual expenses exceeded income and had to be made up by the poor rates, which ate up one-half of the revenue of the Crown.[3] In the early seventeenth century, this situation made people believe the country was overpopulated and emigration to the colonies was welcomed; but in the latter part of the century, and in the next, the overpopulation theory gave way to the desire to hoard a satisfactory labor surplus. Yet the strong outflow of population did not by any means cease. From the large body of poor drifters, many of them diseased, feckless, or given to crime, came a great part of the labor supply of the rich sugar islands and the American mainland. From the London of Pepys and then of Hogarth, as well as from many lesser ports and inland towns, the English poor, lured, seduced, or forced into the emigrant stream, kept coming to America for the better part of two centuries. It is safe to guess that few of them, and indeed few persons from the other sources of emigration, knew very much about what they were doing when they committed themselves to life in America.

Yet the poor were well aware that they lived in a heartless world. One of the horrendous figures in the folklore

3. Christopher Hill, *The Century of Revolution* (1961), 206.

of lower-class London in the seventeenth and eighteenth
centuries was the "spirit"—the recruiting agent who way-
laid, kidnapped, or induced adults to get aboard ship for
America. The spirits, who worked for respectable merchants, were known to lure children with sweets, to seize
upon the weak or the gin-sodden and take them aboard
ship, and to bedazzle the credulous or weak-minded by
fabulous promises of an easy life in the New World. Often
their victims were taken roughly in hand and, pending
departure, held in imprisonment either on shipboard or in
low-grade hostels or brothels. To escaped criminals and
other fugitives who wanted help in getting out of the
country, the spirits could appear as ministering angels.
Although efforts were made to regulate or check their
activities, and they diminished in importance in the
eighteenth century, it remains true that a certain small
part of the white colonial population of America was
brought by force, and a much larger portion came in response to deceit and misrepresentation on the part of the
spirits.

With the beginnings of substantial emigration from the
Continent in the eighteenth century the same sort of
concerted business of recruitment arose in Holland, the
Rhenish provinces of Germany, and Switzerland. In Rotterdam and Amsterdam the lucrative business of gathering
and transshipping emigrants was soon concentrated in the
hands of a dozen prominent English and Dutch firms. As
competition mounted, the shippers began to employ
agents to greet the prospective emigrants at the harbor
and vie in talking up the comforts of their ships. Hence
the recruiting agents known as *Neülander*—newlanders—
emerged. These newlanders, who were paid by the head
for the passengers they recruited, soon branched out of

the Dutch ports and the surrounding countryside and moved up the Rhine and the Neckar, traveling from one province to another, from town to town and tavern to tavern, all the way to the Swiss cantons, often passing themselves off as rich men returned from the easy and prosperous life of America in order to persuade others to try to repeat their good fortune. These confidence men— "soul sellers" as they were sometimes called—became the continental counterparts of the English spirits, profiteers in the fate of the peasantry and townspeople of the Rhineland. Many of the potential emigrants stirred up by the promises of the newlanders were people of small property who expected, by selling some part of their land or stock or furnishings, to be able to pay in full for their passage to America and to arrive as freemen. What the passage would take out of them in blood and tears, not to speak of cash, was carefully hidden from them. They gathered in patient numbers at Amsterdam and Rotterdam often quite innocent of the reality of what had already become for thousands of Englishmen one of the terrors of the age—the Atlantic crossing.

2

In 1750 Gottlieb Mittelberger, a simple organist and music master in the Duchy of Württemberg, was commissioned to bring an organ to a German congregation in New Providence, Pennsylvania, and his journey inspired him to write a memorable account of an Atlantic crossing. From Heilbronn, where he picked up his organ, Mittelberger went the well-traveled route along the Neckar and the Rhine to Rotterdam, whence he sailed to a stopover at Cowes in England, and then to Philadelphia. About four

hundred passengers were crowded onto the ship, mainly
German and Swiss redemptioners, men pledged to work
off their passage charges. The trip from his home district
to Rotterdam took seven weeks, the voyage from Rotterdam to Philadelphia fifteen weeks, the entire journey from
May to October.

What moved Mittelberger, no literary man, to write of
his experiences was first his indignation against the lies
and misrepresentations used by the newlanders to lure his
fellow Germans to America, and then the hideous shock
of the crossing. The voyage proved excruciating and there
is no reason to think it particularly unusual. The long trip
down the Rhine, with constant stops at the three dozen
customs houses between Heilbronn and Holland, began to
consume the limited funds of the travelers, and it was
followed by an expensive stop of several weeks in Holland.
Then there was the voyage at sea, with the passengers
packed like herring and cramped in the standard bedsteads measuring two feet by six. "During the journey,"
wrote Mittelberger, "the ship is full of pitiful signs of
distress—smells, fumes, horrors, vomiting, various kinds
of sea sickness, fever, dysentery, headaches, heat, con-
stipation, boils, scurvy, cancer, mouth-rot, and similar
afflictions, all of them caused by the age and the highly-
salted state of the food, especially of the meat, as well as
by the very bad and filthy water, which brings about the
miserable destruction and death of many. Add to all that
shortage of food, hunger, thirst, frost, heat, dampness,
fear, misery, vexation, and lamentation as well as other
troubles. Thus, for example, there are so many lice, especially on the sick people, that they have to be scraped off
the bodies. All this misery reached its climax when in
addition to everything else one must suffer through two or

three days and nights of storm, with everyone convinced that the ship with all aboard is bound to sink. In such misery all the people on board pray and cry pitifully together." [4]

Even those who endured the voyage in good health, Mittelberger reported, fell out of temper and turned on each other with reproaches. They cheated and stole. "But most of all they cry out against the thieves of human beings! Many groan and exclaim: 'Oh! If only I were back at home, even lying in my pig-sty!' Or they call out: 'Ah, dear God, if I only once again had a piece of good bread or a good fresh drop of water.'" It went hardest with women in childbirth and their offspring: "Very few escape with their lives; and mother and child, as soon as they have died, are thrown into the water. On board our ship, on a day on which we had a great storm, a woman about to give birth and unable to deliver under the circumstances, was pushed through one of the portholes into the sea because her corpse was far back in the stern and could not be brought forward to the deck." Children under seven, he thought (though the port records show him wrong here), seldom survived, especially those who had not already had measles and smallpox, and their parents were condemned to watch them die and be tossed overboard. The sick members of families infected the healthy, and in the end all might be lying moribund. He believed disease was so prevalent because warm food was served only three times a week, and of that very little, very bad, very dirty, and supplemented by water that was often "very black, thick with dirt, and full of worms . . . towards the end of the voyage we had to eat the ship's biscuit,

---

4. For the voyage, Mittelberger, *Journey to Pennsylvania* (edn. 1960), ed. and trans. by Oscar Handlin and John Clive, 10–7.

which had already been spoiled for a long time, even
though no single piece was there more than the size of a
thaler that was not full of red worms and spiders' nests."

The first sight of land gave heart to the passengers, who
came crawling out of the hatches to get a glimpse of it.
But then for many a final disappointment lay in wait: only
those who could complete the payment of their fare could
disembark. The others were kept on board until they were
bought, some of them sickening within sight of land and,
as they sickened, losing the chance of being bought on
good terms. On landing some families were broken, when
despairing parents indentured their children to masters
other than their own.

Not even passengers of means who paid their way,
moved more or less freely about ship, occupied cabins or
small dormitories, and had superior rations could take an
Atlantic crossing lightly. In addition to the hazards of
winds too feeble or too violent, of pirates, shipwrecks, or
hostile navies, there were under the best of circumstances
the dangers of sickness. Travelers in either direction frequently died of smallpox or other diseases on board or
soon after arrival. Anglican colonials often complained of
the high mortality rate among their young would-be
clergymen crossing to England to be ordained. The Dutch
Reformed preacher Theodorus Frelinghuysen lost three
of his five sons on their way to be ordained in Amsterdam.
The evangelist George Whitefield on his first crossing to
the colonies in 1738 saw a majority of the soldiers on board
afflicted with fever and spent much of his time "for many
days and nights, visiting between twenty and thirty sick
persons, crawling between decks upon his knees, admin-
istering medicines and cordials" and giving comfort. On
this voyage the captain's Negro servant died, was wrapped

in a hammock and tossed into the sea. In the end all but a handful of the passengers took the fever, including Whitefield, who survived treatment by bleeding and emetics. The ship on which he returned a few months later was afflicted by a "contrary wind," drifted for over a week to the point at which crew and passengers were uncertain where they were, and took so long to arrive at Ireland that water rations, which had been cut to a pint a day, were just about to run out.[5]

When paying passengers were exposed to such afflictions, how much worse must have been the sufferings of the servants and redemptioners packed into the holds, frequently at a density that violated the laws, and without adequate ventilation. Food provisions were calculated to last fourteen weeks, which was normally sufficient, but the rations deteriorated rapidly, especially in summer. Water turned stale, butter turned rancid, and beef rotted. If Mittelberger's voyage ranked among the worst, Atlantic crossings were frequently at or near the worst, and many more disastrous ventures were recorded.[6] With bad luck, provisions could give out. The *Love and Unity* left Rotterdam for Philadelphia in May 1731 with more than 150 Palatines and a year later landed with 34, after having put in toward the end at Martha's Vineyard for water and food. On the way rations became so low that water, rats, and mice were being *sold*, and the storage chests of the dead and dying were broken open and plundered by the captain and crew. A ship called the *Good Intent*—the names of eighteenth century vessels often reek with irony —arrived off the American coast in the winter of 1751

5. Quoted in Luke Tyerman, *The Life of the Rev. George Whitefield* (1876), I, 124–5, 144–5.

6. See Geiser, chapter v; F. R. Diffenderfer, *German Immigration into Pennsylvania* . . . (1900), chapter v, esp. 63–7.

but found herself unable to make port because of the
weather; she was able to put in to harbor in the West
Indies only after twenty-four weeks at sea. Nearly all of
the passengers had died long before. The *Sea Flower*,
which left Belfast with 106 passengers in 1741, was at sea
sixteen weeks, and lost 46 passengers from starvation.
When help arrived, six of the corpses had been canni-
balized.

It is true that given adequate ventilation, a stock of
lemon juice and vegetables, and good luck with the winds,
decent sanitary arrangements were possible. The philanthropic Georgia Trustees, who were concerned about the
health of their colonists, "put on board turnips, carrots,
potatoes, and onions, which were given out with the salt
meat, and contributed greatly to prevent the scurvy." Out
of some fifteen hundred people who had gone to Georgia
at the public expense, it was claimed in 1741, not more
than six had died in transit. A traveler to Jamaica in 1739
reported that the servants on his ship "had lived so easily
and well during the voyage, that they looked healthful,
clean and fresh, and for this reason were soon sold," yet
he saw another vessel arrive not long afterward with "a
multitude of poor starved creatures, that seemed so many
skeletons: misery appeared in their looks, and one might
read the effects of sea-tyranny by their wild and dejected
countenances." [7]

3

The situation in which the indentured servant or the redemptioner found himself upon his arrival depended in
large measure upon his physical condition. There would

7. Smith, 217–18.

be a last-minute effort to clean up and appear presentable, and in some ports the healthy were separated from the sick, once colonial officials adopted quarantine measures. Boston, the most vigilant of the ports, had long kept a pesthouse on an island in the harbor and fined captains who disregarded the regulations. "As Christians and men," the governor of Pennsylvania urged in 1738, "we are obliged to make a charitable provision for the sick stranger, and not by confining him to a ship, inhumanly expose him to fresh miseries when he hopes that his sufferings are soon to be mitigated." [8] Pennsylvania then designated Province Island for quarantine and built a pesthouse to harbor sick immigrants. In 1750 and again in 1765 it passed laws to bar overcrowding on ships. Laws passed by Virginia and Maryland in the 1760's providing for the quarantine of convict ships were frowned upon in London, and Virginia's law was disallowed.

Buyers came on shipboard to take their pick of the salably healthy immigrants, beginning a long process of examination and inspection with the muscles and the teeth, and ending with a conversational search for the required qualities of intelligence, civility, and docility. At Philadelphia buyers might be trying to find Germans and eschew the Scotch-Irish, who were reputed to be contumacious and work resistant and disposed to run away. Some buyers were "soul drivers" who bought packs of immigrants and brutally herded them on foot into the interior where they were offered along the way to ready purchasers. On the ships and at the docks there were final scenes of despair and frenzy as servants searched for lost articles of indenture, or lamented the disappearance of

8. Diffenderfer, 82.

baggage, unexpected overcharges, the necessity of accepting indentures longer than their debts fairly required, the
separation of families.

The final crisis of arrival was the process we would call
acclimatization, in the eighteenth century known as "seasoning." Particularly difficult in the tropical islands, seasoning also took a heavy toll in the Southern colonies of
the mainland. People from cities and from the mild English climate found the summer hard going in any colony
from Maryland southward, especially on plantations where
indentured servants were put to arduous field labor by
owners whose goal it was to get a maximum yield of labor
in the four or five years contracted for. Fevers, malaria, and
dysentery carried many off, especially in their first years
of service. Seasoning was thought to be more or less at an
end after one year in the new climate, and servants who
had been wholly or partly seasoned were at a premium.

During the voyage, thoughtful servants might have recalled, quite a number of persons had battened on their
needs—the spirit or the newlander, the toll collectors and
the parasites of the seaports, the ship captain or merchant; now there was the master. Any traffic that gave
sustenance to so many profiteers might well rest on a
rather intense system of exploitation. A merchant who
would spend from six to ten pounds to transport and provision an indentured servant might sell him on arrival—
the price varied with age, skill, and physical condition—for
fifteen to twenty pounds, although the profits also had to
cover losses from sickness and death en route. The typical
servant had, in effect, sold his total working powers for
four or five years or more in return for his passage plus a
promise of minimal maintenance. After the initially small
capital outlay, the master simply had to support him from

day to day as his services were rendered, support which was reckoned to cost about thirteen or fourteen pounds a year. In Maryland, where exploitation was as intense as anywhere, the annual net yield, even from unskilled labor, was reckoned at around fifty pounds sterling.[9] The chief temptation to the master was to drive the servant beyond his powers in the effort to get as much as possible out of him during limited years of service. The chief risk was that the servant might die early in service before his purchase price had been redeemed by his work. That he might run away was a secondary risk, though one against which the master had considerable protection. Still, hard as white servitude bore on servants, it was nevertheless not always a happy arrangement for owners, especially for those with little capital and little margin for error: shiftless and disagreeable servants, as well as successful runaways, were common enough to introduce a significant element of risk into this form of labor.

Indentured servants lived under a wide variety of conditions, which appear to have softened somewhat during the eighteenth century. Good or bad luck, the disposition of the master, the length of the term of work, the size of the plantation or farm, the robustness or frailty of the worker—all these had a part in determining the fate of each individual. Servants in households or on small farms might be in the not uncomfortable situation of familiar domestic laborers. Tradesmen who were trying to teach special skills to their workers, or householders who wanted satisfactory domestic service, might be tolerable masters. The most unenviable situation was that of servants on Southern plantations, living alongside—but never with—

9. Raphael Semmes, *Crime and Punishment in Early Maryland* (1938), 80, 278; *cf.* Samuel McKee, Jr., *Labor in Colonial New York* (1935), 111.

Negro slaves, both groups doing much the same work, often under the supervision of a relentless overseer. One has to imagine the situation of a member of the English urban pauper class, unaccustomed to rural or to any sustained labor, thrust into a hot climate in which heavy field labor—including, worst of all, the backbreaking task of clearing new land of rocks, trees, and shrubs—was his daily lot. Even as late as 1770 William Eddis, the English surveyor of customs at Annapolis, thought that the Maryland Negroes were better off than "the Europeans, over whom the rigid planter exercises an inflexible severity." The Negroes, Eddis thought, were a lifelong property, so were treated with a certain care, but the whites were "strained to the utmost to perform their allotted labour; and, from a prepossession in many cases too justly founded, they were supposed to be receiving only the just reward which is due to repeated offenses. There are doubtless many exceptions to this observation, yet, generally speaking, they groan beneath a worse than Egyptian bondage." Yet in Virginia, as the blacks arrived in greater numbers, white laborers seemed to have become a privileged stratum, assigned to lighter work and more skilled tasks.[1]

The status and reputation of Southern indentured laborers were no doubt kept lower than elsewhere because there were a considerable number of transported convicts among them. Colonies to the north were not completely free of convict transportees, but the plantation system regularly put honest unfortunates alongside hardened criminals and lumped all together as rogues who deserved no better than what was meted out to them. Among the by-products of English social change of the seventeenth

1. William Eddis, *Letters from America* (1777), 69–70; J. C. Ballagh, *White Servitude in the Colony of Virginia* (1895), 89–92.

and eighteenth centuries was a very substantial pool of criminal talents. The laws devised to suppress the criminal population were so harsh—scores of crimes were defined as felonies and hanging was a standard punishment for many trivial offenses—that England would have been launched upon mass hangings far beyond the point of acceptability had it not been for two devices that let many accused off the penalties prescribed for felons. One was the benefit of clergy—a practice inherited from the Middle Ages and continued until the early nineteenth century—which permitted a convicted felon to "call for the book" and prove his literacy. On the ancient assumption that those who could read were clerics and thus exempt from severe punishments by the secular state, the relatively privileged class of literate felons could be permitted to escape with the conventional branding on the thumb.

A second practice, the predecessor of convict transportation, was to secure royal pardons for ordinary offenders deemed by the judges to be worthy of some indulgence. Until the end of the French wars in 1713 it was customary to send them into the army, but in peacetime England did not know what to do with felons and drifters. In 1717 Parliament passed an act which in effect made royal clemency contingent upon transportation to the colonies for a term of labor; in consequence the large-scale shipping of convicts began which continued to the time of the American Revolution. To America at large, including the island colonies, around thirty thousand felons were transported in the eighteenth century, of whom probably more than two-thirds reached Virginia and Maryland, where they were readily snapped up by the poorer planters.[2]

The whole procedure, though clearly intended to be a

2. See Smith, 116–19; *cf.* Lawrence H. Gipson, *The British Empire before the American Revolution,* II (1936), 69, 79.

humane and useful alternative to wholesale hangings, was
dreadfully feared by convicts, who may have guessed,
quite rightly, that whoever bought their services would
try to get the most out of them during their seven-year
terms (fourteen years in the case of transmuted death
penalties) of hard labor. In transit felons probably were
fed somewhat better than they were used to, but usually
they were kept below deck and in chains during the entire voyage, and on the average perhaps one in six or
seven would die on the way. "All the states of horror I
ever had an idea of," wrote a visitor to a convict ship, "are
much short of what I saw this poor man in; chained to a
board in a hole not above sixteen feet long, more than
fifty with him; a collar and padlock about his neck, and
chained to five of the most dreadful creatures I ever
looked on."[3] Mortality could run very high: on one ship,
the *Honour,* which arrived in Annapolis in 1720, twenty
of the sixty-one convicts had died. Merchants transporting
felons on government contracts pleaded for subsidies to
cover losses that hit them so hard.

While some planters rushed to the seaports to find
convicts for their field labor supply, others were disturbed
by the effect they expected criminals would have on the
character of the population. These hazardous importations
caused most anxiety in the colonies that received masses
of transported felons. Pennsylvania subjected the importation of convicts to constant statutory harassment after
1722. Virginia at mid-century seems to have thought herself in the midst of a crime wave. The Virginia *Gazette*
complained in 1751: "When we see our papers fill'd con-
tinually with accounts of the most audacious robberies,

3. Smith, 125.

the most cruel murders, and infinite other villainies per-
petrated by convicts transported from Europe, what
melancholy, what terrible reflections it must occasion!
What will become of our posterity? These are some of thy
favours Britain. Thou art called our Mother Country; but
what good mother ever sent thieves and villains to accom-
pany her children; to corrupt some with their infectious
vices and murder the rest? What father ever endeavour'd
to spread a plague in his family? . . . In what can Britain
show a more sovereign contempt for us than by emptying
their jails into our settlements; unless they would likewise
empty their jakes [privies] on our tables!" [4] The concluding metaphor seems to have come quite naturally to the
colonials: Franklin also used it, although he is better remembered for his suggestion that the Americans trade
their rattlesnakes for the convicts.[5] But all laws rejecting
transported convicts were disallowed in England by the
Board of Trade and the Privy Council, while subterfuge
measures designed to impede or harass the trade were
looked at with suspicion.

4

The system of indenture was an adaptation, with some
distinctively harsh features, of the old institution of apprenticeship. In fact, a few native-born colonials, usually
to discharge a debt or answer for a crime but sometimes
to learn a trade, entered into indentures not altogether
unlike those undertaken by immigrants. In law an indenture was a contract in which the servant promised faithful

4. Ibid., 130.
5. Cheesman A. Herrick, *White Servitude in Pennsylvania* (1926),
131–2.

service for a specified period of time in return for his
housing and keep and, at the end of his term of work,
that small sum of things, known as "freedom dues," which
his master promised him upon their parting. The typical
term was four or five years, although it might run anywhere from one or two years to seven. Longer terms were
commonly specified for children, and were calculated to
bring them to freedom at or just past the time they reached
majority. Most indentures followed a standard pattern: as
early as 1636 printed forms were available, needing only
a few details to be filled out by the contracting parties.
Often an emigrant's original indenture was made out to
a merchant or a ship's captain and was sold with its holder
to an employer on arrival. Indentures became negotiable
instruments in the colonies, servants bound under their
terms being used to settle debts, even gambling debts. In
theory the contract protected the servant from indefinite
exploitation, but in practice it had quite limited powers.
It was a document vulnerable to loss, theft, or destruction,
and when one considers both the fecklessness and inexperience of most indentured servants and the lack of
privacy under which they lived, it is little wonder that
their contracts often disappeared.

During the eighteenth century, however, circumstances
began to alter the prevailing system of indentures and to
lessen its severities, particularly when a special class of
bonded servants, the redemptioners, became numerous.
The redemptioner appeared at the beginning of the
century, coming largely from the Continent, often emi-
grating with a family and with a supply of tools and furnishings. The passengers who traveled with Mittelberger
were mostly redemptioners. Indentured servants were simply a part of a ship's cargo, but redemptioners were

low-grade, partially paid-up passengers. The redemptioner embarked without an indenture, sometimes having paid part of the money for his own and his family's passage, and arranged with the shipping merchant to complete payment within a short time after landing. Once here, he might try to find relatives or friends to make up his deficit; failure to pay in full meant that he would be sold to the highest bidder to redeem whatever part of his fare was unpaid. The length of his servitude would depend upon the amount to be redeemed. It could be as short as one or two years, although four years seems to have been much more common. Redemptioners would try to go into service as a whole family group. Although redemptioners were often swindled because of their lack of English and were overcharged for interest, insurance, and the transportation of their baggage, it was less profitable to carry them than indentured servants. Still, merchants were eager to fill their ships as full as possible with a ballast of redemptioners.[6]

All bonded servants, indentured and redemptionist, were chattels of their masters, but the terminability of their contracts and the presence of certain legal rights stood between them and slavery. A servant could be freely bought and sold, except in Pennsylvania and New York where laws required the consent of a court before assigning a servant for a year or more. His labor could be rented out; he could be inherited on the terms laid down in his master's will. Yet he could own property, although he was forbidden to engage in trade. He could also sue and be sued, but he could not vote. It was expected that he would be subject to corporal punishment by his master for vari-

6. Smith, 41.

ous offenses, and whipping was common; but a master risked losing his servant on the order of a court for a merciless or disfiguring beating. The right of a servant to petition the courts against abuse was more than a negligible protection. Penniless servants were, of course, at a disadvantage in courts manned by representatives of the master class: in effect they were appealing to the community pride, compassion, or decency of the magistrates, and the sense that there were certain things that ought not be done to a white Christian. Yet the frequency of complaints by servants makes it clear that the prerogative of appeal was widely used, and the frequency of judgments rendered for servants shows that it was not used in vain. No colony recognized the validity of agreements between master and servant made *during* servitude unless both parties appeared before a magistrate and registered their consent. Statutes regulated the terms of servitude in cases in which no papers of indenture existed.

For many thousands of servants their term of indentured servitude was a period of enforced celibacy. Marriage without the consent of the master was illegal, and the crimes of fornication and bastardy figure importantly in the records of bound servitude—not surprisingly, when we realize how many of the servant population were between the ages of eighteen and thirty. The sexuality of redemptioners, since they commonly came in families, was a much less serious problem for them and their masters. Among indentured servants as a whole, however, there were many more men than women. The situation of maidservants was full of both opportunities and hazards. Their services were considerably prized, and a clever or comely woman, as mistress or wife, might escape from the dreariest exactions of servitude. Still, women were also vulnerable to sexual abuse, and the penalties for simply following their own inclinations were high. Masters were unwilling to undergo the loss of time, the expense of rearing a child, or the impairment of health or risk of death in childbirth, and thus were unlikely to give consent to marriage. But the laws contrived to give masters the chance to turn such events to their own account. For fornication and bastardy there were ceremonial whippings, usually of twenty-one lashes; more to the point, sentences of from one to two or three years of extra service were exacted, an overgenerous compensation for the loss of perhaps no more than a few weeks of work. From Pennsylvania southward, Richard B. Morris has concluded, the master was often enriched far beyond his actual losses. Where a manservant fathered a child, he could be required to do whatever extra service was necessary to provide for its maintenance. Merely for contracting unsanctioned marriages, servants could be put to a year's extra service. If a maidservant identified her master as the father of her child, he could be punished for adultery, and she removed from him and resold. A keen disrelish for miscegenation provided an additional term of punishment: for bearing a mulatto bastard a woman might get heavy whipping and seven years of extra service. Despite such restraints, there were a substantial number of illegitimate births, mulatto and otherwise.

However, the commonest crime committed by servants, not surprisingly, was running away—not an easy thing to get away with, since in the colonies everyone had to carry a pass, in effect an identity card, and stiff penalties ranging from fines and personal damages to corporal punishment were imposed upon persons harboring fugitives. Runaways were regularly advertised in the newspapers, rewards were offered, and both sheriffs and the general public were enlisted to secure their return. Returned they often were, and subjected to what were regarded as suitable penalties; captured servants who were unclaimed were resold at public auction. On the whole, and especially in Pennsylvania and colonies to the south, the laws turned the punishment of the recovered runaway into an advantage for the master. The standard penalty in the North, not always rigorously enforced, was extra service of twice the time the master had lost, though whipping was also common. In Pennsylvania, a five-to-one penalty was fixed and commonly enforced, while in Maryland, the harshest of all the colonies, a ten-to-one penalty was authorized by a law of 1661 and very often enforced to the letter. A habitual runaway, or one who succeeded in getting away for weeks, could win himself a dreary extension of servitude. There was one horrendous case of a maidservant in Anne Arundel County, Maryland, who ran off habitually for short terms, and whose master quietly kept a record, true or false, of her absences. Finally taking her to court, the master rendered an account of 133 accumulated days of absence. Since it was impossible for her to deny her frequent absences, she had no shadow of an answer, and was booked for 1,330 days of extra service.[7] Hers was an unusual but not a singular case: there are recorded penalties of 1,530 days, 2,000 days, and even one of 12,130 days, which the master handsomely commuted to an even five years.[8] Virginia assessed double time, or more if "proportionable to the damages" which could be high in tobacco-harvesting time, plus an additional punishment, more commonly inflicted in the seventeenth than

7. Ibid., 268–9.
8. Morris, 452.

the eighteenth century, of corporal punishment. On the
eve of the Revolution, Negro slavery had largely replaced
indentures in the tidewater plantations but indentures
were still important on the accessible and inviting edges
of settlement, and there runaways became a critical problem. In South Carolina, where fear of insurrection had
been a dominant motive, a law of 1691 had authorized a
week's extra service for a day of absence, and for absences
that ran as long as a week, a year for a week—a fifty-two-
to-one ratio that made Maryland seem relaxed. In 1744
the week-for-a-day ratio was still kept, but the maximum
penalty was set at a year's service. Whipping was also
routine.

The problem of preventing and punishing runaways
was complicated by what was held to be the "pirating" of
labor by competing employers—and it became necessary
to establish a whole series of penalties for enticing or dis-
tracting indentured labor. Plainly, if neighbors could
entice bound laborers from their owners for occasional or
even permanent service by offering money or promising
better treatment, a rudimentary subterranean labor market would begin to replace servitude, and property in
servants would become increasingly hazardous. Pirating
was not taken lightly in the law, and enticers of labor
were subject to personal damage suits as well as to criminal prosecution, with sentences ranging from whipping
or sitting in the stocks to fines. The penalties were so
heavy in the tobacco colonies that law-abiding planters
might even hesitate to feed or shelter a servant who had
apparently been deserted by his master. Indeed, innkeep-
ers in these colonies were often fined simply for entertaining or selling liquor to servants. Suits for damages for
brief enticements were hardly worth the trouble in the

case of servants whose work was valued at a few pence a
day. But in New York a skilled cabinetmaker and chair
carver indentured in 1761 was lured away by a com-
petitor at frequent intervals, and a few years later his
master won a smashing judgment of £128.[9]

Plots hatched by several servants to run away together
occurred mostly in the plantation colonies, and the few
recorded servant uprisings were entirely limited to those
colonies. Virginia had been forced from its very earliest
years to take stringent steps against mutinous plots, and
severe punishments for such behavior were recorded. Most
servant plots occurred in the seventeenth century: a con-
templated uprising was nipped in the bud in York County
in 1661; apparently led by some left-wing offshoots of the
Great Rebellion, servants plotted an insurrection in Gloucester County in 1663, and four leaders were condemned
and executed; some discontented servants apparently
joined Bacon's Rebellion in the 1670's. In the 1680's the
planters became newly apprehensive of discontent among
the servants "owing to their great necessities and want of
clothes," and it was feared they would rise up and plunder
the storehouses and ships; in 1682 there were plant-cutting
riots in which servants and laborers, as well as some
planters, took part.

By the eighteenth century, either because of the relaxed
security of the indenture system or the increasing effectiveness of the authorities, disturbances were infrequent,
although in 1707 a gang of runaways planned to seize
military stores, burn Annapolis, steal a ship, and set up as
pirates, but were stopped. Again in 1721 a band of convict servants conspired unsuccessfully to seize military

9. Ibid., 416–29, esp. 421–3.

stores at Annapolis. An insurrection of some consequence did actually break out among white servants under the British regime in East Florida during the summer of 1768, when three hundred Italians and Greeks in that very heterogeneous colony revolted against hard work and stern treatment, seized the arms and ammunition in the storehouse, and prepared to set sail from a ship at anchor in the river at New Smyrna. They were intercepted by a government vessel and promptly surrendered. Three leaders were convicted of piracy, one of whom was pardoned on condition that he execute his two comrades. Discontent and dissension, reaching into the local elite, were still rife in Florida at the time of the Revolution.[1]

A serious threat to the interests of masters, one which gives testimony to the onerousness of servitude, was the possibility of military enlistment. In New England, where there were not many servants, military service was obligatory and seems to have posed no major temptation to escape servitude, but in Pennsylvania and the tobacco colonies, where servants were numerous and essential, the competing demand by the army for manpower in the intercolonial war of the 1740's, and, even more, in the French and Indian War of the 1750's, aroused great anxiety among the masters. In the 1740's, more than a third of the Pennsylvania enlistments were from men in the servant class whose masters were compensated at the colony's expense; in Maryland, during the French and Indian War, Governor Horatio Sharpe reported not only that "servants immediately flocked in to enlist, convicts not excepted," but also that recruits among freemen were extremely scarce, and in Virginia George Washington

---

1. On insurrections, see ibid., 169–81.

urged that servants be allowed to enlist in the Virginia volunteers lest they seize the alternative and join the regular army.[2] The resistance of the Pennsylvania Assembly to enlistments during the 1750's became provocatively stubborn and in Maryland there was armed resistance and rioting against recruitment. Parliament, whose interest it was to increase the army, passed a measure in 1756 authorizing officers to enlist indentured servants regardless of restraining colonial laws or practices. The best that masters could hope for was compensation from their colony's legislature, a practice that was repeated in Pennsylvania in 1763, or suing the recruiting officer for civil damages. During the Revolution, the Continental Congress and some of the states encouraged the enlistment of servants, but Pennsylvania and Maryland exempted them from military service. When despite this recruiting officers in Pennsylvania continued to enlist servants, a group of Cumberland County masters complained with magnificent gall that apprentices and servants "are the property of their masters and mistresses, and every mode of depriving such masters and mistresses of their property is a violation of the rights of mankind. . . ." [3] A good number of servants ran off to the British forces, especially in Virginia, but neither the wars nor the Revolution ended the practice of servitude, which declined but did not die until the nineteenth century.

5

Numerous as are the court records of penalties which lengthened service, most servants did not run afoul of the

2. Ibid., 284n, 286; E. I. McCormac, *White Servitude in Maryland* (1904), 90.
3. Morris, 292; on the enlistment problem generally, see ibid., 278–94; Geiser, 94–101; Smith, 278–84; McCormac, 82–91.

law; their periods of servitude did at last come to an end, entitling them to collect "freedom dues" if they could, and to start in life for themselves. Freedom dues were usually specified by law, but little seems to be known about their payment. Virginia and North Carolina laws of the 1740's required £3 in money, and North Carolina added an adequate suit of clothes. The Crown provided 50 acres of land, free of quitrent for ten years, in South Carolina. A Pennsylvania law of 1700 specified two complete suits of clothes, one of which was to be new, one new ax, one grubbing hoe, and one weeding hoe. Massachusetts long before in the seventeenth century had provided in biblical fashion that servants after seven years' labor should "not be sent away empty," but what this maxim was actually worth to servants is difficult to say. Like the dues of ordinary apprentices, freedom dues may have functioned most importantly as a kind of inducement to servants to carry out in good faith the concluding months and weeks of servitude. Where the labor of a servant was particularly valuable, his master might strengthen that inducement by a cash payment considerably beyond what had been promised.[4]

What was the economic situation of the servant after completing his servitude? It varied, no doubt, from colony to colony, and with the availability of lands. In the mainland colonies, it appears to have been assumed that an ex-servant was to be equipped for work as a free hired man with enough clothes and tools or money to give him a small start. It was assumed that wages for a freeman were high enough to enable him to earn an adequate competence or to provide himself with a plot of land

4. McKee, 95–6.

within a fairly short time. Some ex-servants no doubt went westward and took up new lands. "The inhabitants of our frontiers," wrote Governor Alexander Spotswood of Virginia in 1717, "are composed generally of such as have been transported hither as servants, and being out of their time, settle themselves where land is to be taken up that will produce the necessaries of life with little labour." [5] But it is quite likely that Spotswood erred considerably on the side of optimism. For example, in Maryland, where a freed servant in the seventeenth century was entitled to 50 acres of land upon showing his certificate of freedom at the office of the land office secretary, the records show that relatively few became farmers, though many assumed their land rights and sold them for cash. Abbott E. Smith, in one of the most authoritative studies of colonial servitude, estimates that only one out of ten indentured servants (not including redemptioners) became a substantial farmer and another became an artisan or an overseer in reasonably comfortable circumstances. The other eight, he suggests, either died during servitude, returned to England when it was over, or drifted off to become the "poor whites" of the villages and rural areas. There is reason to think that in most places servants who had completed a term of bondage and had a history of local residence met the prevailing parochial, almost tribal qualifications for poor relief, and were accepted as public charges.[6] Redemptioners, Smith remarks, did a good deal better, but the scrappy evidence that has thus far been found does not yet allow much precision. Sir Henry Moore, governor of New York, thought them so anxious to

5. Smith, 297.
6. See ibid., 251–2.

own land that they made great sacrifices to do so: "As soon as the time stipulated in their indentures is expired, they immediately quit their masters, and get a small tract of land, in settling which for the first three or four years they lead miserable lives, and in the most abject poverty; but all this is patiently borne and submitted to with the greatest cheerfulness, the satisfaction of being land holders smooths every difficulty, and makes them prefer this manner of living to that comfortable subsistence which they could procure for themselves and their families by working at the trades in which they were brought up." [7] An Englishman who traveled in America in the opening years of the nineteenth century noticed "many families, particularly in Pennsylvania, of great respectability both in our society and amongst others, who had themselves come over to this country as redemptioners; or were children of such." [8]

As for the indentured servants, the dismal estimate that only two out of ten may have reached positions of moderate comfort is an attempt to generalize the whole two centuries of the experience of English servitude, taking the seventeenth century when the system was brutal and opportunities were few with the eighteenth, when it became less severe. [9] In the early years more servants returned to England, and mortality was also higher. But it will not do simply to assume that freed servants, especially those from the tobacco fields, were in any mental or physical condition to start vigorous new lives, or that long and ripe years of productivity lay ahead for them. If we

7. McKee, 112–13.
8. Geiser, 108–9.
9. See Smith, 288–9, on later conditions.

consider the whole span of time over which English indentured servitude prevailed, its heavy toll in work and
death is the reality that stands out.

The Horatio Alger mythology has long since been torn
to bits by students of American social mobility, and it will
surprise no one to learn that the chance of emergence
from indentured servitude to a position of wealth or re-
nown was statistically negligible. A few cases to the contrary are treasured by historians, handed down from one
to another like heirlooms—but most of them deal with
Northern servants who came with education or skills. The
two most illustrious colonial names with servitude in their
family histories are Benjamin Franklin and the eminent
Maryland lawyer Daniel Dulany. Franklin's maternal
grandfather, Peter Folger of Nantucket, a man of many
trades from teacher and surveyor to town and court clerk
and interpreter between whites and Indians, had bought
a maidservant for £20 and later married her. Dulany,
who came from a substantial Irish family, arrived in 1703
with two older brothers; the brothers melted into the
anonymity that usually awaited indentured arrivals, but
Daniel was picked up by a lawyer who was pleased to buy
a literate servant with some university training to act as
his clerk and help with his plantation accounts. The closest thing to a modest, American-scale family dynasty to
come out of servitude was that of the New England
Sullivans. John Sullivan and Margery Browne both came
to Maine as indentured servants in the 1720's. After Sullivan earned his freedom he became a teacher, bought
Margery out of servitude, and married her. Their son
John became a lawyer, a Revolutionary patriot, one of
Washington's leading generals, and governor of New
Hampshire. His younger brother, James, also a lawyer,

became a congressman from Massachusetts and in time governor of the state. In the third generation, John's son, George, became a Federalist congressman and the attorney general of New Hampshire; James's son, William, pursued a successful legal career in Boston, played a prominent role in state politics, and was chosen to be one of the three delegates to take the manifesto of the Hartford Convention to Washington. John Lamb, a leader of the Sons of Liberty and later an officer in the Revolution, was the son of Anthony Lamb who had followed an improbable career: an apprentice instrument maker in London, Anthony became involved with a notorious burglar who ended on the gallows at Tyburn; as a first offender, Lamb was sentenced to be transported, served out an indenture in Virginia, moved to New York, and became a reputable instrument maker and a teacher of mathematics, surveying, and navigation. Charles Thomson, one of six children orphaned by the death of their father on shipboard in 1739, began his American life as an indentured servant and became a teacher in Philadelphia, a merchant, a Revolutionary patriot, and Secretary of the Continental Congress. Matthew Thornton, whose parents came to Maine in the Scotch-Irish emigration of 1718, began life under indenture, became a physician, a patriot leader in New Hampshire, and a signer of the Declaration of Independence. Matthew Lyon, who won notoriety as a peppery Republican congressman from Vermont and as a victim of the Sedition Act, emigrated from Ireland in 1765 and paid off his passage by three years of indentured service on farms in Connecticut before he bought his own farm in Vermont. And there were others, brands snatched from the burning, triumphs of good fortune or strong character over the probabilities.

6

Thoreau, brooding over the human condition in the relatively idyllic precincts of Concord and Walden Pond, was
convinced that the mass of men lead lives of quiet desperation. His conviction quickens to life again when we
contemplate the human costs of what historians sometimes lightly refer to as the American experiment. It is
true that thousands came to the colonies in search of
freedom or plenty and with a reasonably good chance of
finding them, and that the colonies harbored a force of
free white workers whose wages and conditions might
well have been the envy of their European counterparts.
Yet these fortunate men were considerably outnumbered
by persons, white or black, who came to America in one
kind of servitude or another. It is also true that for some
servants, especially for those who already had a skill, a
little cash, or some intelligence or education or gentility,
servitude in America might prove not a great deal worse
than an ordinary apprenticeship, despite the special tribu-
lations and hazards it inflicted. But when one thinks of
the great majority of those who came during the long
span of time between the first settlements and the disappearance of white servitude in the early nineteenth
century—bearing in mind the poverty and the ravaged
lives which they left in Europe, the cruel filter of the Atlantic crossing, the high mortality of the crossing and
the seasoning, and the many years of arduous toil that lay
between the beginning of servitude and the final realization of tolerable comfort—one is deeply impressed by the
measure to which the sadness that is natural to life was
overwhelmed in the condition of servitude by the stark

miseries that seem all too natural to the history of the poor. For a great many the journey across the Atlantic proved in the end to have been only an epitome of their journey through life. And yet there must have seemed to be little at risk because there was so little at stake. They had so often left a scene of turbulence, crime, exploitation, and misery that there could not have been much hope in most of them; and as they lay in their narrow bedsteads listening to the wash of the rank bilge water below them, sometimes racked with fever or lying in their own vomit, few could have expected very much from American life, and those who did were too often disappointed. But with white servants we have only begun to taste the anguish of the early American experience.

CHAPTER III

The
Slave Trade

1

THE largest stream of immigration into the thirteen colonies at mid-century was that of black slaves. Although slavery had taken a firm legal and social form in the colonies before the end of the seventeenth century, in 1700 its economic role was still minute. We have no complete records of slaves and free Negroes, but for a period when well over 95 per cent of Negroes in America were slaves, the number of Negroes gives a rough measure of the slave population. But how many Negroes were there? Colonial population figures are still in a nebulous state, especially for the period before the 1760's, and those now set down with deceptive finality in the census volume, *Historical Statistics of the United States*, will someday undergo substantial revision. They now show a Negro population for all the colonies of about 28,000 in 1700. But since it has been pointed out by Wesley Frank Craven that this total includes an estimate for Virginia that may exaggerate by as much as 7,000 or more, the whole number may be much too high.[1] If, however, in the absence of more certain data

1. Wesley Frank Craven, *The Colonies in Transition* (1968), 290.

we tentatively accept the 28,000 estimate, it would represent 11 per cent of the whole population. By 1770, the black portion of the population, standing at 21.8 per cent, was at its highest in American history. Over seventy years the black percentage had roughly doubled, and the whole Negro population had grown to 459,000.

Before American slavery is examined, it is important to see hemispheric slavery as a whole. The growth of slavery in the English mainland colonies was only a small part of an immense world historic process in which over a span of three centuries African kings and chieftains, Portuguese, Spanish, Genoese, English, French, Dutch, and Danish slave traders, Yankee merchants from the Northern colonies, Portuguese, Spanish, English, Dutch, and French planters in Latin America and the Caribbean islands, and the planters of the rice and tobacco colonies of the North American continent were all knit together in a far-flung fraternity of the unfraternal, engaged in the business of creating, supplying, and exploiting a vast empire of slavery in the New World. The plantations of the Western Hemisphere and the slave trade were the foundation of the colonial industry and the commerce of the European nations in the eighteenth century, and the slave trade itself was a central factor in their domestic economies and their political life, a major piece on the international chessboard of diplomacy and war.

The North American colonies were only on the fringes of the immense South Atlantic system of slave trading and slave exploitation, which was mainly an affair of Central and South America and the sugar islands of the Caribbean. The precise dimensions of the slave trade are unknown, but the most educated guess, which has emerged from the impressive researches of Philip Curtin, is that over the cen-

turies of the slave trade the territory of the United States
received less than 5 per cent of all slaves brought to the
Western Hemisphere. The primary development of Negro
slavery took place in tropical America, starting with Brazil
in the late sixteenth century and proceeding into the
Caribbean where it reached its peak two hundred years
later. During the forced migration of the staggering numbers of persons required to man the plantations, the largest
intercontinental migration before the era of modern industry, about 9 to 10 million Africans, according to Curtin,
were brought to the New World. Of these the thirteen
colonies and later the United States took only a small
part—probably less than 400,000, surely not more than
500,000.[2]

Europeans had an almost insatiable demand for tropical
staples—for cocoa, coffee, cotton, and above all, early and
late, for sugar—and had the physical power to seize the
land and to conscript the labor to produce them. There
were barriers to this production in Africa that were sur-
mounted in the Western Hemisphere. Tropical America
not only had better agricultural land than Africa, but it had
a climate in which whites, though at some toll in mortality,
could live and manage plantations. It was commonly believed that only blacks could do heavy labor in the hot
climates of the sugar islands and the Deep South; yet the
real limiting factor was not, as men then thought, climatic
but medical and epidemiological. When European whites,
African blacks, and New World Indians met in the Western Hemisphere, they all entered into a new disease environment with different relative immunities. The mortality of the Europeans themselves in the disease climates

2. Philip Curtin, *The Atlantic Slave Trade: A Census* (1969), 88–9.

of the Western Hemisphere was well below the forbidding rates experienced by soldiers and sailors in Africa. The Indian natives, who had had contact with few epidemic diseases, were the most vulnerable: they were decimated at a horrendous rate, and the possibility of continuing New World production with their labor was cut off by vast strokes of natural catastrophe. Smallpox, typhus, and measles carried Indians off on such an appalling scale that the indigenous population of the Spanish colonies, which at the beginning of European contact may have been as much as 50 million, fell to about 4 million in the seventeenth century, after which it once again began to rise.[3]

While the natives were being decimated, Europeans looked more and more to Africa as a source of labor. The Africans, living on the fringes of European and Mediterranean society, had acquired some immunity both to Old World temperate diseases and to Old World tropical diseases. Hence, even though their toll in transit and upon arrival was quite high, it was actually somewhat lower than that of Europeans migrating to the tropical New World who had almost no immunity to malaria and yellow fever. In consequence of their comparative hardihood and the ability of African kingdoms to deliver substantial numbers of slaves to European traders on the west coast of Africa, there developed a great intercontinental system in which a huge labor supply was brought from tropical Africa to tropical America, where it was supervised and controlled by white planters and overseers, administrators and soldiers.[4]

3. Charles Gibson, *Spain in America* (1966), 116–17; *cf.* 63–4.
4. Philip Curtin, "Epidemiology and the Slave Trade," *Political Science Quarterly*, 83 (1968), 190–216.

2

The first African slave traders were Arabs and Moors who, contrary to the notions of modern ideologues, showed no tenderness for their neighbors to the south. After they spread across North Africa during the eighth century, they developed a rich trade across the Sahara in pepper, gold, palm oil, ivory, and slaves bought from native traders in Timbuktu and other market centers, driven northward in coffles hundreds of miles along caravan trails marked by skeletons, across burning deserts and icy mountaintops, and delivered to Mediterranean ports. This, one of the most callous and murderous phases of the slave trade, long supplied the Mediterranean Basin, Asia Minor, and Turkey with black slaves; indeed, far into the nineteenth century, and even in the early twentieth, long after the European slavers had at last been suppressed, Arab slavers were still plying their trade.[5]

The European phases of the slave trade began with the Portuguese, who, as they edged their way down the west coast of Africa, established economic contacts with African tribes. About the middle of the sixteenth century and after, Portuguese control of African trade was challenged by traders from Holland, England, France, Sweden, and Brandenburg. By the end of the sixteenth century a trade of some regularity had been established, and at a rough estimate perhaps 125,000 slaves had been imported into Spanish America and Brazil.[6]

In the early seventeenth century, as the African trade proliferated, Englishmen entered it, and in 1663 an English

5. Archibald Lewis, *Naval Power and Trade in the Mediterranean, A.D. 500–1100* (1951); Christopher Lloyd, *The Navy and the Slave Trade* (1968); Jerome Dowd, "Slavery and the Slave Trade in Africa," *Journal of Negro History*, II (1917), 1–20.
6. Curtin, *The Atlantic Slave Trade*, 116.

company, the Company of Royal Adventurers of England Trading to Africa, was founded. Its trading posts were lost in the second Dutch War, 1664–5, when the Dutch swooped down on the Guinea Coast and captured all but one of the English centers. The English did not give up the slave trade, however, but began building new African forts, and in 1672 founded the Royal African Company which, in return for a monopoly of the trade, undertook to maintain the posts. In 1698, in response to the clamor from planters in the sugar islands for more and cheaper Negroes, the Royal African Company's monopoly was dissolved and, as Eric Williams put it, "the right of a free trade in slaves was recognized as a fundamental and natural right of Englishmen." [7]

Up to the time the Royal African Company was founded, the slave trade to the colonies of the English North American mainland was negligible, although during the first half of the seventeenth century Dutch New Amsterdam, the chief North American slaving port, was thriving. After the founding of the Royal African Company in 1672 the slave trade to the English mainland colonies began to grow, but the great boom began after the 1713 Treaty of Utrecht, in which England won the *asiento*, the monopoly of the Spanish slave trade which the Spaniards, who did relatively little slave trading for themselves, awarded to others.

It seems appropriate that the guinea, a coin identified with luxury trades in Britain and until recently the standard unit of price for elite goods, took its name from the Guinea Coast. The slave trade had a large if incalculable part in the prosperity of eighteenth-century England, as the lush

7. Eric Williams, *Capitalism and Slavery* (1944), 32.

profits from growing sugar and selling slaves spilled over into banking, insurance, textiles, and heavy industry. The ports of London, Liverpool, and Bristol were deeply involved in the slave trade by the early years of the century, and by the 1760's the prosperity of Liverpool, whose ships carried more than half the English part of the trade, was commonly thought to rest on the slavers. It was reported that an actor there, hissed for appearing drunk on the stage, recovered his dignity, drew himself up, and announced: "I have not come here to be insulted by a set of wretches, every brick in whose infernal town is cemented with an African's blood." [8]

Although slave trading was less important for the economies of the Northern colonies than of England, they too took to it, and early in the century Yankee slavers, operating chiefly out of Newport and Bristol in Rhode Island and in much smaller volume out of Boston, Salem, and Providence, with a sprinkling of vessels out of Portsmouth, New London, and New York, entered the business. In the main, they supplied the West Indies rather than the mainland; the vast majority of slaves brought to American shores came in British hulls. Yet if colonials held only a marginal place in the North American slave trade, the trade itself was more than marginal to the growing fortunes of many Northern traders, distillers, and shipbuilders.

The West Indies was the hub of the commerce of the Northern colonies. American traders went only in limited numbers to the Guinea Coast, where they had to compete with the English and the French; they usually preferred to engage in the less dangerous and less speculative trade to southern Europe, the Wine Islands, and above all to the

8. Quoted in ibid., 63.

West Indies and colonial coastal ports. Still, many ships cleared Newport or Bristol with a combined cargo of the best grade of fish for Mediterranean Europe and rum for the Guinea trade, where a prime male worker could be bought for about one hundred gallons. Rum was considered essential for befuddling the African traders. The slaves would then be sold in the West Indies, whence the ships would head home with a cargo of molasses for the distilleries of Rhode Island and Massachusetts and some bills of credit drawn on London. However, all slave traders considered carrying slaves incidental to the larger commerce of selling colonial timber, fish, rum, meat, and grain products, in return for molasses to make rum and coin to pay their English trade balances. It was above all the West Indies that paid off, and many a Northern ship that never saw the Guinea Coast cleared regularly for the Caribbean carrying refuse fish for slaves, along with timber and a variety of foodstuffs, and returned with heavy cargoes of sugar and molasses and light cargoes of slaves. Stop-offs might be made at Charles Town or the Virginia estuaries, where in the course of other trading the slaves would be sold, a few choice domesticated West Indian Negroes being reserved for Northern markets, where they could be sold as domestics or artisans.

Newport, the leading slave port, had at mid-century perhaps as many as 170 vessels, or roughly half its merchant fleet, engaged in slaving. Rev. Samuel Hopkins, one of the first Congregational ministers to denounce slavery, charged in 1787 that Newport had been "built up and flourished in times past" on this trade and that by it the inhabitants had "gotten most of their wealth and riches." [9] The Rhode

9. John R. Spears, *The American Slave Trade* (1900), 20.

Island rum-and-slaves traffic yielded £40,000 a year for re-
mittances to England.[1] In 1768, when 97,000 blacks were
estimated to have been taken from Africa by Europeans,
they were carried as follows: 53,000 in British vessels,
23,500 in French, 11,300 in Dutch, 6,300 in American, and
small numbers carried by Portuguese and Danes.[2] Of the
American total Rhode Island doubtless had by far the
major share.

American slavers were among the smallest and least
seaworthy in the trade, with exceptionally little headroom
for the slaves. Shipowners believed that small ships were
more profitable than large ones—certainly they did provide a way of spreading the risks—and most of the colonial vessels engaged in the trade were of about forty or
fifty tons, or about one-third the size of typical British
slavers. They were commonly manned by crews of no
more than nine, including the master, who sailed with the
anxious knowledge that if sickness ran through his small
crew there might not be enough able-bodied men to secure his ship against mutiny. Many of these ships were
cheaply built and barely seaworthy. "We can see daylight
all round her bow under deck," wrote the master of the
Sanderson in 1752. "However I hope she will carry me safe
home once more."[3] That she did, and at great profit to her
owners.

In later generations Southern spokesmen liked to portray the eighteenth-century South as having been supplied

1. W. B. Weeden, *Economic and Social History of New England*
(1890), II, 459.
2. Leila Sellers, *Charleston Business on the Eve of the American Revolution* (1934), 124, citing David MacPherson, *Annals of Commerce*, III,
484.
3. Lawrence H. Gipson, *The British Empire before the American
Revolution*, III (rev. edn. 1960), 64; Spears, 23–4, cf. 82–3; cf. also
American Historical Record, I (1872).

with its slaves by Yankee traders, whose hypocritical descendants afterward pilloried the South for the institution their forebears had fastened upon it. The truth is that roughly nine out of ten Negroes imported into the Chesapeake area were imported in British vessels,[4] and probably the same proportion in Charles Town. Of the 10,548 slaves brought into Virginia during the years of 1751–63 only 1,293 came in colonial ships; New England's role in Virginia's slave supply was always small.[5] Moreover, Southern merchants and planters eagerly entered into the trade themselves, rarely by owning ships but commonly by buying an interest in an African voyage in partnership with English merchants. Some Southerners, including members of notable Virginia and Maryland families, regularly received consignments of slaves brought in British ships, using local connections to resell them at a very satisfactory commission. Carolina planters also traded in slaves, notably Henry Laurens, who, though sometimes troubled by the evil of it all, in his later years indignantly denied that he had withdrawn from the trade out of "goodness of heart." It was Laurens who instructed his West Indian correspondents to feed the slaves well and to tell the captain who would bring them to Charles Town "to beat them with humanity and keep up their spirits." [6]

Although some white men raided and kidnapped blacks along the African coast, such violence was neither prudent nor necessary. The vast majority of slaves were bought from native African slavers at or near the West African coast. Whites knew almost nothing about Africa farther

---

4. Arthur P. Middleton, *Tobacco Coast* (1953), 136.
5. Ibid., 137–8.
6. Sellers, 146, 144. *Cf.* the letters of Laurens reprinted in Elizabeth Donnan, ed., *Documents Illustrative of the Slave Trade* (1965), IV.

than fifty or a hundred miles into the interior, and for the most part the European trading companies were content to operate from coastal forts to which the efficiently organized African societies were capable of delivering a steady supply of slaves. Before the arrival of Europeans the peoples of West Africa had lived under a number of remarkable empires of considerable diversity. Many of these peoples were pastoral, some were agricultural; they fished, they traded extensively, they developed skilled craftsmen, well-articulated codes of law, and highly sophisticated sculpture and music. Some African cities, such as Benin, Djenné, and Timbuktu, were complex societies, particularly Timbuktu, which was a notable center of Muslim learning. But the Africans had not developed their own written languages, and their isolation from Europe, protective though it was, shut them off from the scientific thought and mechanical invention of the early modern world. Their great cities were built of clay and wood, and in time they crumbled; a considerable portion of their history and institutional lore was lost for lack of records; their artifacts were carried off to museums. In the early contacts of the sixteenth and seventeenth centuries, however, some of the white men who did business with them were, for all their ethnocentrism, deeply impressed by African culture.

Africa had a system or systems of slavery long before white men came to the Guinea Coast, and had regularly enslaved war captives and criminals. Once the European trade opened, the profits to be made from a large external slave market provoked more wars and instigated more rigorous punishment of crime by native chiefs.[7] Other persons sold themselves or their families for food during

7. Donnan, II, 396; Thomas Buxton, *The African Slave Trade* (1840), 52–9.

famine, or were kidnapped by native gangs. Many native kings ran profitable slave businesses, and responded eagerly to opportunities for greater profits. The slave trade became a recognized and entirely legal form of business in Africa.

Moreover, the Africans took to guns and gunpowder with a rapidity which, while lamentable in many respects, was highly self-protective in others. Africans had no more impulse toward racial solidarity than Europeans did toward Christian unity. But three things stood between the Africans and those voracious white territorial conquests to which they would succumb at last in the nineteenth century. The first was their facility with firearms, which enabled African kings to charge Europeans substantial rents for permission to build trading forts, yet deny them the power to dominate any more land than the immediate territories around the forts. In 1693, for example, the soldiers of Akwamu seized the Danish fort of Christiansborg in Accra, held it for a year, and returned it to the Danes only for a substantial ransom in gold. The second, and perhaps most formidable, protection was tropical disease—yellow fever, malaria, dengue—which gave to portions of Africa the name of "white man's grave." The third was the slave trade itself: it was labor, not territory, that the whites wanted from Africa, and the African kings, through their commissioned merchants, were usually pleased to sell laborers, accustomed as they were to selling, exchanging, and sometimes giving away their own slaves. At the beginning they probably did not know what they were selling their slaves into, and in the end apparently did not much care. The slave trade, which corrupted everyone connected with it, soon became a systematic, entirely legal, and largely amicable business, in which the Europeans in return for slaves and ivory brought to Africa rum, guns, gunpowder, iron and copper, jewelry and trinkets, swords, knives, kitchen-ware, cheap cotton fabrics, and expensive Asian silks.

White men, confined to coastal areas, rarely saw or knew much about the African interior from which most slaves were supplied. Slave-trading tribes penetrated deep into the interior, waging wars which were hardly more than slave-raising expeditions. Coffles of slaves were driven to market in shackles, sometimes over very long distances. Mungo Park, the famous Scottish explorer, once made his way out of the deep interior by attaching himself to a coffle of thirty-five slaves being driven about 550 miles by several native merchants to a post on the Gambia River. His account of this journey is impressive not for the cruelty of the human agents but for the rigors of the experience in itself. The slaves, fettered to each other, were afraid of being eaten; although attempts were made to cheer them and give them diversion and relief, many were often sunk in melancholy. During the journey everyone in the party, slave or free, suffered great fatigue, was plagued by brown ants, tormented by blistered feet, and burned by the sun. A woman and a girl broke down with fatigue, were se-verely whipped for it, and began eating clay, perhaps as an attempt at suicide. Raiding a beehive for honey, everyone in the party was badly stung, one woman so severely that she stiffened, was unable to walk, and, after the others made some efforts to carry her, was abandoned by the merchants to the wild animals, despite pleas from her companions that her throat be cut. The coffle passed through many villages, and saw the charred ruins of two that had been burned in wars. They hid in the tall grass to escape from a pack of marauders, and after a second such encounter the leaders hired mercenaries to protect them.

At last, after seven weeks, the slaves were delivered to the trading post, the next phase of their ordeal.[8]

On arriving at the coastal trading posts, slaves were examined by physicians, selected, branded with the mark of the company that bought them, and then marched to the beach. Many of those coming from the distant interior had never seen the ocean, and were terrified by the pounding of the surf and the sight of the strange and coarse white traders and the tall masts of the waiting ships. Members of some tribes, believing with a certain sense for metaphorical truth that the white men were cannibals who would eat them, were thrown into a state of terror. Desperately they threw themselves on the beach, clawed at the sands of their own land, attempted at times to strangle themselves, and had to be whipped, beaten, pushed, and dragged into the canoes which would carry them through the rough surf to the ships. One captain reported: "The negroes are so wilful and loth to leave their country, that they have often leaped out of the canoes, boat and ship, into the sea, and kept under water till they were drowned, to avoid being taken up and saved by our boats, which pursued them; they having a more dreadful apprehension of Barbadoes than we can have of hell, tho' in reality they live much better there than in their own country. . . . We have likewise seen divers of them eaten by sharks, of which a prodigious number kept about the ships in this place, and I have been told will follow her hence to Barbadoes, for the dead negroes that are thrown overboard in the passage."[9]

---

8. Mungo Park, *Travels in the Interior Districts of Africa* (2nd edn., 1799), chapters 24–6.
9. Daniel Mannix and Malcolm Cowley, *Black Cargoes* (1962), 47–8; *cf.* 87.

Once secured on board, the slaves began the next part
of their ordeal, the Middle Passage, so called because the
voyage from the Guinea Coast to the West Indies was the
middle leg of the triangular trade. Here one has to imagine
the situation of slaves—often separated from every human
connection they had known since birth and half convinced
that they were being taken off to be eaten—shackled in
pairs, hand to hand and wrist to wrist, and packed on bare
and abrasive wooden floors into sleeping spaces that left
them less room than a corpse has in a coffin. Except for
moments of feeding and exercise, the men were kept in
the hold; women were often permitted to go on deck,
where, if the captain so allowed, they were fair game for
the crew. A mercantile company might instruct: "Be careful of and kind to your Negroes and let them be well used
by your officers and seamen." [1] But captains were frequently incompetent, and the circumstances of the trade
tended to undermine their humanity and morale. They
were also faced with a tremendous hygienic problem for
which they had no solution: was it better to pack slaves
tightly and risk higher mortality or to pack them loosely
and count on arriving with a higher proportion alive?
Cupidity and tight packing usually won. Slaves were
jammed together back to face like spoons in a drawer, or
sometimes virtually sitting in each other's laps. Extra
shelves were attached to the holds of some ships which
cut headroom to the point at which slaves could not sit
up. Relief from these cramped positions was given only
twice a day in good weather when the slaves could be
fed on deck; in bad weather they were fed in the holds.
Since feeding times were the most likely moments of

1. Donnan, II, 371.

mutiny, those of the sailors who were not busy distributing food would stand throughout the mealtime with lighted matches at guns loaded with small shot and trained on the slaves.

Lassitude and despondency as well as disease threatened the safe delivery of a cargo. The sensitive Ibos were particularly noted for falling into suicidal despondency. As a supposed remedy for both despondency and scurvy, forced dancing was inflicted after the morning meal, a bleak ritual in which sailors snapped cat-o'-nine-tails at the slaves, who jumped and bounced in irons which tore at their flesh. Sometimes the slaves were also ordered to sing, and they responded with songs laden with melancholy. The task of keeping the hold at all clean was revolting to the crews but indispensable to the operation. While some sailors were supervising the slaves on deck, others were sent below to air, scrape, and wash the slave quarters, and douse them with large quantities of vinegar. The problem of toileting was never very satisfactorily solved. Some captains attempted to provide latrines of a kind. Dr. Alexander Falconbridge, a ship's surgeon, reported: "In each of the apartments are placed three or four large buckets, of a conical form, near two feet in diameter at the bottom and only one foot at the top, and in depth about twenty-eight inches, to which, when necessary, the negroes have recourse. It often happens that those who are placed at a distance from the buckets, in endeavouring to get to them, tumble over their companions, in consequence of their being shackled. These incidents, although unavoidable, are productive of continual quarrels in which some of them are always bruised. In this distressed situation, unable to proceed and prevented from getting to the tubs, they desist from the attempt, and as the necessities of nature are not to be repelled, ease themselves as they lie." [2] Some captains did not even bother to clean up the accumulated filth, leaving their slaves to wallow in their own dung until the voyage was over.

The worst moments came in bad weather when the portholes had to be shut. On such occasions, Falconbridge recalled: "I frequently went down among them till at length their apartments became so extremely hot as to be sufferable for a very short time. But the excessive heat was not the only thing that rendered their situation intolerable. The deck, that is, the floor of their rooms, was so covered with the blood and mucus which had proceeded from them in consequence of the flux, that it resembled a slaughterhouse. It was not in the power of the human imagination to picture to itself a situation more dreadful or disgusting. Numbers of the slaves having fainted, they were carried upon deck, where several of them died and the rest were, with great difficulty, restored. It had nearly proved fatal to me also. The climate was too warm to admit the wearing of any clothing but a shirt, and that I had pulled off before I went down; notwithstanding which, by only continuing among them for about a quarter of an hour, I was so overcome with the heat, stench and foul air, that I nearly fainted; and it was not without assistance that I could get upon deck. The consequence was, that I soon fell sick of the same disorder, from which I did not recover for several months." [3]

The suicidal impulse among the slaves had constantly to be combated. Some slaves believed that on their death they would be returned to their country and their friends.

2. Alexander Falconbridge, *An Account of the Slave Trade on the Coast of Africa* (1788), 25–6.
3. Ibid., 32.

On one voyage in 1788 the captain learned that the slaves were expressing this desire; he therefore hinted that they would be beheaded when dead and would return headless. The slaves were brought on deck to witness the beheading of a corpse. One wrenched himself loose, rushed overboard, and went down into the sea. A surgeon on one slaver reported that a woman found some rope yarn with which she strangled herself. On another a male slave tried to cut his throat, and when the surgeon sewed up the wound, tore out the sutures and attempted to cut his throat again; the second wound was repaired and his hands were tied, but the man refused food and starved himself to death in a little more than a week. Attempts at self-starvation were so common that a sort of clamp was devised with which the mouth of the slave could be pried open and food poured into the gullet through a funnel.

When one considers the odds against successful mutinies and the precautions taken to prevent them, the number and ferocity of revolts on shipboard, especially near the Guinea Coast, are ample testimony that the Africans did not go docilely into transatlantic slavery. There are circumstantial records of fifty-five mutinies between 1699 and 1845, and references to scores of others.[4] The odds, of course, were heavily against the slaves. On the high seas mutiny was futile if not suicidal, since the slaves knew nothing about navigation. Only near the shore, should they succeed in killing the crew, did they have a chance to drift ashore in the ship by cutting its anchor cables. Even if they could swim to shore the odds were against them. Captain William Snelgrave, who saw several mutinies, recalled one in which those slaves who had not already

---

4. Harvey Wish, "American Slave Insurrections before 1861," *Journal of Negro History,* 22 (1937), 300–6; Mannix and Cowley, 108–12.

jumped overboard were warned that to reach the shore would be of no use to them because their own countrymen would only catch them and sell them to other ships. This truth was enough to quiet them for a time.[5]

One captain gave his slaves knives to eat their meat which they used to hack pieces of iron from the forecastle door and to break their shackles; they then killed the guard at the hatchway entrance and launched a battle which cost twenty-eight of them their lives. On another occasion in 1790, an English slave ship went to the help of a French vessel on which slaves had hidden while it was at anchor. By the time the English seamen in their boats reached the French ship there were one hundred slaves in control of the deck and others coming up from the hatches. When the English reached the decks, the slaves fought furiously. "I could not but admire," reported an English survivor, "the courage of a fine young black who, though his partner in irons lay dead at his feet, would not surrender but fought with his billet of wood until a ball finished his existence. The others fought as well as they could but what could they do against firearms?" [6]

Even a greater hazard to the trade was disease, which if it began among the slave cargo spread to the crewmen as well. No one knows the entire toll of lives lost in the slave trade, but the total would have to embrace the great numbers of enslaved blacks and enslaving whites who died of disease on shipboard. Some information on losses at sea is available. Men weakened by scurvy sickened with yellow fever, malaria, dengue, blackwater fever, amoebic dysentery, smallpox, measles, ophthalmic infections, and venereal diseases, from any or all of which a captain might

5. William Snelgrave, *A New Account of Guinea and the Slave Trade* (1754), 171.
6. Mannix and Cowley, 110–11.

lose half or more of his cargo in transit. The captain of the *Briton* was warned by his surgeon that smallpox had been brought aboard by the last slave loaded into the cargo. The captain refused to believe it, and, in the words of an observer on the voyage, smallpox "soon broke out amongst the slaves. I have seen the platform one continued scab. We hauled up eight or ten slaves dead of a morning. The flesh and skin peeled off their wrists when taken hold of, being entirely mortified." [7]

3

Eric Williams, the black Marxist historian, has written that "the 'horrors' of the Middle Passage have been exaggerated." [8] Although it is hard to see how the horrors of the psychic experience can be much exaggerated, he is probably right about the rate of death in transit as a matter of comparative mortality. Not only have the losses been exaggerated by some writers, but the necessary comparisons with the mortality of slave ship crews and of such other victims of the crossing as indentured servants are not usually made. In fact, average mortality among crews appears to have been somewhat greater than that among slaves and that of transported convicts quite comparable. Figures are lacking on indentured servants, but their losses are known to have been quite high.

Scholars' estimates of slave mortality during the Middle Passage have run as high as one-quarter or one-third of the cargo to as low as 13 per cent. What limited samples we have strongly suggest that time was an important factor, since losses fell quite steadily during the eighteenth and nineteenth centuries. A sample of mortality on slavers of

7. Ibid., 122.
8. Williams, 34.

the Royal African Company from 1680 to 1688 shows a
mean loss in transit of 23.4 per cent. Two samples a century
later give 8.7 per cent and 17 per cent. A substantial sample
of French traders operating out of Nantes between 1748
and 1792 showed 15.2 per cent mortality, which equals the
estimated figure for white convicts during transportation.
Among ships known to the British Foreign Office during
the years of illegal trade 1817–43, there was a mean loss
of 9.1 per cent. Among other things, the duration of the
voyage correlates closely with mortality. The high death
rate per voyage among the crews reflects the vulnerability
of white men to the tropical disease environment, a fact
demonstrated by the contemporaneous mortality records
of military units posted in the tropics, and with records of
Europeans at the trading posts on the Gulf of Guinea.
There, among newly arrived Europeans, a death rate of
about 50 per cent in the first year of residence was common. A slave trader from Nantes, the *Marie Gabrielle*, lost
thirty-one sailors out of thirty-nine on a voyage of 1769.[9]
And when crews were depleted by disease, the slaves knew
their chances of successful mutiny had increased.

The multiple dangers to seamen are illustrated in an account written from Barbados by the captain of the *Rain-
bow* to her Liverpool owners reporting a voyage of 1757–8.
On a fifty-two-day voyage from the African coast, the
captain wrote, "I have buried all my officers, except my first
and third mates and gunner. Having lost since left Liverpool, 25 white people and 44 negroes. The negroes rose on
us after we left St. Thomas's [São Tomé]; they killed my
linguister [interpreter] whom I got at Benin, and we then
secured them without farther loss. We have an account of

9. Curtin, *The Atlantic Slave Trade*, 275–86.

five privateers being to windward of Barbadoes, by a re-
taken vessel brought in here this day, so that we shall run
a great risk when we leave Barbadoes." [1]

Such was the nature of this enterprise: always in danger
from privateers and pirates; an internal routine of hard
bargaining and hard drinking on the Guinea Coast, of
disease and mutiny, of brandings, whippings, beheadings,
and suicides. The dehumanization of captains and crews
was predictable, and made the trade gratuitously cruel for
its ultimate victims, the slaves. There were, to be sure, in-
teresting and exceptional men in the business like the
surgeon Falconbridge, whose account of the trade, written
after his decision to fight it, is one of the best sources of
our knowledge of it; or Captain Hugh Crow, who somehow commanded the respect and loyalty of both crews and
slaves, who delivered one cargo without a single loss of
life, and boasted that he could do so repeatedly; or the
foulmouthed and sententious John Newton, who abandoned the trade after nine years, underwent a conversion,
became rector of St. Mary Woolnoth and a friend of the
abolitionist William Wilberforce, and during his slaving
days wrote a famous hymn, "How Sweet the Name of Jesus
Sounds." It was Newton who said: "I know of no method
of getting money, not even that of robbing for it, upon the
highway, which has a more direct tendency to efface the
moral sense, to rob the heart of every gentle and humane
disposition, to harden it, like steel, against all impressions
of sensibility." [2]

Service in the slave trade was not a thing men usually
chose to do. All maritime work was hard, but the slave
trade was the worst not simply because of its threats to

1. Mannix and Cowley, 133.
2. John Newton, *Thoughts Upon the African Slave Trade* (1788), 14.

life but because the captains, tyrannical on all ships of
the time, were of necessity most absolute here. Crews were
mustered from men down on their luck, adventurers, kid-
nappees and escapees, scapegraces and dimwits, and slaving fed whatever tendencies toward the perverse that
were brought to it. Hugh Crow, humane though he was
with his sailors by the standards of the time, thought them
"the very dregs of the community," [3] said they were frequently insubordinate and often wholly untrained to the
ways of the sea. Still, this was a way of life worse than
anyone deserved, and in the end the human toll among the
crews was one of the most persuasive arguments used by
the British crusaders against the trade. Crews' rations were
sometimes poorer and leaner than those doled out to the
slaves, and there are records of instances when crewmen
cadged handouts from kindly blacks. Beatings with the
cat-o'-nine-tails, which cut out bits of flesh and left unmistakable scars, were common, and some captains used
salt to exacerbate the wounds. One crippled captain, a
nightmare figure, tore at the flesh of sailors with his finger-
nails as he was carried past them, and would order men to
be flogged at his bedstead so that he could record the pain
in their faces. After scenes of such force and cruelty, re-
venge could be wreaked upon the slaves by crewmen
whose inhibitions, such as they were, were often broken
down by drink. Yet for the seamen themselves life in the
Guinea trade was so rough that impressment into the rigorous service of a man-of-war, should it befall them, was
welcomed as a way out. One final recourse was to jump
ship: as black men ran away from slavery, white men ran
away from the slave trade.

3. Mannix and Cowley, 142.

CHAPTER IV

✥

Black
Slavery

1

W̲E now turn from the vast theater of the South Atlantic system to the small corner occupied by the American colonies. Because we are concerned first with the slaves themselves, and slavery in the mainland colonies was primarily a Southern institution, Southern slavery demands our initial attention. In 1760, as colonial slavery was nearing its peak, about 284,000 Negroes lived in the Southern colonies from Maryland to Georgia, while about 41,000 lived in the colonies from Delaware and Pennsylvania northward to Massachusetts and New Hampshire. Nearly 60 per cent of all Negroes worked in the two tobacco colonies, Virginia and Maryland, and nearly 30 per cent in North Carolina, South Carolina, and Georgia. Virginia, with 140,000 Negroes, led all the colonies in absolute numbers, followed by South Carolina and Maryland. In the proportion of blacks to whites, however, South Carolina, being 60 per cent black, was the only province with a Negro majority; Virginia followed with 41 per cent. Georgia and North Carolina were slightly more than one-third black, Maryland slightly less. In the North the only colony with more than one Negro out of ten was New York (13.7 per cent), which was followed by Rhode

Island (7.6 per cent), New Jersey (7 per cent), and Delaware (5.2 per cent). In Pennsylvania and each of the remaining New England colonies blacks numbered only about 2 per cent of the population.

In the course of time a steady stream of slaves, sometimes varying in volume with the state of the market for staples, was brought by slavers to Savannah, Charles Town, Norfolk, and the Patuxent River region in Maryland. In Virginia, some slaves were carried in small vessels well up the tidal rivers and sold directly to planters at their own wharves, others were delivered in the larger vessels of the Bristol traders to commission merchants at Yorktown, Hampton, or Bermuda Hundred, who would then sell them at auction. Most slaves brought to the Northern colonies were reimported from the West Indies, but the vast majority of those brought to the South came directly from Africa.[1] To Africans, stunned by the long ordeal of the Middle Passage, the auctions could only have marked a decrescendo in fright and depression; the first sight of their new homes, the realization that the assurances they had received that they would not be eaten were really true, the glimpses of other blacks who had found a viable pattern of life and labor, must have been at least slightly reassuring. But as one tries to imagine the mental state of the newly arrived Africans, one must think of people still sick, depleted, and depressed by the ordeal of the voyage, the terror of the unknown, the sight of deaths and suicides, and the experience of total helplessness in the hands of others. What they had been and known receded rapidly, and the course of their experience tended to reduce their African identity to the withered husks of dead memories.

1. *Historical Statistics,* Table 2, 281–93 and 294–7.

Many years ago in his *The Myth of the Negro Past,* an inquiry into African survivals in American Negro culture, Melville J. Herskovits tried to show that under slavery the conditions for perpetuating many elements of language, legends, religion, and music were not entirely destroyed. He pointed to a number of cultural survivals that were or could have been of African provenance. But the observation of E. Franklin Frazier, the Negro sociologist, in his classic work *The Negro Family in the United States,* seems more persuasive: "In America there was no social organization to sustain whatever ideas and conceptions of life the Negro slave might have retained of his African heritage." And of the family itself, the primary agency by which this heritage might have been conserved, Frazier concluded: "There is no reliable evidence that African culture has had any influence on its development." [2] African survivals, in fact, were more commonly to be observed in Latin America and the Caribbean islands, where the depletion of the slave population was so rapid that a constant heavy influx of new captives kept a fresh awareness of African practices alive. In the American colonies, where there was a natural increase of slaves, the new immigrants were in a smaller proportion to native-born Negroes, and the course of tutelage ran heavily the other way—that is, there appears to have been more substantial indoctrination of the newly arrived in the ways of the New World than there was refreshment of African practices in the memories of American Negroes.

Even when one takes full account of the evidence for various survivals—the memories, habits, and occasional legends to which Herskovits refers—the totality of what the African had been deprived of is far more impressive:

2. E. Franklin Frazier, *The Negro Family in the United States* (rev. edn., 1948), 17, 8.

besides his native soil, which meant a great deal to him, he had been ripped away from all, or almost all, of his familiar associations and his family and tribal connections. In some cases he had been stripped of an important rank or title and in all cases of his customary function; very often he lost his opportunities for sex, and more often still for a sustained tender erotic attachment; he no longer had the implements and materials of his craft; except for his voice, he had lost the implements of his music. Once bought and settled, he had to learn the ways of a system of slavery different and much harsher than some of the slave systems of Africa, he had to respond to the orders and whims of a new master or overseer, had to learn a new system of labor in the cultivation of the unfamiliar crops of tobacco, corn, rice, and indigo. If he had been a craftsman in Africa, and was so fortunate as to ply a craft in America, he had to adapt his skills to new demands and materials and follow unfamiliar instructions. He had to learn a new language; he had to devise a new code of behavior for himself. The blacks who had preceded him might be kind and helpful, but they might also look down on him as a greenhorn. However, there seems to have been no parallel on the American mainland to the tragic reception of the *Prince of Orange* at St. Kitts in 1737, when an acclimatized Negro came on board and, thinking to tease the arriving slaves, told them that they would be blinded, tormented, and then eaten, driving more than a hundred to jump overboard, thirty-three of whom were drowned.[3]

In the best of cases, after the ordeal of the crossing, those slaves who had survived the sicknesses and the

3. Daniel Mannix and Malcolm Cowley, *Black Cargoes* (1962), 127.

temptations of suicide had a complex adjustment to make —not merely in learning new ways of labor, but in testing the limits of the system of slavery under which they were to live, sounding out the intricate and one-sided system of racial etiquette, learning how far one might go in withholding labor or expressing resentment, finding modes of dissimulation, responding to incentives, entering the subtle if limited bargaining that sometimes went on between master and slave, in some cases treasuring plans or hopes for gaining freedom. It is impossible not to be impressed by the measure of physical hardihood, patience, and mental agility that went into this reluctant adaptation. The Africans had endured the unendurable; they survived; they made for themselves such a life as life would allow them.

Some slaves, of course, made their way into domestic service and craftsmanlike occupations, either on the plantations or in the towns and villages all along the seaboard; others, owned in twos and threes, labored alongside their masters on small farms in a situation not unlike that of underprivileged familiar laborers. Normally the agricultural units on which slaves worked were small enough for them to surmount the difficulties of their diverse native languages and to know each other. Although a small number of wealthy planters owned one hundred or two hundred slaves or even more, most of them broke up their labor force into scattered plantation units. The vast majority of slaveholders held twenty slaves or fewer, often only three or four. For example, even in Lancaster County, Virginia, which had a large Negro population and where almost seven out of every ten white farmers owned slaves, in 1745 there were only three plantations with between twenty-one and thirty taxable slaves, and none were any

larger. Eighty per cent of the Lancaster County slaveowners held five taxable slaves or fewer. On the eve of the
Revolution, after some concentration had occurred, 63 per
cent of its slaveowners remained in this class.[4] With few
exceptions, then, most Africans slaved on the plantations,
large and small, in what can be described only as a system
of driven labor. The economy of the plantation required
that a staff of slaves, who had to be housed and provisioned
throughout the year and could not be laid off in slack
times, be kept fully and productively occupied in all sea-
sons. Southern staples were in fact year-round crops, requiring an unbroken routine of labor. On plantations
devoted to the production of a crop which called for a
large concentration of labor on a relatively small area of
land, the routinization of operations was easier than on
large, general farms, and a simple system of supervision
became possible, even when the labor force was reluctant
to work and unfamiliar with the tasks. Planters could thus
compensate for the inefficiency of slave labor by keeping
costs low—maintaining slaves at a bare subsistence and
working them a full day through a full year. Large planters
normally divided their slaves into gangs of twenty or
thirty and put them under the supervision of overseers
who worked on salary or shares or both. The slaves faced
lashes from a driver if they did not seem to be doing the
stint of labor assigned for their age, sex, and strength, and
could thus be forged, even without incentives, into a work
force of tolerable productivity.[5] There might be resistance
among the new arrivals, sullenly disguised as an incapacity

4. Robert E. Brown and B. Katherine Brown, *Virginia 1705–1786:
Democracy or Aristocracy* (1964), 75.
5. Lewis Cecil Gray, *History of Agriculture in the Southern United
States* (1932), I, 463, 468, 479, 545 ff.

for learning. "*A new negro*," wrote a traveler in 1740, "if he must be broke, either from obstinacy, or, which I am more apt to suppose, from greatness of soul, will require more hard discipline than a young spaniel. You would be surprised at their perseverance; let a hundred men show him how to hoe, or drive a wheelbarrow, he'll still take the one by the bottom and the other by the wheel; and they often die before they can be conquered." [6] Yet the lash was there when needed, and if such stubbornness had been universal or long lasting the plantations could not have been made to pay.

Governor Gooch once wrote to the Bishop of London that despite a few harsh masters most slaves lived "much better than our poor laboring men in England." [7] It is a statement we may be permitted to doubt. Slaves were often housed in barrackslike structures, without furniture except for a few rude cots, and their weekly food allowance would most likely be a peck of corn and a pound of pork. It is true that in the fields of the typical small farm and plantation they would often find themselves toiling alongside white indentured servants and even at times the sons of their masters. It is easy to believe that the pace of work was tolerable, but the days were long, and the relentless hand of control, compulsion, and quick retribution lay heavily over them at all times.

Sound and enterprising management, though it would never make slave labor highly productive, did not fail to find year-round work for slave gangs. Tobacco culture, which flourished from Virginia and Maryland to the northern counties of North Carolina, was particularly demanding, and required a heavy concentration of hands per acre. In

the winter, around mid-January, seeds had to be sown in
carefully prepared beds, and in April or May, when the
seedlings had reached a certain height, they had to be
carefully transplanted on an opportunely wet day to the
fields, which then needed repeated hoeing and plowing to
keep the soil loose and eliminate weeds. During this time
the plants needed regular topping—cutting off new leaves
to prevent excessive growth. The newly developing suckers
growing at the base of the leaf stems also had to be lopped
off, and the plants had to be checked for hornworms. In
the late summer, as the crops yellowed, their stalks were
split and cut, left for a time in the fields to wilt, then
taken to tobacco sheds for hanging and curing—a laborious process, since the curing leaves had to be carefully
spaced.

At the peak of the harvest season, a day's labor began
before sunup and might last fifteen hours; while the curing
was still going on, the ground was being prepared for the
next crop. Something like a fifteen-hour day might be
standard in a peak season, and the laws of some of the
Southern colonies—Georgia's of 1755 setting a maximum
of sixteen hours and South Carolina's setting fifteen for
spring to early autumn and fourteen for the rest of the
year—though presumably unenforceable, represent a statement of the community's sense of the proper limits. Sundays were free, as were several days at Christmas. But it
was the prevailing conception of good managers that the
day on the plantation should be long and full. George
Washington summed up the accumulated wisdom of such
managers near the end of his life when he wrote: "To request that my people may be at their work as soon as it is
light, work till it is dark, and be diligent while they are at
it, can hardly be necessary, because the propriety of it

must strike every manager who attends to my interest, or regards his own character, and who, on reflecting, must be convinced that lost labor is never to be regained. The presumption is, that every laborer does as much in twenty-four hours as his strength, without endangering his health or constitution, will allow." [8]

Rice, cultivated with success in South Carolina and the Georgia low country, required that swamps be converted into productive fields by the elaborate systems of banks, ditches, and sluices which made periodic flooding and draining possible. Much labor went into extending and repairing these banks and sluices. The work of cultivation kept slave gangs busy in winter raking fields, burning stubble, and then breaking ground. In the early spring seeds were planted; then fields were flooded, and labor was diverted for a time to other crops and chores. Next the fields were drained, dried, hoed, and weeded, and after a second flooding and drying came the final harvest flooding. In September the slaves cut the rice with sickles, sheaved it, sacked it to dry, carried it to the plantation mill for threshing, pounded it to remove husks, winnowed and screened it, and packed it in barrels.

Indigo, which caught on rapidly in South Carolina after mid-century thanks to the ingenious experiments of Eliza Pinckney and the eagerness with which England sought it, was an important crop until the end of the Revolutionary era. Its cultivation, however, was carried on under considerable difficulties. Work began with early spring sowing, and in June or July the grown plants were cut from the roots and laid in shallow vats under water to ferment the dye out of the leaves. The water was then drained

8. Gray, I, 556–7; this was written in 1799.

off and the plants beaten for hours with paddles to renew fermentation. Limewater was stirred in to precipitate the blue color, the water was then drawn off, the residual paste collected, drained in bags, kneaded and pressed, cubed, dried, and packed. All this labor was hardly finished when the gangs had to cope with the second crop which sprouted out of the roots of the first, and was harvested in August and September. In addition, during the entire growing season, the furrows had repeatedly to be weeded and caterpillars had to be picked off the plants. Finally, the leaves had to be carried to the vats with great care to avoid rubbing off their blue bloom, and the fermentation process needed careful watching.

The demanding annual round of cultivation of the three staple crops left the plantation work force only limited intervals in which to perform other equally necessary tasks. In the tobacco country, for example, where a field could usually be planted to the staple crop only once in three years, the arduous clearing of new fields was a constant chore; in the rice country the banks and sluices always needed tending and repair. On any plantation labor was needed for tending corn and other food crops, since the planters, though mainly intent on their staples, found it economic to raise food for their hands; men were needed also for mending fences, building hogsheads, and miscellaneous chores. In the rhythms of these year-round schedules the slaves lived and worked, driven by the force of necessity and finally by habit. Incentives, occasionally given to craftsmen, were rare for the field hands: they might avoid the lash, but the fruit of their labor was not theirs, and although most had been born into industrious tribal societies they now gave their labor grudgingly and erratically.

2

North of Maryland slavery was not vital to the economy as it was in the South; the treatment of slaves in the North, therefore, illuminates many of the social differences between the two sections, and has a distinct interest for the social and moral history of the Northern colonies. The North, however, cannot be treated as a unit, since in some colonies, such as New York, slaves were relatively numerous while in others, notably in New England, they were few. New York was slow in drawing white settlers until after mid-century, and the shortage of labor led to a considerable use of slaves; indeed it is possible that in the early Dutch days it was slave labor that enabled the colony to survive. Most of the first slaves were not from Africa but were reimported from Curaçao in the Dutch West Indies. It was a profitable system: in the 1640's it cost only a little more to buy a slave than to pay a free worker's wages for a year. Although the slave system in the Dutch West Indies was brutal, in New Netherland the institution was not particularly harsh. Many slaves there had a kind of half freedom under which they enjoyed personal liberty in return for an annual payment to the West India Company and an occasional stint of labor for it. They were allowed to testify in court, an effort was made to convert them to Christianity, and free Negroes were permitted to own freeholds and to intermarry. Still, the desire of slaves for liberty did not flag, and a considerable number of runaways, sometimes assisted by whites, fled to the neighboring English colonies.

After the English took control of New Netherland in 1664, a brisk and highly profitable trade in skilled slaves was carried on. Most slaveholders in the province were flourishing small farmers or small artisans who, in the absence of an adequate supply of free labor, needed moderately skilled help, and were able to pay the rising prices for slaves. A partial census of 1755 showed a widely diffused slave population, most owners having only one or two slaves, only seven New Yorkers owning ten or more. Among the largest lots held were those of the elder Lewis Morris with 66 slaves on his large estate and the first Frederick Philipse, an affluent landowner, with about 40. Such men could work gangs of slaves on their manors, but slaves were also sought by other wealthy men for the comfort and prestige a substantial staff of domestic servants would bring. William Smith, for example, was reputed to keep a domestic staff of 12 or more to run his New York City household, and other leading citizens traveled with Negro footmen. But the main body of slaves was employed by small proprietors, and, learning a wide variety of skills, worked chiefly in the towns, in the service trades and the shipyards, in the shops of coopers, tailors, bakers, weavers, masons, and other craftsmen. From the first the competition of black labor was resented by whites. Competition in the labor market was intensified by the slave owners' widespread practice of putting out their slaves for hire, under-cutting white laborers who were paid twice the slaves' wages. On most New York farms slaveholding was uneconomical: the growing season was relatively short, and idle slaves would have to be maintained during the long winter months. Small proprietors also had little space to house a slave family, and on small premises slave children would be a liability rather than an asset. In New York sterility in a female slave was at a premium. Nonetheless, slavery persisted; white labor was in short supply, and selected black labor was skillful and productive.

Miscegenation, which began in New York under the Dutch, yielded such a number of persons of mixed blood in the colony that by the end of the seventeenth century slave status had to be defined not by color but by the status of the mother. Some light-colored runaways won freedom by passing into the white population. Bargaining between blacks and their white lovers inevitably took place, as slaves found themselves in a position to ask for money or goods, even in some cases for manumission. Yet even under the relatively open system of slavery that prevailed, family structure was weak and there were a large number of broken and female-headed families.

The New York slave, suspended in an awkward equipoise between complete bondage and half freedom, was often restive. Slave controls, reflecting persistent nervousness in the white population, were quite rigid. Aside from private punishments that could be administered by masters, such public controls were meant to put sharp limits on the temptations slaves would face. After 1702, flogging was prescribed if three slaves gathered together on their own time. They were not permitted to gamble or to buy liquor, though liquor was often sold to slaves by tavern keepers, nor could they engage in trade without their masters' consent. Fires were a frightening problem in the eighteenth-century towns, and blacks were commonly suspected of arson. With hired-out slaves coming and going in the city, the opportunities for arson were considerable; the perpetrators of arson were always hard to trace, and arson could be used to conceal theft. The penalty for committing arson, consequently, was death.[9]

A special cause of slave restiveness arose from the

---

9. Edgar J. McManus, *A History of Negro Slavery in New York* (1966), 85. See J. J. Goebel, Jr., and T. R. Naughton, *Law Enforcement in Colonial New York* (1944).

presence in New York of a considerable number of Spanish Negroes, captured in the wars with Spain, condemned as prizes, and sold into slavery without regard to their prior status. Apparently some of the Spanish Negroes had been freemen. They were resentful and rebellious at having been re-enslaved, and some played a role in the New York slave conspiracy of 1712. Although slaves were entitled to and indeed usually received real and not *pro forma* trials, serious offenses were punished with harsh sentences intended to be effective deterrents. The killing of a white person by a black was punished by torture followed by execution, a sentence which courts did not hesitate to impose. Yet for lesser offenses, slaves in New York as in several other colonies enjoyed an exemption which grew out of their value as property: whites could be executed for certain categories of theft, but slaves could not.[1]

New England was more important as the major carrier of the slave trade to the mainland colonies than as a user of slave labor. Principle was not, however, at issue. From the very beginning the Puritans had sought to solve their labor shortage by enslaving Indians for limited terms of service, or Negroes, and in 1645 Emanuel Downing, John Winthrop's brother-in-law, expressed the hope that slaves could be supplied because the colony would never thrive "until we get . . . a stock of slaves sufficient to do all our business."[2] In the early days even Roger Williams condoned slavery; at the peak of the eighteenth-century slave trade, the New England slavers were men of great wealth and respectability in their communities. Small numbers of

1. McManus, 96.
2. Lorenzo J. Greene, *The Negro in Colonial New England 1620–1726* (1942), 60.

slaves were brought to such major ports as Boston, Newport, and Salem and some were sent into the communities
of the interior. The typical New England slaveholding was
one or two slaves per family, although there were a few
large owners in the Narragansett country, farmers who
engaged in dairying and stock raising on parcels of
land ranging from three hundred to two or three thousand acres and employing from a half-dozen to forty
slaves, indispensable for such large-scale enterprises. For
comfort and convenience, as well as for status, leading
village families might own a domestic slave or two, and
the generality and respectability of the practice is under-
lined by the presence of slaves in such prominent and
upright ministerial families as those of Jonathan Edwards,
Ezra Stiles, and the Mathers. Even Judge Samuel Sewall
who wrote an early and prophetic anti-slavery tract held
slaves. John Adams, who found the practice repugnant
and held no slaves, recalled: "The best men in my vicinity
thought it not inconsistent with their character." [3] Besides
domestic service and family farm labor, slaves were employed in a wide variety of occupations, skilled and unskilled, in the shops of blacksmiths, tanners, and carpenters, the offices of printers, in distilleries, ropewalks, iron
forges, lumbering, shipbuilding, and other industries.
Partly in the hope of escaping slavery, Negroes also went
to sea. As a source of cheap and reasonably skilled labor,
Negroes were probably more important to the New England economy than their small numbers would lead one
to expect.

In the small-scale slaveholding pattern of New England,
blacks were often the familiar associates of their masters,

3. Ibid., 109.

and New England slavery, with this pattern of intimacy and an ethos of personal restraint, lacked the harshness of slavery in the Southern colonies or New York. New England masters, though on occasion they became nervous about their slaves, did not suffer the constant terror of Negro uprisings that afflicted planters in the South and the West Indies. There were, to be sure, some rumors of insurrection, some slaves plotted to burn Charlestown, Massachusetts, in 1741, and there were occasional panics over arson.[4] And many slaves ran away. The desire for freedom that was so generally manifest among the slaves of the colonial era was not quenched by the comparative mildness of New England slavery.

The machinery of control in New England, though less rigid than elsewhere, was elaborate enough. On pain of being classified as runaways, slaves were forbidden to wander beyond the town limits without a pass from their masters or some other authority. Ferrymen were prohibited from transporting slaves across rivers, householders from entertaining them, tavern keepers from selling them liquor. Slaves were forbidden to remain on Boston Common after sunset, and a law of 1728 in Massachusetts prevented them from buying provisions from country people. Small thefts were punishable by whipping, not more than twenty lashes, and if the amount stolen was large, the guilty slave, especially in Rhode Island, might be punished by banishment—a dire penalty, because it usually meant that the slave would be sold into the West Indies. Slaves were subject to a nine o'clock curfew. They were forbidden to build bonfires, out of fear of arson. Striking a white person was punished by severe whipping. To prevent

4. Ibid., 160–1.

masters from freeing old and decrepit slaves who would then have to be supported at the public expense, laws required them to support their former slaves and not permit them to become public charges.

In spite of laws against miscegenation, it was quite common in New England. While there is no accurate general measure, some sense of the prevalence of miscegenation is given by the records of Rhode Island, which show that in 1782 the 3,806 Negroes in the colony included 464 mulattoes, or nearly one-eighth of the Negro population.[5]

As elsewhere, the Negro family was gravely injured by slavery, even though many masters attempted to accommodate slaves by sanctioning marriages. Sometimes a mother and her children were sold away from their husband and father, sometimes children were sold or even given away from their parents. A petition to the Massachusetts legislature by a group of Boston Negroes in 1773 expressed their plight poignantly and with an adroit appeal to Christian pieties: "The endearing ties of husband and wife we are strangers to for we are no longer man and wife than our masters or mistresses think proper. . . . Our children are also taken from us by force and sent many miles from us where we seldom see them again there to be made slaves of for life which sometimes is very short by reason of being dragged from their mothers' breasts. How can a slave perform the duties of a husband to a wife or parent to his child? How can a husband leave master and work and cleave to his wife? How can the wife submit themselves to their husbands in all things? How can the child obey his parents in all things?"[6]

5. Ibid., 210.
6. Ibid., 217.

3

It has to be remembered, when we consider the English during the period when they were beginning to have numerous contacts with Africans, that we are dealing first with the Elizabethan men and then with men of the era of the Great Rebellion—that is, with the English in one of the most tumultuous, aggressive, and triumphant phases of their history, an expanding and militant people with a curious mixture of intense sensitivity, robust violence, deep moral persuasion, and acute rapacity, men who were living in the throes of religious rebellions and wars, violent political and religious prejudices, civil insurrection, fierce persecutions, rising national vendettas, and enormous destructive energy. Moreover, there was little at work in England, or anywhere in western Europe, to counter the most primitive ethnocentric impulses. There was not, of course, and would not be for centuries, any intellectual countertradition of cultural relativism—an enormously sophisticated and very modern idea—to check the welling tide of brute prejudice. And, what is of still greater importance, there was, despite some flickerings and stirrings in the Church, no strong cultivated tradition of humanitarianism to limit racial revulsion and bridle the drive toward human exploitation. A few white men who saw Benin may have been impressed by its grandeurs, and a few who bartered with Africans on the Guinea Coast may have known that they were dealing with formidable men. But like the Portuguese and Spaniards before them, the English were soon branding Africans, shunting them about like cattle, often in fact referring to them as such. The Negro as beast: it is always convenient and comfortable to believe that those who are about to be either killed or exploited mercilessly are something less than human, and hence available to be used for the benefit of humans. The dehumanization of the object is an important psychological precondition of destruction, and it is convenient to make the victim the embodiment of evil, indeed to project upon him one's own worst and most feared impulses, to make him an externalization of one's own beast. The primary limiting factor upon the white man in the long history of African slavery arose not out of humanitarian compunction but out of self-interest: the white man came not to destroy altogether, but to capture and sustain life, to be able to put it under virtually total domination for the sake of his own comfort or profit. His was a savagery contained chiefly by the desire to exploit; and his approach to the African built a historical monument of ruthlessness plastered over with condescension.

From the time of his first contacts with the African what the Englishman saw was a black heathen, or, perhaps more correctly, a heathen black. Blackness, as Winthrop D. Jordan has amply documented, was a term loaded with pejorative meaning well before many Englishmen realized that there were men with black skin. Even before the sixteenth century, *black* in common usage suggested not simply a color but dirtiness, dark and deadly purposes, death, disaster, disgrace, censure, and wickedness.[7] And for men to be cursed with blackness must somehow be their punishment for dire sin; blackness betokened in itself an exceptional inner evil. Such implications were confirmed by what Englishmen reported of the actual conditions of the African. One of the earliest accounts of the Guinea Coast, written in 1554, describes

7. Winthrop D. Jordan, *White over Black* (1968), 7.

Negroes as "a people of beastly living, without a God, law, religion, or commonwealth"—in short, as different from Englishmen as night and day, or indeed as black from white.[8] To the curse of blackness was added the curse of heathenism and of lechery. The Englishman could not see in the religions of the African any religion at all, and what he thought he beheld in him was simply a naked savage. Naked and libidinous: for the white man's preoccupation with Negro sexuality was there at the very beginning, an outcome not only of his own guilt at sexual exploitation—his easy access to the black woman was immediately blamed on *her* lasciviousness [9]—but also of his envious suspicion that some extraordinary potency and ecstatic experience were associated with primitive lust. The rape complex, the fear of sexual retaliation, would follow upon this as soon as the two races were living in the same society. In *Othello* Desdemona endures what Roderigo calls "the gross clasps of a lascivious Moor"; Iago imagines that the Moor has been in his own bed, and taunts Brabantio with the thought that "an old black ram/Is tupping your white ewe."

Against these deep feelings about blackness there was no counterpoise to stop the English colonials from reaching the extremes of prejudice. A measure of what extremes were reached was the difference in their attitude toward Negroes and Indians, especially toward their conversion to Christianity. From the first, the English colonials made extensive, if largely unsuccessful, efforts to convert Indians. But for a long time—in many places until the middle or late eighteenth century or even afterward—they

8. Ibid., 24.
9. Ibid., 35.

held back from teaching their religion to Negroes until they were finally convinced that Christianity did not imply emancipation and did not necessarily contribute to slave discontent. In the face of English racial prejudice, the Christian impulse toward universalism, which held up relatively well in Catholic colonies, was allowed to flag. Conversion was left for a while by the Anglican church to the feeble efforts of some of the dissenters, and when taken up was pursued against much resistance from masters. Slaveowners, particularly in the Southern colonies, feared at first the logic of the traditional idea that if in Christ all men are brothers, then the enslavement of another Christian is unthinkable. Then, by the beginning of the eighteenth century, in all Southern and two Northern colonies (New York and New Jersey), they had reassured themselves by statute that no slave could become free by virtue of Christian conversion. Even after this, those early-eighteenth-century missionaries who concerned themselves with the faith of the Negro still met resistance from masters—this was true in the mainland colonies as it had been earlier in the West Indies—who argued on one hand that slaves needed their free Sundays not for worship but for time to cultivate their subsistence gardens, and on the other, as one missionary reported in 1730, that "the Negroes had no souls; [or] that they grew worse by being taught and made Christians." [1] To admit Negroes to Christian fellowship, the overwhelming majority of masters initially believed, would give them disturbing notions about the parity of white and black souls, a sentiment caricatured almost too perfectly by the South Carolina lady who asked

1. Quoted in Edwin S. Gaustad, *Historical Atlas of Religion in America* (1962), 148.

an Anglican minister: "Is it possible that any of my slaves could go to Heaven and must I see them there?" [2] Even by the time of the Revolution most slaves were not Christians, though when conversion was offered them they often responded with alacrity.

In secular tradition, the Negro, unlike the Indian, was never romanticized as "the noble savage"—but it is hard to say to what extent this arose from a different response to the Indian's ruddy brown skin, and to what extent from the fact that the Indian was never successfully enslaved on a large scale. The white colonials might make war with and come to hate and fear Indians, but they had to deal with them as resistant nations, buy their lands, make treaties and cope with them as collective powers. They dealt with Negroes as individuals who were nearly helpless. "It was no mere luck of the toss," writes Winthrop D. Jordan, "that placed the profile of an American Indian rather than an American Negro on the famous old five-cent piece. Confronting the Indian in America was a testing experience, common to all the colonies." To conquer the Indian, a formidable and worthy adversary, was an act and a symbol in the ongoing conquest of the wilderness, and became a part of the civilizing mission of colonization. The Negro had no such lofty place in the white man's experience and imagination.[3]

English colonials never considered treating Negroes as equals, even those who happened to attain freedom, or

---

2. Jordan, 183; on resistance to conversion see ibid., 180–7; and for the West Indies, Frank Tannenbaum, *Slave and Citizen* (1946), 82–91. For the Northern colonies, Arthur Zilversmit, *The First Emancipation* (1967), 7–10, 24–8; see Marcus W. Jernegan, "Slavery and Conversion in the American Colonies," *American Historical Review*, XXI (1916), 504–27; Frank J. Klingberg, *An Appraisal of the Negro in South Carolina* (1941).
3. Jordan, 91; attitudes toward Negroes and Indians, 89–91, 21–4, 27.

making Negro slavery contractual, terminable, and non-heritable, as was white indentured servitude. There was, to be sure, a certain awkwardness in their heritage which early English colonizers had to overcome, since slavery had no status in English law, and the closest thing to it, villeinage, had long been defunct. But it is impressive how rapidly colonial slavery sprang up on the mainland and in the islands, and congealed into the form it was to keep until the mid-nineteenth century. What shaped it was the white man's attitude toward blacks, his commanding need for subordinated labor, his sternness under the rigors of the wilderness, and his nervousness in the presence of a restive and sometimes rebellious labor force of another race that in some places outnumbered him. In most of the colonies, there was little doubt from the beginning what slavery would be like. From a very early point in the history of Barbados Negroes were treated as slaves for life, and the Barbadian approach to slavery, brought by emigrants from that island to South Carolina, helped to make the slave system of that colony the harshest on the mainland. The first English slave code in New York (1665) recognized slavery for life. New Englanders too enslaved Negroes for life from the beginning, also taking their image of slavery from the West Indies. One law against enslavement was piously passed by Rhode Island in 1652, but never became operative. In the tobacco colonies, by contrast, slavery developed gradually; it became a reality in practice before it had a distinct legal form; and some of the early uncertainties about the legal status of slaves there have given rise to debates among historians as to whether the first Negroes were not on a footing comparable to white indentured servants. There is little evidence, for example, to tell exactly how Negroes were

treated in Virginia before 1640, when there were only a few
hundred, some of them apparently free.[4] Whatever their
status in this early period, however, they were not treated
as equals; for example, blacks were not permitted to bear
arms, while white servants were.[5] And it is certain that after 1640 they were held as slaves doomed to hereditary
lifetime service. By the 1660's lifelong slavery had been
codified as an institution. By 1705 Virginia had embodied
her slave laws in a fully worked-out code similar to those of
the nineteenth century.[6] Hence, when slaves began to be imported into the colonies in truly large numbers, the stern
pattern of American slavery had everywhere been set.

4

Of decisive long-run importance for the Negro and for
American civilization was the system of attitudes and practices within which the institution of slavery was encased.
Here a comparison with Latin-American slavery is instruc-
tive. It has often been argued that in Latin America, because limitations were set by church and state on violations
of the slave's personality by his owners, slavery was a
"milder" institution than in the Anglo-American colonies.
Some serious questions have been raised about this view:
checks laid down by the church and laws decreed by the
Iberian monarchs cannot be assumed to have worked the
way they were intended across the Atlantic. As C. R. Boxer
has shown, they did not prevent the slavery of colonial

4. Ibid., 72 ff.
5. Carl Degler, "Slavery and the Genesis of American Race Prejudice,"
Comparative Studies in Society and History, II (1959), 49 ff.
6. John C. Hurd, *The Law of Freedom and Bondage in the United
States* (1858), I, 231–2; for the 1705 code, ibid., 238–41.

Brazil from becoming "a hell for blacks." [7] One powerful consideration suggests that slavery was less onerous on the North American mainland than to the south: if the ability of a population to survive and multiply can be taken as a basic test of well-being, the facts of demography argue that slavery in North America was milder than in most other parts of the New World. Over the decades, the Negro population of the mainland colonies, and later of the United States, showed the largest natural increase in the hemisphere. As of 1950 the United States had almost a third of the Afro-American population of the Western Hemisphere, although in the days of the slave trade only less than 5 per cent of the Negroes had been sent there. This may be compared with the dismal record of the Caribbean islands, which had imported an estimated 43 per cent of the slaves and had only 20 per cent of the population of African descent in 1950.[8] No one, white or black, seems to have doubted that the resale of a slave to the West Indies, which was often resorted to as a punishment for a serious crime, was punishment of the most terrible sort. Still, so many factors besides work load, housing, diet, and the nature of punishment enter into the natural growth rate of the slaves—such factors as sex ratio, population density, and disease environment—that it is as yet impossible to be sure that in fact milder work and better treatment account for the great natural increase of North American slaves. What is true is that North American mainland slaves increased steadily, whereas in many other places in the Western Hemisphere, including the

7. C. R. Boxer, *Race Relations in the Portuguese Colonial Empire, 1415–1825* (1963), 114.
8. Philip Curtin, *The Atlantic Slave Trade: A Census* (1969), 91–2.

West Indies and parts of Latin America, the slave trade had to be relied on to replenish a natural decrease of blacks.[9] On many of these latter plantations as many as fifteen men were employed to each woman; but this sexual ratio was based upon those planters' assumption that the burden of work was too heavy for women, an assumption that does not appear to have been regularly made anywhere on the North American mainland.

However, when one turns from the working system of slavery itself to the social atmosphere that surrounded it, slavery in such Latin-American countries as Brazil and Cuba had certain advantages in the form of a more fluid and open social system. While the Latin-Americans developed a complex system of race and class which admitted gradations and compromises, the Anglo-Americans of the North American mainland quickly became committed to sharp race separation, took a forbidding view of manumission, defined mulattoes simply as Negroes, and made outcasts of free Negroes. Hence there was as little upward mobility from slavery as possible, especially in the Southern colonies and states, and even where masters chose to manumit slaves. The purchase of liberty, quite within the grasp of slaves in some parts of Latin America, was for a long time close to impossible here. Mulattoes, usually the offspring of white men and black women, were given the status of their mothers and forced to stay in the ranks of Negro slaves. Free Negroes were underprivileged outcasts, disfranchised, closely regulated, and watched lest they stir up slaves or assist fugitives, and encouraged or sometimes required to leave a province upon achieving freedom, even when it was not clear where they could go. (It is testimony

9. Tannenbaum, *Slave and Citizen,* 35–9; David B. Davis, *The Problem of Slavery in Western Culture* (1966), 232–3.

to the strength of the desire of slaves for freedom that
they sought it even when they could see how hard the lot
of the free Negro was.) Hence, in North America, especially in the plantation colonies and states, there would be
no gentle gradations in society, no mestizo culture, no escape through money or mating from the degradation put
upon blackness, no accepted and respected class of free
Negroes and mulattoes to stand as an intermediate segment of society between enslaved blacks and privileged
whites, no effective reassurance against the constant fear
lurking in the white mind—the fear that emancipation
would mean not merely the end of a labor system but the
very end of civilization itself. The North American white
man in the colonial era thus laid down an institutional
framework which, however modified later, created a lasting frame of mind. The idea of emancipation and racial
coexistence on terms of equality or near-equality became
a monstrous, demonic, haunting, apocalyptic image. And
worst of all, something of a self-fulfilling prophecy.

Virginia, chosen here for representativeness rather than
notable severity, illustrates the way in which certain op-
tions were foreclosed at an early date. In 1662 a statute
provided that all children were to be free or slave according to the condition of the mother—not an unusual
legal practice, but one which guaranteed, in a society where
interracial sex usually involved the access of white men to
black women, that without other provisions to the contrary
the mulatto population would be slaves. An act of 1682
provided that Negro, mulatto, and Indian slaves who were
Christian converts could not have their lifelong slavery
converted to a term of indentured servitude even if their
masters so desired. An act of 1691, which provided that
any English man or woman who married a Negro, mulatto,

or Indian should be banished forever from the province, was modified in 1705 by a provision for fine and imprisonment for such intermarriage. Another law of 1691 forbade a Negro or mulatto to be set free by anyone, unless the benefactor also paid to transport him out of the colony. The code of 1705 denied to Negroes, mulattoes, and Indians the right to hold office or to be witnesses in any cases in law. A law of 1723 forbade the manumission of persons in any of these three classes, except for meritorious services to the province, so judged by the governor and the Council. Other laws of that year deprived these classes of the vote, and specified that they could not serve in the militia except as "drummers or trumpeters in servile labor but are not to bear arms." [1]

The racial attitudes of American colonials were not altogether comprehensible in London, and we are fortunate to have from the hand of Governor William Gooch an attempt to explain them which casts a sharp little shaft of light on the way in which the plantation experience was bringing colonial Englishmen to depart from their home heritage in the matter of racial justice. The year was 1723. For whatever reason, perhaps because the number of free Negroes was still negligible, Virginia had not yet taken action to deprive them of the right to vote. Now, because of restlessness among the slaves and the discovery of the alleged plot (as Gooch very vaguely phrased it) to "cut off the English," the Assembly passed a number of slave laws, including the aforementioned one denying the vote to free Negroes, mulattoes, and Indians. [2] The London government queried Gooch about the necessity of this disfranchisement, whereupon he explained it in terms that

1. Hurd, I, 231–42, *passim*.
2. Ibid., I, 242.

show how well he had come to understand the Virginia point of view.

During the recent disturbed period, Gooch explained, the free Negroes and mulattoes were suspected to have been involved in the plot of the slaves, even though there was no legal proof that would convict them. And "such was the insolence of the free Negroes at that time that the next Assembly thought it necessary, not only to make the meetings of slaves very penal, but to fix a perpetual brand upon free Negroes and mulattoes by excluding them from that great privilege of a freeman, well knowing they always did, and ever will, adhere to and favour the slaves. And 'tis likewise said to have been done with design, which I must think a good one, to make the free Negroes sensible that a distinction ought to be made between their offspring and the descendants of an Englishman, with whom they never were to be accounted equal. This, I confess, may seem to carry an air of severity to such as are unacquainted with the nature of Negroes, and the pride of a manumitted slave, who looks on himself immediately on his acquiring his freedom to be as good a man as the best of his neighbours, but especially if he is descended of a white father or mother, let them be of what mean condition soever; and as most of them are the bastards of some of the worst of our imported servants and convicts, it seems no way impolitic, as well for discouraging that kind of copulation, as to preserve a decent distinction between them and their betters, to leave this mark on them, until time and education has changed the indication of their spurious extraction, and made some alteration in their morals." The numbers denied the vote, Gooch added, were so "inconsiderable" that the new disabilities imposed on them did not amount to much, since by earlier acts they were already barred from being jurymen or witnesses in any law case, "and so are as much excluded from being good and lawful men, as villeins were of old by the laws of England." [3]

What was involved, of course, was not simply a difference in prejudice, but a difference in social systems. It is impossible to measure the prejudices of colonial Englishmen against those of Frenchmen, Portuguese, and Spaniards. Color prejudice in varying degrees existed in all the colonial societies. But in large parts of Latin America, and on some English West Indies islands, very few white women were available, and what happened only rarely in North America happened there with frequency: men took Negro or mulatto concubines and produced families of mulatto or quadroon offspring. In some parts of the New World the aging, lonely planter whose only relatives were children or grandchildren of color became a common phenomenon. Such men often showed a good deal of affection and concern for their offspring and made some effort, through general or special acts of legislatures, to provide for them a condition of freedom or comfort and to prevent them from being forced, by virtue of their color, into the degradation of quite brutal systems of slavery.[4] In addition to the caste of colored freemen created by this process, there was a larger class of freemen created by frequent manumission, which was much easier in Latin America than it was, at least in the beginning, in the English colonies of North America,[5] and by purchase. For example, at the beginning of the nineteenth century, about 33 per cent of the whole colored population of Cuba was free; in

3. Herbert S. Klein, *Slavery in the Americas* (1967), 232–3.
4. Davis, 262–88.
5. See Davis, 262–8, and Tannenbaum, 53–71.

Virginia, despite a rash of recent manumissions, it was less than 6 per cent.[6]

Parts of Latin America thus were far ahead of the American colonies in creating a numerous class of free Negroes, and were accustomed to the idea of a society in which considerable numbers of blacks would enjoy positions of comfort and status. In such societies, though abolitionism was often bitterly resisted, the idea of ultimate and complete emancipation was not usually accompanied by the apocalyptic sense of horror that always enshrouded it in the United States. In the English colonies of the mainland, the physical condition of the slave might in fact have been considerably better than in the countries to the south. But his prospects for a life of comfort and acceptance as a freeman were also much poorer. And even though the pattern of North American society softened noticeably in the nineteenth century, the chances of the United States for achieving emancipation without going through a catastrophic convulsion and retaining a lingering heritage of racial hatred were correspondingly lessened.

5

Slavery is an economic regime and a scheme of human relations. As neither blacks nor whites could forget, it is also a system of power. In the eighteenth century little was said about the natural docility of the black man or his contentment as a slave. Since an abolitionist movement had not yet arisen, no such defenses were necessary; and since a pattern of slave control was not fully worked out, and slaves were arriving in alarming numbers, anxiety about

6. Klein, 202, 236; *cf.* 194–202, 235–8.

the system was too close to the surface of consciousness to be denied.

In fact, American slavery was never characterized by large numbers of slave revolts, but this reality needs to be reconciled to what appears to have been equally true: blacks, especially in the earliest decades, were far from being docile or contented and whites did not assume they were. Even though the slave revolt that proved most deadly for both races did not occur until Nat Turner's uprising of 1831, it is important in understanding the slave system to remember that violent resistance to enslavement was much more intense in its beginning than in its more established years. Most slave rebellions at sea took place when the ships were hardly out of sight of the Guinea Coast. Most slave rebellions which occurred on the North American mainland, from beginning to end, took place before 1812. The striking restiveness of newly imported blacks indicates that the horrors of the Middle Passage had not stunned them into complete pliability and acquiescence. Planters, who valued tractability, commonly preferred native or "country born" blacks to new arrivals. Perhaps the best evidence that blacks resented their condition and yearned for freedom was that no white man seems to have doubted this was so. Whites could have been mistaken, of course, misled by their fear and guilt; but across the immense gulf that separated them whites and blacks observed each other with a certain sullen but pragmatic intentness, demanded by the intimacy in which they would live, and a thousand subtly shaded actions and glances could express resentment. Nineteenth-century Southerners, fending off antislavery men, would speak of the contentment of the slave and his affection for his master. In the eighteenth century, such matters were discussed with greater candor.

There remains the undeniable fact that even in the eighteenth century slave rebellions were very few. Historians so minded have been able to swell their number by counting, as though they were full-fledged, consummated rebellions, all cases of aborted rebellions or alleged plots, all those in which a few blacks ran away together carrying stolen weapons, and all instances of white panic over rumors of plots. The whole question of the reality of aborted plots or rumored plots is a thicket of difficulties. Some planned revolts probably were aborted, betrayed by disloyal blacks who were tempted by the prospect of receiving their freedom from governor and council for meritorious service to the colony. However, in explaining the relatively small number of overt rebellions one must reckon with a certain common sense among the blacks, many of whom were familiar with warfare and most of whom may be imagined to have had a sense of the odds against them. Near the Guinea Coast, where it might be feasible to capture and direct a white pilot or simply to drift back to shore, blacks mounted many mutinies. But once on the American strand, and situated in communities where they were usually divided into small groups (the two big colonial revolts, significantly, were urban), denied all communication and outnumbered, where every white man had the use of a gun and there were slave patrols on the roads, they seem to have understood the hopelessness of an insurrection aimed at the capture or maintenance of independent power. Their only chance for freedom was to fight their way across the borders to Spanish ground or possibly to Canada, or to join some Indian tribe and take their chances on how they would be received. Otherwise to rebel required a suicidal desperation—and this too was by no means lacking, from the moment slaves threw themselves overboard from the slave ships to the occasions when they shot themselves or cut their throats to avoid recapture. Rebellion was a desperate venture which commonly needed the help of some unusual agency—rum, as was the case in the Stono Rebellion of 1739, or faith in a magic powder given them by their leaders, which may have activated the New York uprising of 1712.[7]

But there were less drastic alternatives: there were ways in which resistance to slavery could be expressed short of rebellion and with some prospect of minor tactical success, ranging all the way from withholding effort in labor, feigning sickness (a difficult problem for planters) to destroying equipment or stock, arson, or running away, either for a term of days or with the hope of final escape. Under great provocation, there was self-mutilation, suicide, or the murder of an owner or overseer.

Despite stringent controls and punishments, there were enough revolts and actual plots to keep white fears alive. Whites, moreover, were exercising a dominion as total as they could contrive over a people they saw not as potential equals but—so a South Carolina law of 1712 put it— as men of "barbarous, wild, savage natures," [8] and any sign of slave self-assertion that might indicate a disposition to rebel they had to interpret not as a desire for freedom on terms of equality, a condition which they could not conceive of, but as an evidence of what a Virginia governor

7. Kenneth Scott, "The Slave Insurrection in New York City in 1712," *New York Historical Quarterly* (1961), 49.
8. Hurd, I, 299.

called "the lust of domination," a desire first to rape and plunder their owners and then to establish a black tyranny over them.

All white plans to put down slave restiveness were affected by this idea. In the Europe of the time, cruel punishments—branding and the cropping of ears, for example, for relatively minor crimes—were still common; and there the conviction prevailed among the elite classes that it was not possible for the masses to live a fully human life. In a world in which there was so little charity and humanity for the mass of whites, it is not surprising that harsh responses to black crime or rebellion were commonplace, or that in rare instances punishments went to such extremes as roastings and burnings, hanging men in chains, dismemberings, and severing heads and impaling them in public as a warning.

Hector St. John de Crèvecoeur has left an unforgettable reminder of the horror that might lurk in the American Eden. Walking through a pleasant wood on the way to dinner with a planter, presumably near Charles Town, he suddenly came upon a Negro suspended in a cage and left to die, his pinioned arms already attacked in many places by birds, his eyes picked out of now hollow sockets, his body covered with wounds and blood, the whole scene a sudden testament to the savagery of man and nature. Crèvecoeur could do no more than find some water for a man who begged for poison. At his host's he was informed that the slave had killed the plantation overseer, and that "the laws of self-preservation rendered such executions necessary." [9]

The laws of self-preservation were incarnated in firm

9. Hector St. John de Crèvecoeur, *Letters from an American Farmer* (Everyman's edn., 1912), 173.

civil laws. Long before the end of the seventeenth century,
Virginia had provided that a master who killed a resisting
slave in the course of "correction" should not be guilty of a
felony, on the presumption that a man would not inten-
tionally "destroy his own estate"; also that no Negro could
go off a plantation without a pass, that any "Negro lifting
his hand against any white person" should get thirty
lashes, and that it was lawful to kill in the attempt to recapture any runaway who had injured an inhabitant. The
colony's code of 1705 specified the circumstances under
which a criminal slave might be dismembered by order of
the court. A law of 1723 decreed that there should be no
penalty imposed upon a white tried for the murder of a
slave and found guilty only of manslaughter.[1]

The laws of South Carolina were somewhat more severe
than those of Virginia. By a statute of 1690 it was made no
crime to deprive a runaway slave of life or limb, though
the wanton murder of an orderly slave might bring three
months in jail and required compensatory payment to the
owner. In 1712 and again in 1714 South Carolina codified its
slave controls and punishments, provided for patrols, and
prescribed death for running away. In 1740, after an insurrection, these provisions were strengthened. Georgia, which
adopted slavery over the resistance of its philanthropic
founders only in 1747, ultimately enacted South Carolina's
slave code. In North Carolina runaways were defined as
outlaws liable to be killed, and a conspiracy by any three
slaves was made a felony. Maryland's laws were similar to
Virginia's, though an act of 1723 provided for cropping the
ears of blacks who struck whites and allowed that fugitive
and resisting Negroes be "shot, killed, or destroyed," while

1. Hurd, I, 232 ff.

an act of a few years later provided that a Negro or slave should be hanged on conviction of certain serious crimes and the body quartered and exposed.[2] In the North, New England laws were relatively mild, those of New York and New Jersey severe. New York permitted barbarous public executions and private punishments short of deprivation of life or limb. Early in the eighteenth century both New Jersey and Pennsylvania passed laws permitting castration—in the first case for rape or even willing intercourse with a white woman, in the second for attempted rape—but both measures were disallowed by the Crown. In the case of New Jersey it was remarked that such punishments were "never . . . allowed by or known" in English law.[3] Although the harshest laws were not often invoked, they cast light on a society and a state of mind.

Although the problem of slave control was recognized in the seventeenth century, the testing period came with the rapid influx of slaves that followed the Peace of Utrecht, especially in the years 1720–40. Leading men in the Southern colonies were aware of disturbances in the Caribbean, particularly tumultuous in the 1730's, where Jamaica alone endured more than a dozen bloody slave insurrections; [4] they must also have known about the revolt of 1712 in New York. Southern whites lived in anxious conflict between their desire for ample slave labor and their fear, most notably in South Carolina, that the high ratio of blacks to whites would endanger white society. The proportion of newly arrived Africans among the slaves was at its peak then, and the South was receiving considerable

2. Ibid., 253.
3. Zilversmit, 9, 16; *cf.* 7–24 on Northern laws; *cf.* Greene, chapter 6.
4. Lowell J. Ragatz, *The Fall of the Planter Class in the British Caribbean 1763–1833* (1928); Frank W. Pitman, *The Development of the British West Indies, 1700–1763* (1917).

numbers of hardy male slaves who had been warriors. The minds of educated colonials turned readily to thoughts of Roman slave insurrections. "We have already at least 10,000 men of these descendants of Ham, fit to bear arms," said William Byrd in 1736, "and these numbers increase every day, as well by birth as by importation. And in case there should arise a man of desperate courage amongst us, exasperated by a desperate fortune, he might with more advantage than Cataline kindle a servile war. Such a man might be dreadfully mischievous before an opposition could be formed against him, and tinge our rivers wide as they are with blood." [5]

Even in the late seventeenth century Virginia had once been disturbed by rumors of a slave conspiracy in the Northern Neck, and then again by the activities of armed runaways.[6] In 1710, after one planned insurrection had been aborted and two potential rebels executed, the newly arrived Governor Spotswood argued that the Virginia militia was far too weak—"so imaginary a defence," he said, "that we cannot too cautiously conceal it from our neighbours and our slaves, nor too earnestly pray that neither the lust of domination, nor the desire of freedom may stir these people to any attempts." The Negroes, Spotswood thought, "by their daily increase seem to be the most dangerous." Fearing an insurrection that would "surely be attended with most dreadful consequences," he proposed that "we cannot be too early in providing against it, both by putting ourselves in a better posture of defence and by making a law to prevent the consultations of these Negroes." In the same year Governor Robert Gibbes urged the South

5. Jordan, 111.
6. On early Virginia slave discontent, see Herbert Aptheker, *American Negro Slave Revolts* (1943), 165–8, 170–1.

Carolina Assembly to consider "the great quantities of negroes that are daily brought into this government, and the small number of whites that comes amongst us, and how many are lately dead and gone off," and "how insolent and mischievous the negroes are become." As a remedy and as part of a more effective system of warning he proposed to erect gibbets on which executed bodies could be displayed.[7]

The first serious revolt in the mainland colonies took place in New York City in 1712, when about two dozen slaves, thinking themselves protected by sorcery, set fire to a building and ambushed the whites who came to put it out, attacking them with guns, clubs, and knives, killing and wounding several. The uprising was suppressed within twenty-four hours by soldiers called from the fort, and after trial a score were acquitted or reprieved but twenty-one slaves were executed. "Some were burnt," reported Governor Robert Hunter to the Lords of Trade, "others were hanged, one broke on the wheel, and one hung alive in chains in the town, so that there has been the most exemplary punishment inflicted that could possibly be thought of. . . ."[8] A generation later, in 1741, a year of war and discontent, a series of unexplained fires threw New Yorkers into a startling fit of mass hysteria over rumors of a slave conspiracy, and many even fled the city. Although no evidence of any slave plot has ever been unearthed, nor any connection found between the Negroes and the fires, the crowds clamored for convictions. After trial, eleven Negroes were burned to death and fifty de-

7. Quoted in Jordan, 111; quoted in Aptheker, 171n.
8. Aptheker, 173; on New York conspiracies see McManus, chapter 7; Scott; T. Wood Clarke, "The Negro Plot of 1741," *New York History,* 25 (1944), 167–81.

ported to the West Indies. Nothing like this had happened in the colonies since the Salem witchcraft panic a half century before.

Virginia rumbled in the 1720's with abortive plots and rumors of plots. In 1722 three blacks were accused of urging other slaves to rise up and destroy whites, though some doubt about their guilt is suggested by the relative restraint of the penalty: three years' imprisonment, or, on the promise of their masters to comply, resale and transportation out of the colony. The following year another supposed plot was uncovered, and seven Negroes were sentenced to sale and transportation. In 1729 a number of slaves ran off to the Blue Ridge Mountains with stolen guns, ammunition, and agricultural tools, and were recaptured after a pitched battle. The next year the charge that several Negroes were agitating for an insurrection was evidently taken with full seriousness by the officials of the province, since four slaves were tried and executed for this crime.

South Carolina was alarmed in 1711 by a group of armed blacks who plundered a number of houses and plantations before their leader was tracked down and killed. Many South Carolinians believed that conspiracies, whose actuality seems hazy, had also been aborted in 1713 and again in 1720. But in 1739 the province suffered the full-fledged rebellion it had long feared. A certain carelessness in the treatment of Negroes on the part of the easygoing people of Charles Town may have had something to do with making it possible, since it was not uncommon for one or two hundred Negroes to hold drinking parties in the city. In any case, this revolt was set off when the governor of Spanish Florida, anticipating the war with England which in fact soon came, published in 1738 a royal edict offering freedom to slaves who escaped from the English planters to Saint Augustine, once more stimulating the familiar Negro hope of escape by flight to the Spanish colony. The revolt which broke out in the fall of 1739 was simply an attempt by slaves to fight their way to freedom across the border. One night twenty slaves led by a Negro named Jemmy broke open a warehouse near the Stono River, helped themselves to guns and ammunition, killed ten whites, and burned several houses. Then, after having recruited about sixty more blacks, they set out toward Saint Augustine. After several hours, the militia summoned by Lieutenant Governor William Bull caught up with them. After a desperate battle, in which the Negroes, many of them rum sodden, were considerably outnumbered, the "insurrection" was suppressed with forty blacks and twenty whites killed.[9]

The following year another conspiracy, apparently of serious dimensions, was crushed when a slave betrayed it, and a group of over 150 slaves who gathered for the event were easily put to flight. About 50 were caught and hanged. Later in the year damaging fires broke out in Charles Town, and, whatever their source, some slaves were executed for arson.[1] The Stono revolt led to a new codification of slave laws in South Carolina which, in order to prevent masters from "exercizing too great rigour and cruelty over them," prohibited them from working their slaves on Sunday or more than fourteen or fifteen hours a day, and other minimally protective standards imposed some limitations. Gatherings of slaves were outlawed, selling alcohol to them was forbidden, as well as teaching them to write, and the patrol system was strengthened by

9. M. Eugene Sirmans, *Colonial South Carolina*, 207–8.
1. Aptheker, 189–90.

turning it over to the militia. The Assembly also tried to cut slave importations by raising the tax on them, but this measure was disallowed a few years later by the Board of Trade.[2] With the Stono Rebellion the major uprisings of the colonial period came to an end, though signs of slave restiveness did not. Uncomfortably, but at great profit, the South had become entrenched in the slave system.

2. M. Eugene Sirmans, "The Legal Status of the Slave in South Carolina, 1670–1740," *Journal of Southern History,* 28 (1962), 462–73.

CHAPTER V

‌✣

The
Middle-Class
World

1

"T HE people of this province," said the *Pennsylvania Journal* in 1756, "are generally of the middling sort, and at
present pretty much upon a level. They are chiefly industrious farmers, artificers or men in trade; they enjoy and
are fond of freedom, and the *meanest among them* thinks
he has a right to civility from the greatest." [1] As always,
when class relations are discussed in America, one catches
a note of exaggeration. Yet what is exaggerated is only the
truth, here a profound truth. What we must envisage in
order to comprehend eighteenth-century America is a
middle-class world. When one speaks of the middle class in
a society so imperfectly measured by economic historians,
one speaks inevitably with imprecision. As a first approxi-
mation, the middle class can be defined only as a stratum
of propertied people who were neither conspicuously rich
nor distressingly poor, and the definition can be made
progressively more explicit only by enumeration and description.

1. Quoted in Clinton Rossiter, *Seedtime of the Republic* (1953), 106.

There are, of course, some qualifications that must in-
stantly be made when this society is described as middle
class. It was, as we shall see, a middle-class society gov-
erned for the most part by its upper classes. Some of the
qualifications are regional: there were sharper divisions in
the towns than in most of the countryside, and especially
in New York and South Carolina one has to reckon with
potent provincial aristocracies. There were everywhere
significant differences of wealth and opportunity, and
there is some evidence to suggest that in most places
wealth at mid-eighteenth century was becoming somewhat
less evenly distributed. In any case, when one speaks of a
complex society as being substantially middle class, one
conveys an implicit comparison with other societies that
are less so; and the comparison made here is not with some
imaginary, uniformly middle-class utopia, but with the
actual societies that have appeared on the globe, and in
particular with contemporaneous European societies,
whose travelers here were so often struck by the middle-
class quality of American life.

In this society, as in all complex societies, there were the
rich and the poor, and as in all such societies the poor were
disproportionately miserable and the rich disproportionately powerful. What distinguished the colonial world of
the mainland was that here, much more than elsewhere,
the thoughts of both rich and poor were so much directed
toward the middle. Here, more than elsewhere, the poor
man, if white, could really hope to edge his way into the
middle class. And here, more than elsewhere, the rich man
had to exercise his power in the knowledge that his way of
doing so must not irritate a numerous, relatively aggressive, and largely enfranchised middle-class public. Here
there were harassed governors, but no Court; there were

rich men and influential councillors, but no nobility; there
were churches, two of them with the thin legal claims of
establishments, but no Church with a full hierarchical
panoply and a deeply rooted place in the texture of the
society; here there were struggling colleges, competently
educating the future rulers and ministers of the provinces,
but no ancient universities fit to serve as the hiving places
of boisterous young aristocrats; here there were stunningly
large tracts of lands put at the disposal of favorites and
speculators, but on them were no magnificent estates
manned by scores of servants and capable of feeding
scores of brilliant and fashionable guests. This was a scene
in which the basic institutions of Old World society were
represented by shadowy substitutes, but in which the
simpler agencies of the middle class were in strong evidence: the little churches of the dissenting sects, the
taverns (then known as "ordinaries"), the societies for self-
improvement and "philosophical" inquiry, the increasingly
eclectic little colleges; the contumacious newspapers, the
county courthouses and town halls, the how-to-do books,
the *Poor Richard's Almanack*.

Eighteenth-century colonials recognized classes in their
own realistic way by speaking quite routinely of "the better sort," "the middling sort," and "the meaner sort." Still,
what made colonial mainland society a preponderantly
middle-class world was not the absence of other classes
but the overwhelming weight and presence of the middle
class, by the standards of the time—a weight and presence
measured not only in numbers and in exemplary influence,
but in politics and the suffrage, in the prevalent manners
and political ideas. The qualities of an aristocracy were, to
be sure, not altogether missing: there were pockets of inherited family pride and privilege and, with allowances

for the American scale of things, of aggrandized wealth. There was also a significant measure everywhere of elite solidarity and control. But there was only a slender sense of the personal prerogative, the code of honor, or the grand extravagance in life-style that goes with a hereditary aristocracy. What one saw in constant evidence—and one saw it even among the upper classes and the lower—was the disciplined ethic of work, the individual assertiveness, the progressive outlook, the preference for dissenting religions, and the calculating and materialistic way of life associated with the middle class.

Middle-class aspirations not only caused the upper classes to temper their ways, but penetrated white society at its less affluent levels. And not unrealistically: eighteenth-century French observers of England commented with surprise and envy at the readiness with which an Englishman of vigor and resourcefulness could move from one class to another; but English observers of the colonies, as well as boastful natives, made the same comparisons between the colonies and the home country. In the colonies goodly numbers of those starting life below the middle class not only shared its aspirations but had a significant chance to realize them within a lifetime. And in this America was supreme. Open the work of an English historian writing a general history of the eighteenth century, and you will soon be in the midst of a strong and necessary preoccupation with the grinding, unremitting poverty of the small farmer or the pestiferous, deadly squalor of the urban poor. Open the work of his American counterpart, and you are as likely as not to find an equally strong preoccupation with the process by which the propertyless man or the small farmer arrived at more comfortable circumstances.

But of course this was a middle-class world with a difference, which sets it off from post-industrial worlds: it was a middle-class *rural* society, peopled mainly by farmers and small planters and by those who bought from them, supplied them, worked for or slaved for them. Perhaps eight out of ten of its people made their living from farming, the rest as artisans or in extractive industries. Its middle class was based less upon shopkeeping, industry, or urban services than upon the widespread ownership of the land, which in America was easier to get and keep, to work and inherit, than anywhere else in the world. Still a harsh society for those without land, skill, and freedom, the society of the mainland colonies put land in remarkable quantities into the hands of a sizable proportion of its people, paid more for industrial skills than it desired to, and honored freedom more generously the more it exploited its slaves.

The colonial world was no more homogeneous in regional economies than it was in religious and ethnic stocks. The five substantial towns of the seaboard marked its most significant urban enclaves; and in addition to these we can distinguish a number of major variations on the basic rural theme: the New England villages, the Hudson River estates, the Chesapeake society, the South Carolina planting society, and the backcountry.

2

The major urban enclaves in rural America, the five seaboard cities, throve by exporting rural surpluses. Philadelphia, which grew fastest, did so because of the richness of the interior it served in exportable wheat, flour, bread, beef, pork, butter, iron, lumber, and furs—goods which

were conveyed by its merchants to the West Indies and to
northern and southern Europe. Boston, by contrast, serving an interior without an abundance of surpluses, failed
to grow at all; the other ports, New York, Newport, and
Charles Town, grew moderately. By mid-century each of
these cities had developed its own commercial gentry,
knowledgeable in the ways of the world's markets, busy
in coastal trade with each other, and engaged in strengthening their familial and cultural ties. Visitors were often
impressed by these cities. Peter Kalm noted in 1748 that
Philadelphia had come into existence within the lifetime
of one man: "And yet its natural advantages, trade, riches
and power, are by no means inferior to any, even of the
most ancient towns in Europe." "The nobleness of the
town," confessed an English naval officer eight years later
concerning New York, "surprised me more than the fertile
appearance of the country. I had no idea of finding a place
in America, consisting of near 2,000 houses, elegantly built
of brick, raised on an eminence and the streets paved and
spacious, furnished with commodious keys and ware-
houses, and employing some hundreds of vessels in its
foreign trade and fisheries—but such is this city that very
few in England can rival it in its show." [2]

In cities so highly developed it was impossible for candid observers to pretend that there was no class system.
Arthur Browne, an Anglican clergyman who had lived in
Newport, Boston, and Portsmouth, New Hampshire, took
pleasure in pointing out that utopian aspirations toward
classlessness were belied even by American experience:
"The inhabitants of the town by more information, better

2. Carl Bridenbaugh, *Cities in Revolt* (1955), 3, 42.

polish and greater intercourse with strangers, insensibly acquired an ascendancy over the farmer of the country; the richer merchants of these towns, together with the clergy, lawyers, physicians and officers of the English navy who had occasionally settled there, were considered as gentry: even being a member of the Church of England gave a kind of distinctive fashion. A superior order thus formed by better property and more information existed even to a degree sufficient to excite jealousy in the agricultural system, and to be a gentleman was sufficient in some parts of the country to expose the bearer of the name to mockery and rudeness. . . ." [3]

There is a reason, moreover, to suppose that during the century preceding the Revolution urban inequalities increased in some respects. James Henretta's researches, based on Boston's tax records for 1687 and 1771, show that the proportion of its adult males without taxable property had increased over this long span of time from 14 per cent to 29 per cent. The standard of living of craftsmen, small shopkeepers, and laborers had undoubtedly improved considerably with the economic development of the community as a whole, but their relative position vis-à-vis the richer merchants was somewhat poorer. In 1687 the richest quarter of the taxable population had had 66 per cent of the assessed wealth; by the eve of the Revolution it had 78 per cent. The mercantile elite was growing more prominent and somewhat more exclusive.[4] Whether this trend, mapped out in a static city whose population declined between the early 1740's and 1760 and did not sig-

3. Ibid., 137.
4. James A. Henretta, "Economic Development and Social Structure in Colonial Boston," *William and Mary Quarterly*, 22 (1965), 75–92.

nificantly rise again until after the Revolution, was dupli-
cated in the more dynamic cities of the seaboard is still
uncertain.

Yet when all this is said, it must be remembered that
the mercantile upper crust in the American cities was an
open class with few other barriers to acceptance beyond
wealth, and that wealth acquired through a series of good
strokes of business or a fortunate marriage could bring a
family from obscurity to prominence in two generations or
even in one. "A man who has money here," said a Rhode
Island sea captain in 1748, "no matter how he came by it,
he is everything, and wanting that he's a mere nothing,
let his conduct be ever so irreproachable. Money is here
the true fuller's earth for reputation, there is not a spot or
stain but it will take out." [5] This is rather like what Defoe
had written about England a half century earlier:

> *Wealth, howsoever got, in England makes*
> *Lords of mechanics, gentlemen of rakes:*
> *Antiquity and birth are needless here;*
> *'Tis impudence and money makes a peer.*

In Europe, especially in England, the aristocracy modified itself over time by intermarriage with the business
class. In America the aristocracy, such as it was, *constituted* itself out of the business class—a proposition which
is true even of the South when full regard is given to the
entrepreneurial ways of most planters. And the emergent
middle class carried its pristine bourgeois standards upward with it. The middle-class search for comfort and convenience was more in evidence than the search for ele-

5. Bridenbaugh, *Cities in Revolt*, 140.

gance and display, and so were its rather calculating morals and discipline, its manners, and its political ideas. Cadwallader Colden, who himself held no low station in the society of New York, celebrated not the standards of the upper segment to which he belonged but those of the class just beneath it. "Riches," he pronounced, "are not always acquired by the honestest means, nor are they always accompanied by the greatest integrity of mind, with the most knowledge, or with the most generous sentiments and public spirit . . . the middling rank of mankind in all countries and in all ages, have justly obtain'd the character, to be generally the most honest. . . . And I am likewise fully persuaded that we may much more safely trust our liberty and property with our neighbors of middling rank than with those of the greatest riches who are thereby tempted to lord it over their neighbors." Benjamin Franklin, planning for his son William at sixteen, envisaged for him a way of life rooted not in those topmost colonial strata to which Franklin had access but in the middle ranks from which he had come. "I don't want him to be what is commonly called a gentleman," Franklin wrote a friend. "I want to put him to some business by which he may, with care and industry, get a temperate and reasonable living." [6] Hence the philosophy, the political values, the moral commitments of the townspeople, even into the upper ranks, remained middle class.

The situation of propertyless wage workers is never enviable, and the seaboard cities were filling with a working class subject to all the hazards of the economy. Merchant seamen, though their wages in good times were higher than the average for other workers, followed a particularly

6. Ibid., 148–9; for Franklin, 148.

miserable trade which subjected them to grave mistreat-
ment. Yet by the lights of the time, free labor in every segment in the economy from the seaboard cities to the ham-
lets of the interior was well paid, and had been from the
beginning, justifying the summary verdict of Judge William Allen: "You may depend upon it that this is one of the
best poor man's countries in the world." [7] In the early days
of Massachusetts Bay, John Winthrop had complained
that workmen took advantage of their scarcity to "raise
their wages to an excessive rate," and at the end of the
seventeenth century a Pennsylvania observer reported that
if high wages were refused them, laborers "would quickly
set up by themselves, for they can have provisions very
cheap, and land for a very small matter, or next to nothing
in comparison of the purchase of lands in England." [8]
Hence the working class too could aspire to a proprietary
condition and to joining the ranks of the "middling sort"
with considerably better chances of real success than anywhere else.

The employing classes, living under the guidance of the
prevailing mercantilist theories, had no hesitation about
setting maximum wage rates by law. But such laws were
all but hopeless in America where the machinery of law
was notably feeble. The laws, drawn solely with the interests of employers in mind, put labor at a disadvantage; but
the market was on labor's side, and the market was stronger.
Wages were, by the common estimate of contemporaries,
often two or three times what they were in England, [9] but

7. Ibid., 148.
8. Percy W. Bidwell and John I. Falconer, *History of Agriculture in
the Northern United States, 1620–1860* (1925), 33.
9. *American Husbandry* (1775; ed. by Harry J. Carman, 1939), 66.

even the margin between wages and land costs was so slender that proprietorship was always tempting.[1] This made labor undependable, and enterprises were known to fail not for lack of cheap materials or good markets but because their labor supply evaporated in the open American air. Laws, particularly common in the Southern colonies, requiring men to stick to their trades and not abandon them for farming were another insufficient and unenforceable remedy. Under these circumstances it is hardly surprising that employers seized upon indentured servants who were bound to serve out a term of labor and in the South eagerly imported slaves bound for life.

A labor force relatively free from dire need was also free from a spirit of subservience. "When we hire any of these people," said Crèvecoeur, drawing a contrast between England and America, "we rather pray and entreat them. You must give them what they ask. . . . They must be at your table and feed . . . on the best you have." In New Jersey the teacher Philip Fithian saw "gentlemen, when they are not actually engaged in the public service, on their farms, setting a laborious example to their domestics, and on the other hand we see labourers at the tables and in the parlours of their betters enjoying the advantage, and honour of their society and conversation." A British official reported in 1760 that "under forms of a democratical government, all mortifying distinctions of rank are lost in common equality; and . . . the ways of wealth and preferment are alike open to all men."[2] Patently an exaggera-

1. Jackson Turner Main, *The Social Structure of Revolutionary America* (1965), 166–76.
2. Quotations are from Carl N. Degler, *Out of Our Past* (1959), 46, 49–50.

tion, this statement nevertheless marked out the direction of American society, its deviation from what decent Englishmen thought right. The reports of royal governors on the state of American politics in the 1760's rumble with anxiety about the effects upon civic life of an aggressive and self-confident lower class. Governor William Bull of South Carolina not long before the outbreak of the Revolution found city politics taking a direction "inclined more to the democratical than regal scale." Concerning Boston, Governor William Shirley complained after the anti-impressment riot of 1747 that "the principal cause of the mobbish turn in this town is in its Constitution; by which the management of it is devolved upon the populace assembled in their town meetings; where . . . the meanest inhabitants who by their constant attendance there are generally in the majority and outvote the gentlemen, merchants, substantial traders and all the better part of the inhabitants to whom it is irksome to attend." [3]

3

It is tempting to think of New England simply as a region of obdurate villagers, homogeneously English and Congregationalist. Certainly it showed a more recognizable likeness to the mother country than could be seen anywhere among the more mixed peoples to the south. The anonymous author of *American Husbandry* saw "in many respects a great resemblance between New England and Great Britain," which in the most cultivated parts might make a traveler think himself not far from home, while a

3. Bridenbaugh, *Cities in Revolt*, 224, 116.

British officer after a colonial tour in the 1760's thought Boston "more like an English old town than any in America— the language and manners of the people, very much resemble the old country." [4]

Yet for all this, the New England colonies differed markedly from England and all of Europe in their social structure and class relations; they also differed significantly from each other, not least in their economies. Striking as the social distance might be between a Boston or Newport merchant and the poorest of the inland villagers, New Englanders had quite unwittingly devised an economy as close to egalitarian as anything in the Western world. While the early Puritan ministers and civic leaders had gone on honing their denunciations of democracy to a sharp edge, the religious and communal aspirations, the land policies, and the social composition of their hearers had silently put the society on the path toward a relatively democratic polity.

In 1772 Benjamin Franklin made a tour of Ireland and Scotland, where he was impressed by the state of "landlords, great noblemen, and gentlemen, extremely opulent, living in the highest affluence and magnificence," and at the same time appalled at the condition of "the bulk of the people tenants, extremely poor, living in the most sordid wretchedness, in dirty hovels of mud and straw, and clothed only in rags." In contrast, "I thought often of the happiness of New England, where every man is a freeholder, has a vote in public affairs, lives in a tidy warm house, has plenty of good food and fuel, with whole clothes from head to foot, the manufacture perhaps of his

4. *American Husbandry*, 46; Lawrence H. Gipson, *The British Empire before the American Revolution*, III (rev. edn. 1960), 5n; ibid., 4–5.

own family." [5] "We in New England," wrote Joseph Trumbull of Connecticut from England in 1764, "know nothing of poverty and want, we have no idea of the thing, how much better do our poor people live than 7/8 of the people of this much famed island." [6]

The author of *American Husbandry* agreed. "Respecting the lower classes of New England," he wrote, "there is scarcely any part of the world in which they are better off. The price of labour is very high, and they have with this advantage another no less valuable, of being able to take up a tract of land whenever they are able to settle it. . . . This great ease of gaining a farm, renders the lower class of people very industrious; which, with the high price of labour, banishes every thing that has the least appearance of begging, or that wondering, destitute state of poverty, which we see so common in England." As for substantial farmers, he found those of Britain "incomparably richer" than those of New England, but when he turned to the lower class of farmers, he thought that there was not "a more miserable set of men to be found than the little farmers in Britain . . . whereas in New England, the little freeholders and farmers live in the midst of plenty of all the necessaries of life; they do not acquire wealth, but they have comforts and abundance." [7]

New England had always been set off by certain methods of colonization—a measured approach to the settlement of the western wilderness, the careful preliminary survey of new lands, the creation of new towns under a system in which the lands were divided—though not

5. *The Writings of Benjamin Franklin,* ed. by Albert H. Smyth (1906), V, 362.
6. Chilton Williamson, *American Suffrage* (1960), 39.
7. *American Husbandry,* 52–3, 67; *cf.* 46.

equally—largely among resident proprietors, a soberly
marshaled progression based upon relatively compact settlement. New England village society, with its town
church and its town meeting and its sense of moral community, seemed determined, at least for its first century
and more—there would be grave changes in the eighteenth century—to edge its way slowly into the resistant
wild lands, keeping its old ways as intact as possible. Most
New Englanders were general farmers, very few of them
on a large scale. And although they were tilling a soil that
was—with some notable regional exceptions in Rhode
Island and Connecticut—rocky and relatively infertile,
and tilling it with methods that fell far short of the best
then known, they managed to create and sustain a strikingly peaceful and comfortable rural society. Unlike farmers in other colonies they did so without a substantial
force of indentured servants at their beck—New England
had somehow always been relatively unreceptive to them [8]
—or of slaves.

On the seacoast, of course, New England made good use
of its opportunities in the fisheries, shipbuilding, distilling
(rum, the traders of Massachusetts claimed in 1748, was
"the great support of all their trade and fishery; without
which they can no longer subsist" [9]) and slave trading.
Massachusetts, though a society of farmers, was actually
importing wheat in the 1750's; but Connecticut and Rhode
Island had soil rich enough to produce cereals beyond
local needs and to provide grain and cattle, beef, pork, and
horses for the export trade. All New England had timber,
and New Hampshire had enormous white pine trees suitable for great masts, produced at a striking profit. Yet

8. Abbott E. Smith, *Colonists in Bondage* (1947), 4, 28–9.
9. Gipson, III, 3, 16.

little of the commercial wealth reaped on the seaboard, which was by far the most inegalitarian of the regions of New England, reached the interior. The commonly observed comfort and solidity of the general farming regions of New England must be traced to other foundations. Its broadly shared land must surely be one of them. An outstanding feature of New England rural society was the relatively small proportion of landless men, which, even in the eastern Massachusetts counties, did not usually exceed 20 per cent.[1] This, of course, suggests a common minimum of comfort rather than flat equality. In Massachusetts as a whole, it is estimated that the wealthiest 10 per cent at mid-century and shortly after owned about half the inventoried property—a scale of distribution which, though far from egalitarian, is considerably more so than that which was shown in the United States at the mid-twentieth century.[2] Yet it must be remembered that this figure incorporates the sharp inequalities of the towns, and that the distribution of wealth in rural New England was notably more equitable.

The New England system of compact settlement made it much more feasible for the people of its interior to take advantage of the division of labor than in other colonial regions. In the rural South, by contrast, the vast diffusion of the population through the countryside made it extremely difficult for artisans to find a settled market for their skills, to maintain standards, and to get a satisfactory living from their trades. Rather quickly they drifted into the ranks of the farmers. A few wealthy townsmen and great planters might provide for their needs by importing highly skilled craftsmen as indentured servants, or by

1. Main, 21.
2. Ibid., 42.

training slaves. But the great majority of the smaller planters and farmers had to improvise, do without, or buy expensive imported wares.[3] In New England better markets
were to be had for the craftsman's skills, and the entire
population benefited accordingly. Compact village conditions were more consistently to be found. Connecticut, for
example, in the curiously limited sense in which we must
use the term for the eighteenth century, was the most
"urban" of the colonies, as measured by the number of
towns having about four thousand people.[4] Where a black-
smith, a cooper, a cobbler, a carpenter were lacking, they
were often procured by common town effort, often with
a handsome portion of land as a special inducement. Ingenuity and crafts and skills flourished.[5] What was true in
this respect of New England was also true on the whole of
the more compactly settled areas of the rural North generally; but in New England, where long, closed-in winters
and folkish habits of industry and inventiveness both conspired to develop indoor skills, they flowered.

When a satisfactory account of its early economic development is written, the industriousness of the New England population may well rank along with these other
forces as an explanation of the region's high standard of
comfort. Its work habits were those of a disciplined population which, contemplating its opportunities to get ahead,
had first-rate incentives. New England also had behind it
the moral impulses of a disciplined community which
looked upon work as having a quasi-religious merit and
upon worldly success as a possible token of God's favor.
Comparing New England with New France, the Jesuit

---

3. Carl Bridenbaugh, *The Colonial Craftsman* (1950), 7–32, esp. 29–32.
4. Gipson, III, 74n, 75.
5. Bridenbaugh, *The Colonial Craftsman,* 37–53.

Charlevoix made note of the prudential economics of the New Englanders. In New France, he said, "there reigns an opulence by which the people seem not to know how to profit; while . . . poverty is hidden under an air of ease which appears entirely natural. The English colonist keeps as much and spends as little as possible; the French colonist enjoys what he has got, and often makes a display of what he has not got. The one labors for his heirs; the other leaves them to get on as they can, like himself." [6] Living in a compact community, and surrounded by a large body of grandparents, uncles, and cousins, the young New Englander beginning a search for a livelihood had the props of kinship to assure him of an occasional helping hand and a respectable place in the community. If he chose to cut himself off from these bonds by moving to a newly settled area, he might only be trading them for the significant advantages of the early resident-proprietor of a new town. Finally, even the political structure of the towns was conducive to pride and self-respect: there were so many official functions, major and minor, especially in the early phases of town development, and these were so often rotated, that to exercise at least minor authority and responsibility was part of the experience of an extraordinarily high proportion of the adult males of the New England village.[7]

In the decades following the Peace of Utrecht in 1713, the New England colonies underwent a period of phenomenal growth. By mid-century there were signs of a new and critical phase in the economic development of

6. W. B. Weeden, *Economic and Social History of New England,* II, 512, quoting Parkman, *Old Regime,* 393.
7. Charles S. Grant, *Democracy in the Connecticut Frontier Town of Kent* (1961); Michael Zuckerman, *Peaceable Kingdoms* (1970); see also Sumner Chilton Powell, *Puritan Village* (1963).

older New England, which was now reaching the limits of its internal land supply. Recent demographic studies have all pointed to a similar pattern in the land supply: town lands were ample for the first resident generation, and remained sufficient to accommodate the second; but by the third a pinch was felt, and emigration began to be necessary.[8] For example, the frontier town of Kent, Connecticut, situated in the northwest corner of the state, was founded in 1738. Its land supply accommodated the second generation, the sons of the original residents, as they came of age in the 1750's and 1760's, even though individuals had less land to work than their fathers. The third generation, reaching adulthood after 1770, found themselves inheriting much smaller slices. The pressure of population on the land began to be felt acutely, large numbers emigrated, and those who stayed behind found themselves in declining circumstances.[9] Many villages to the east had gone earlier through a similar cycle of development. As long as their internal supply of ungranted land held out, Connecticut, Massachusetts, and Rhode Island had been able to contain these pressures, but the extraordinary population growth of the early eighteenth century brought them to the point of more or less saturated settlement by about 1755, except for some tracts remaining in northwest Massachusetts.[1] In the 1760's, as soon as the war with France was over on the American continent and frontier uncertainties were removed, a new thrust began into Vermont, Maine, and New Hampshire, but these regions did not

8. Philip Greven, *Four Generations; Population, Land, and Family in Colonial Andover, Massachusetts* (1970); Grant; and Kenneth Lockridge, *A New England Town: The First Hundred Years* (1970).

9. Grant, chapter 6.

1. Lois K. Mathews, *The Expansion of New England* (1909), map facing 98.

long suffice, and in 1781, at the end of the military action of the Revolutionary War, New England settlement once again would begin to make great new leaps that carried it into upstate and western New York, western Pennsylvania, Ohio, and then beyond.

By mid-century land speculation was raging through Massachusetts and Connecticut. The practice of limiting land grants for new towns to congregations had already broken down in Connecticut at the end of the seventeenth century, and government need for income from land sales pushed the process forward, so that it now became increasingly easy for individual speculators to acquire land.[2] Massachusetts followed suit, especially after 1725, and before long land speculation was rampant in New England, undermining the old steady pattern of town settlement and shifting the attention of villagers from cultivating the land to cultivating land values. In 1753 a group of Connecticut entrepreneurs, taking advantage of the broad terms of Connecticut's charter which had promised land from sea to sea, made a questionable purchase of about two hundred square miles in Pennsylvania on the Susquehanna River from the Indians, organized as the Susquehanna Company, and distributed stock shares widely among leading personages in the colony. Large proprietors, of course, benefited from the land rage, though in nothing like the dimensions that prevailed outside New England; but the passion for speculation reached down to the level of the ordinary farmers.[3] The urge to exploit the land was changing the old order, the

2. Richard L. Bushman, *From Puritan to Yankee* (1967), chapters 5 and 6.
3. Grant; James Truslow Adams, *Revolutionary New England* (1941); Bushman.

Yankee entrepreneur was replacing the Puritan villager, and that desire for novelty, for moving from place to place, already so strongly manifested in other colonies and among other stocks, was now becoming characteristic of New Englanders as well.

4

The Hudson River was like a dagger cutting a swath of land monopoly and aristocratic domination between New England and the colonies to the south and west. The Dutch had attempted to import into New York a quasi-feudal system of ownership and control in the huge patroonships of the Hudson Valley, and the early English governors had not only confirmed the patroons' titles but had outdone the Dutch in showing favoritism to land monopolists. Near the end of the seventeenth century, after a short interval during which grants of moderate size were common, Governor Benjamin Fletcher had handed out to favorites grants of such insolent and flamboyant extravagance that his successor, the Earl of Bellomont, found it was now all but impossible to settle the country with inhabitants, "there being no land but what must be purchased from his few grantees." "This whole Province," he complained, "is given away to about thirty persons in effect," and he was not surprised to find settlers flowing out of New York when men could "buy the fee-simple lands in the Jerseys for £5 per hundred acres, and I believe as cheaply in Pennsylvania." [4] Hence, along the eastern and southern borders of New York, there were carved out in a helter-skelter fashion great blocks of land whose bound-

4. Bidwell and Falconer, 64.

aries were drawn by fraud and maladministration as much as by design, the region along the Hudson of Pelham Manor, Scarsdale Manor, Fordham Manor, Morrisania, Cortlandt Manor, Livingston Manor, and others; and, between the Hudson and the east branch of the Delaware, another series of patents running up to as much as 300,000 acres in size. The Hardenburgh Patent in Ulster County was estimated in 1749 at over one million acres. Livingston Manor, one of the best managed of the Hudson estates, had almost 160,000.

New York landlords preferred renting to selling, and tried to hold land prices up to artificial levels which were highly unrealistic by American standards. They were sustained in this practice by the tax policies of the province, which, by not taxing unimproved lands, made it possible to hold on to large tracts for long periods without prohibitive cost. Richard Peters, the Secretary of Pennsylvania, was appalled at the contrasting policy that prevailed beyond his colony's northern border: "I'm vastly surprised that this monstrous monopoly has never been taken notice of when the remedy appears so plain and effectual, nothing more than a tax upon each 100 acres of unimproved land which would render it impracticable for any single man to hold a very large tract, and would very soon divide these vast bodies into more useful parts." [5]

But the manor lords had little difficulty in dominating the Assembly, and, counting tenants, hired laborers, indentured servants, and slaves, New York developed a numerous landless and relatively poor population. Since word had gone out that this colony was no place for a poor man, New York shared but lightly in the population boom

5. Gipson, III, 113.

of the post-Utrecht period, until about 1750 when it began to attract settlers, many of whom were squatters, from New Hampshire, Massachusetts, and New Jersey. New York then entered upon a period of growth and turbulence which arose from the incongruity between its land policies and those of its neighbors. This era was marked by boundary disputes and by memorable land riots which British regulars had to be called in to quell.

In agricultural management New York tended to share the defects of its neighbors, but in industry it was relatively inactive. A modest amount of iron was extracted on Livingston Manor, beaver hats were made, and there were rum distilleries ancillary to the trade with the Indians and Africa. The fur trade, centered in Albany, was an important focus of colonial enterprise, tapping a large area of the north country and Canada, and yielding handsome profits to rich Albany enterprisers. The Albany merchants enjoyed a bad reputation for swilling the Indians with rum so they could buy pelts for cheap trinkets and trifles; they were even accused in the 1740's, not least by Governor George Clinton, of egging on French-allied Indians to plunder New England settlements, hoping to profit from the loot. The traveler Peter Kalm thought: "The avarice, selfishness, immeasurable love of money of the inhabitants of Albany are well known throughout all North America." [6]

South of New York lay the heartland of the rural middle-class society of the colonies—the region of Pennsylvania, New Jersey, and Delaware, an area characterized in the main by agrarian prosperity, and by repeated bursts of self-satisfaction which seem on the whole to have been warranted. Its center, Pennsylvania, was still growing

6. Gipson, III, 119–20.

apace as Germans and Ulstermen overtook the English and Quaker population. As complex ethnically as New England was simple, Pennsylvania was proud of the masterless self-sufficiency of its propertied farmers. It was a saying there, Gottlieb Mittelberger reported, that Pennsylvania was "heaven for farmers, paradise for artisans, and hell for officials and preachers." [7] The geographer and surveyor Lewis Evans attributed the well-being of Pennsylvania to its land policies. "What the world has imputed to the happiness of our constitution, is with more justice to be ascribed to the happy management of the land offices," he wrote. At these offices cheap land could be had through simple procedures, and one could be sure of firm and unchallengeable land titles. "Every man is glad to hold immediately under the Chief Lord of the Soil. And if we add to this the great ease, and dispatch that business has been done with in our offices, we need not wonder to see so many strangers flock thither to partake of our happiness." [8]

Mittelberger credited Pennsylvania's extraordinary heritage of religious freedom with its liberality and well-being. Among the dozen and more distinct religious groups in the province, he reported, he seldom heard or saw a quarrel. "Even strangers trust each other more than acquaintances in Europe. People are far more sincere and generous than in Germany; therefore our Americans live more quietly and peacefully together than the Europeans; and all this is the result of the liberty which they enjoy and which makes them all equal." He found the rural Pennsylvanians quick to share their abundance. One could travel about the province "for a whole year without spending a *kreuzer*,"

---

7. Gottlieb Mittelberger, *Journey to Pennsylvania* (edn. 1960), ed. and trans. by Oscar Handlin and John Clive, 48.
8. Gipson, III, 181–2.

he wrote; upon arrival at a house the traveler "is asked whether he wishes to have anything to eat. Then the stranger is given a piece of cold meat, generally left over from a meal. In addition he is given plenty of bread, butter or cheese, as well as drink. If he wants to stay overnight, he and his horse can do so, free of charge." [9]

Travelers in the rural areas of Pennsylvania and the other Middle Colonies often commented on the absence of great estates and the comfortable condition of those living even on the smallest. In the most commercially successful farming areas of this region, however, as in other regions, there is some reason to believe that settlement and economic development led to somewhat greater inequalities of possession. At least one area, Chester County, with good soil, good markets, and good transportation, appears to have undergone a gradual but steady concentration of wealth during the eighteenth century, though at the same time there may also have been a gradual improvement in the living standards of the poorest farmers. In 1715 the poorest 60 per cent of the taxpayers there owned 36 per cent of the assessed taxable wealth; by 1760 they owned 26.8 per cent, and while their share of the whole continued to go down thereafter the total amount of their income rose.[1]

Delaware and New Jersey shared in large part the character of Pennsylvania, their lands being given over to general small-scale farming, much of it on good soil, with relatively few grand estates. Economically and politically they were both somewhat anomalous, since they were append-

9. Mittelberger, 73–4.

1. James T. Lemon and Gary B. Nash, "The Distribution of Wealth in Eighteenth-Century America: A Century of Change in Chester County, Pennsylvania, 1693–1882," *Journal of Social History*, 2c (1968), 1–24.

ages of Pennsylvania and New York. New Jersey shared the misfortune of having New York's governors until 1738 when it became a separate colony. Economically and culturally it was split in two, East Jersey, oriented economically toward the port of New York and religiously toward New England Congregationalism and New York Presbyterianism, and West Jersey, strongly influenced by its seventeenth-century Quaker proprietors, sharing Pennsylvania's Quaker heritage, and marketing its produce in Philadelphia. Delaware's port was Philadelphia and its governor Pennsylvania's. It could hardly be said that these two colonies were overgoverned. New York's governors were preoccupied with that province, while Delaware's existence as a province separate from Pennsylvania rested on shaky legal foundations. With its Dutch, Swedish, Finnish, English Quakers, Scotch-Irish, and New England émigrés, the area was notably heterogeneous, and yet largely free of sectarian controversy. In 1742 Governor Lewis Morris of New Jersey described the people of his province as "the most easy and happy people of any colony in North America." [2] But if he had lived some years longer (he died in 1746) he would have seen more than a score of riots in East Jersey out of conflicts between squatters and proprietors, a series of emphatic exclamation points appended to the effort, here again unsuccessful, to transplant to America the prerogatives of feudalism.

5

Observers with some knowledge of the Northern Colonies commented on the greater social and economic inequality

2. Gipson, III, 128.

they saw in the upper South.[3] They also noted the extra-ordinarily thin dispersal of the population through this countryside, where self-sufficiency of a sort was the goal of all good managers and where even a modest farm or plantation might occupy two hundred acres. Here, after the compact villages of New England and the pocket-scale urbanity of Boston, New York, and Philadelphia, was a society truly and thoroughly rural. Williamsburg, the capital of Virginia, was a hamlet of some two hundred houses and about a thousand people, white and black. Richmond, a county seat, was a tiny village. Of Annapolis, the capital of Maryland, which was even smaller than Williamsburg, the English vicar Andrew Burnaby, who saw it in 1759, remarked: "None of the streets are paved, and the few public buildings here are not worth mentioning. The church is a very poor one, the stadt-house but indifferent, and the governor's palace is not finished."[4]

Yet here, in the tobacco country, lay the center of gravity of the colonial population, and here were the mainland provinces most prized in the mother country. Chesapeake society—the area that stretched across provincial boundaries from Maryland through Virginia to embrace the Albemarle section of North Carolina—produced the colonies' richest staple, their most valued export. They were also experiencing a most startling and momentous social change, as their white bonded labor was fast receding before waves of blacks. Coming from the Northern colonies, the alert traveler could sense, even though no one yet spoke of Southerners or a Southern accent, the outlines of a distinctly different civilization. The historical image of

3. Main, 227–8.
4. Andrew Burnaby, *Travels Through the Middle Settlements in North-America* (1775; edn. 1960), 47.

the colonial South has been fixed upon the great planters, the large slaveholders, the Dulanys and Carrolls of Maryland, the Carters and Byrds of Virginia. These men, along with their cousins, associates, and allies in the planter class, set the tone of Southern societies, established the articulate traditions, and had the lion's share of making the ruling decisions. But in sheer numbers, even in the tidewater plantation counties, the men who made up the bulk of Chesapeake society were small planters and yeoman farmers, many of the latter holding no slaves, men of slender means but strikingly little social discontent, men who lived limited lives bound to the annual rhythms of the tobacco crop. Passed over by historians, this middle stratum was eminently visible to contemporaries and vital to the economic and political order.

In the older commercial counties of Virginia where lands had undergone much subdivision, only about 5 per cent of the white population could be called great planters. Two-thirds of the whites there had farms of two hundred acres or less.[5] The poorest—those with meager estates worth less than £50—were perhaps a fifth of the whole white population. The majority fell somewhere between, a broad middle layer with varying prospects and a wide range of living standards. In Maryland, whose social strata have been studied in more detail than those of Virginia, nine out of ten planting families at mid-century had estates worth less than £500. These planters would be producing at least some tobacco for sale, but the cash returns of those in the bottom ranks were hardly more than enough to supply the next year's cash needs, and supported little more than a "country living," a crude abun-

5. Main, 62, 65–6; Robert E. and B. Katherine Brown, *Virginia, 1705–1786; Aristocracy or Democracy?* (1964), 12, 15.

dance based on home-grown cows and pigs, corn and vegetables. Moving upward on this scale, one passes gradually from this rude sufficiency to solid comfort, to planters who had bonded labor to serve them, substantial and amply equipped houses, and sufficient income to permit savings and investment and to offer some assurance that their children could be launched upon equally comfortable lives.[6]

As for the planters near the top, they were by this time beginning to feel the pressure of a voracious staple that had now been cultivated for well over a century, and that usually could be planted only one year in three on one patch of soil. The ceaseless clearing of fresh lands enforced by the nutritional demands of the tobacco plant had driven the Virginians deep into the interior and had strained the backs of generations of indentured servants and now of slaves. The lavish ways of the leading families, inherited from the days of fresher soils and better markets, were already putting many of them in debt, and those who relied on tobacco alone to finance their high standard of living were in serious trouble. In Maryland the large planting fortunes had always depended to a considerable degree on something besides tobacco—land speculation, mercantile activities, moneylending, iron manufacturing, flour milling. The practice of law was a steady and valuable source of cash in itself, but, more important, led to personal connections and to knowledge of business trends and conditions, of the drift of the land market, all of which could be converted into speculative profits.[7] By

6. Aubrey C. Land, "Economic Base and Social Structure: The Northern Chesapeake in the Eighteenth Century," *Journal of Economic History*, 25 (1965), 639–54.
7. Ibid., see also Land's *The Dulanys of Maryland* (1955), esp. chapter 2.

1750 Virginia was well launched into a final burst of pre-Revolutionary expansion and speculation: between 1743 and 1760 its Council granted over three million acres of western land to groups and individuals. Wealth and status were converted into office and political influence, which in turn was converted into privileged access to the land. Speculators leased some of their lands over long terms to tenants in return for contractually specified improvements—a practice enormously profitable to landlords. Otherwise, speculators could hold a portion of their lands for appreciation, selling parcels of several hundred acres to new planters when prices reached an acceptable level. Representative patents of the period ran to 50,000 and 100,000 acres. In 1745, a provincial councillor, Thomas Lee, along with a group of associates and one prominent London merchant, organized themselves as the Ohio Company of Virginia, and were given the right to receive and survey a tract of 200,000 acres along the Ohio; they were promised another 300,000 if within seven years they would build a fort and garrison it and settle a hundred families. In 1749 grants to the Loyal Land Company totaled 800,000 acres.[8]

But land so easily come by could not, as it turned out, be sold extortionately; there was simply too much competition. Over a period of thirty-two years the Beverley family sold 71,000 acres at an average price of less than a shilling an acre. William Byrd sold land at one or two pounds for a hundred acres. Since land was available at such prices and on installment, men of moderate skill could acquire a substantial acreage with the proceeds of a few months' labor.[9] Land speculation touched small

8. Gipson, II, 4–7.
9. Brown and Brown, 16–22.

owners as well as large patent holders. Not only craftsmen and artisans but merchants and professionals were drawn into the land boom. The case of Jonathan Boucher, known to history chiefly as a Loyalist spokesman, typifies the nature of the opportunities and the appeal of the land. Six years of work in England had brought him only to the position of a tutor at £30 a year, but when he came to Virginia as a schoolmaster in 1759 he received £60 sterling together with room and board and the privilege of taking four extra students at his own price. By 1763, now an Anglican minister, Boucher also had bought a plantation and ran a small school. Shortly thereafter he reported an annual income of £250 and a net worth of £700. Land was so readily acquired that during the 1740's and 1750's the governors complained periodically that they could not recruit men for the army because there was no class of landless idlers to draw from. Explaining his failure to raise men in 1759, Governor Francis Fauquier of Virginia complained: "Every man in this colony has land and none but Negroes are laborers." [1]

Thus, between the dominant and flamboyantly wealthy upper crust of planters and, on the lowest level, the modest number of poor whites and the mass of blacks stood a broad class of white farmers, moderately prosperous or at least comfortable, many owning their own slaves and all feeling the decisive bond of whiteness in a society rapidly growing blacker. The problem of class in Virginia was complex, and class relationships and manners were changing. Probably the best description of the common people of Virginia was written by the Reverend Devereux Jarratt, a notably successful Anglican revivalist in the later dec-

1. Ibid., 9.

ades of the century. Born in 1732 in the Piedmont,
Jarratt was the son of a country carpenter whose family
lived in a rural abundance quite bare of luxuries. Simple
and uneducated, they thought of themselves as occupying
a very low station in the social hierarchy, although
Jarratt's paternal grandfather owned and his father inherited 1,200 acres. The Jarratts thought of gentlefolk as
superior beings. "A *periwig,* in those days, was a distinguishing badge of *gentle folk*—when I saw a man rid-
ing the road . . . with a wig on, it would so alarm my
fears . . . that, I daresay, I would run off, as for my life." [2]
Significantly, this sense of awe of the gentry, which Jarratt
thought universal among his rank and age, had so changed
by the end of his life when he wrote his memoirs that he
thought the opposite pattern had come to prevail. And
certainly a kind of deference had long been carefully paid
by the upper class to the lower class of whites, in part
as a necessity of politics, in part as a way of cementing
the social bonds of white men.[3]

For if the gentry had learned, as Virginia's political
practices suggest, to defer in their manner to the enfranchised small planters and farmers, it was not solely to
win office but to hold white society together. One other
aspiration that surely held it together was the desire to
arrive at the point, already reached by so many and surely
within the reach of many more, at which one's life was
eased and fattened, made more endurable, by owning
bonded labor—a desire curiously put by one Virginian
who disliked slavery but conceded: "This is part of our

2. Gipson, II, 44.
3. Brown and Brown, 34; *cf.* Charles S. Sydnor, *Gentleman Freeholders, Political Practices in Washington's Virginia* (1952), esp. chapters
3 and 4.

grievance, but to live in Virginia without slaves is morally impossible." [4] No one can say how much the incoming tide of blacks, setting desire and fear on the same side of the scale, eliminated friction between whites. But it can be said that Maryland and Virginia, which had had their full share of turbulence in the seventeenth century, were notably tranquil in the middle of the eighteenth. The energies of the people now went into personal advancement rather than class or group conflict. And the ways of this world were readily accepted by white newcomers. A group of Maryland Germans, writing to urge their countrymen to join them, reported in 1746: "We here enjoy full liberty of conscience . . . the law of the land is so constituted, that every man is secure in the enjoyment of his property, the meanest person is out of reach of oppression from the most powerful, nor can anything be taken from him without his receiving satisfaction for it." [5] In the Chesapeake society, under a ruling gentry reasonably united and enjoying the support and acceptance of the lesser planters, there were suppressed anxieties based upon problems of economic solvency and of race, but there was a notable absence of tumult and mordant discontent. [6]

6

"The planters," said Henry Laurens in 1750, "are full of money," [7] and if the South Carolina Assembly had taken the trouble to provide itself with a statehouse instead of meeting in private homes, this might have been a suita-

4. Gipson, II, 14n.
5. Ibid., 56. See Dieter Cunz, *Maryland Germans: A History* (1948).
6. *Cf.* Carl Bridenbaugh, *Myths and Realities* (1952), 18.
7. Ibid., 67.

bly emblematic phrase to put over its entrance. South Carolina in its heyday enjoyed a prosperity that surpassed anything seen in the other colonies, its leaders rejoicing in their well-being at a time when Virginians were beginning to worry about their debts. As compared with Virginia, South Carolina was a new colony, an upstart, whose first permanent settlement had been made when Virginia had been growing for more than sixty years. Even in 1730 South Carolina had only about 12,000 inhabitants, and at the time Laurens spoke it was still filling with newcomers, its upper ranks swelling with the newly rich. Profitable rice culture on a considerable scale began only with the eighteenth century and the indigo crop in the 1740's; the economy had only lately grown rich on these staples and on its trade in deerskins, livestock, and timber.

By comparison with Charles Town's elite, old Boston's upper crust looked poor and flimsy,[8] and the hedonistic life of the South Carolina capital put the other seaboard towns in the shade. Josiah Quincy, Jr., looking at South Carolina with the cool eye of an alien New Englander, found it "divided into opulent and lordly planters, poor and spiritless peasants and vile slaves."[9] But he missed the secret of the province's strength: it lacked the vigorous middle class of several of the other colonies, but it compensated for that lack in good measure by the extraordinary size of its upper class, and by the uncommon prosperity that percolated down through the lower ranks of its whites. At mid-century Governor James Glen estimated that the white population of the province embraced 5,000 people who had "plenty of the good things of life," another 5,000 who had "some of the conveniencies of life,"

8. Main, 57 ff.
9. Ibid., 227.

10,000 with the "necessaries of life," and about 5,000 or 6,000 who had a "bare subsistence."[1] A modern student of its social structure, looking at the colony on the eve of the Revolution, substantially confirms this estimate, finding a wealthy class that controlled nearly 60 per cent of the personal property, but also a poor white class that constituted "scarcely one-seventh of the white population."[2] Three out of five whites were farmers; and four out of five farmers held property worth at least £200; of the typical poor low-country planters, half held slaves.[3] It was, of course, upon the slaves, who considerably outnumbered the whites, that all this generalized white prosperity rested. But South Carolina had other advantages. It was selling its rice in relatively noncompetitive markets. Its taxes were extraordinarily low, and despite the rigors of their labors, its slaves were rapidly multiplying. The grain and pork produced by its inland farmers gave it a balanced economy. Even the costs of its defense were undertaken by backcountry troops paid out of the royal treasury.[4]

A foreign traveler, taking a more indulgent view of the Carolinians than Quincy, found that the secure planter class appeared to "think and act precisely as do the nobility in other countries."[5] South Carolina had been much influenced in its beginnings by a strong influx of Barbadian émigrés, who brought with them the slave-driving ways of the West Indians and the upper-class aspirations common alike to the English gentry and the

---

1. M. Eugene Sirmans, *Cultural South Carolina* (1966), 228.
2. Main, 64.
3. Ibid., 64–5; Sirmans, 227.
4. Gipson, II, 130–8, 150–1.
5. Bridenbaugh, *Myths and Realities*, 66, quoting from Johann D. Schoepf, *Travels in the Confederation*, ed. Andrew J. Morrison (1911), II, 205.

West Indian planters. Even when the colony became more heterogeneous, with an influx of Huguenots, Swiss, Ulstermen, and Germans, the English and Barbadian tradition still held. South Carolina, as it fattened on its slaves and staples, developed the most lordly and most leisured ruling class in America. Rice planters found it most economic to set up relatively small units, cultivated by about thirty slaves and one overseer, and the richest of them might have a dozen or more such establishments. Putting their overseers in charge, they enjoyed a good deal more leisure than the normally hardworking planters of the Chesapeake country, and this leisure went into the pleasurable life of Charles Town. Unlike the would-be grandees of New York, perhaps their closest parallel in the colonies, they had no sharply feuding elite factions in politics; unlike the Virginians, they developed no passion for politics and government, and very little sense of civic responsibility. Where, for a Virginian, much of masculine social life was beginning to be centered in politics and the county courthouse, the South Carolinian found the clubs, theaters, races, and balls of Charles Town enormously engrossing. Although the province's broad suffrage gave ample opportunity for the lower class to mount an opposition in the Commons House, it was an opportunity that was not seized, and the top families fell rather easily into control of politics. So lax were they, however, that many planters were not eager to have the honor of serving, and it was hard to persuade them to fill the seats.[6] Local government simply failed to develop under this pervasive negligence; the vestries and the parish road commissions were the

6. Sirmans, 245, 255.

only functioning local officials. Outside Charles Town there were no courts or judges except for justices of the peace with authority over trifling matters. It was not until the Regulator movement of the 1760's, which was brought about in large part by the failure of local government, that the South Carolina elite was wakened from its political somnolence.

South Carolina was flanked north and south by provinces that bore little resemblance to it. Among the southernmost colonies, North Carolina was closest to the farming country of the North, though it probably had more marginal and impoverished farmers. At the end of the colonial period it was probably the most rural of all the colonies; only about 2 per cent of its population (or less than 5,000 persons) lived in urban settlements, and its leading metropolis, New Bern, was a thriving town with about 150 buildings.[7] Three enclaves of enterprise stood out among its general farms: in the northeast, the Albemarle country, there was an area which seemed like an extension of the Chesapeake tobacco economy though its planters were smaller and less pretentious; in the southeast, the Cape Fear region was given over, like South Carolina, to rice and indigo cultivation; and in the west, the pine barren belt, rich in forests of longleaf pine, was the base of a rich and distinctive naval store industry and put North Carolina in the lead in producing resin, pitch, tar, and turpentine. Slaves were employed extensively in all three of these regions, but even in the rice-indigo region where concentrations were greatest, it was a very rare household that held more than twenty slaves. In the western por-

7. R. H. Merrens, *Colonial North Carolina in the Eighteenth Century* (1964), 142, 147–9.

tions of the colony only about one of ten households had slaves, and even they had only a few each.[8]

Its cheap land, and the health and beauty of its interior regions, gave North Carolina a far-flung reputation which brought down from the North that horde of settlers which almost trebled its population between 1750 and 1770. In other quarters, however, especially among officials, the colony was long disdained as a refuge of debtors and criminals, and for its turbulence and anarchy. Land titles were often in a state of confusion, squatters abounded, and uncertainties attending the enormous Granville Grant, an inheritance of the proprietary period, added to the difficulties. Even as early as the 1720's an unlucky Anglican minister who had been assigned to the Albemarle region was relieved, when he left, to get away from "an obscure corner of the world inhabited by the dregs and gleanings of all other English colonies."[9] When George Burrington took his commission as governor in 1724, Colonel William Byrd warned him that he was taking over a "people accustomed to live without law or gospel"; and wished him good luck "in bringing the chaos into form and reducing that anarchy into a regular government." And as late as 1775 Governor Arthur Dobbs complained to the Assembly that armed deserters who had run off from the militia or had stolen horses appeared boldly and with impunity in public, "and the jails are so weak without any jailor or person to guard them, that no criminal can be secured."[1]

Yet the majority—the ubiquitous Germans and Scotch-Irish, the English Quakers and sober Moravians—came to

8. Ibid., 74–81, 129–30.
9. Ibid., 33.
1. Gipson, II, 115.

the colony simply in quest of farms on which they could honestly support their families; and the interior was filled, by and large, with farms that were sold or allotted by headright in parcels of one hundred to three hundred acres. A holding of more than six hundred acres there was a rarity indeed; and although good soils and good grazing lands supported a system of productive general farming, interior North Carolina reared a population of husbandmen who were richer in land than in most other goods. Indeed, the presence of an unusually large rural middle class, and a comparatively even distribution of wealth, made North Carolina decidedly different from the other Southern colonies.[2]

The history of the youngest colony, Georgia, showed that a neo-classic utopia was no better a model than a feudal estate for resisting the unregulated rural bourgeois order that held sway in America. Planted as a social experiment, and at the same time expected to act as a buffer state between Spanish Florida and English South Carolina, Georgia was the offspring of a strange marriage of humanitarian enthusiasm and imperial strategy. When an English law of 1729 released a large number of unfortunate debtors from prison, General James Oglethorpe and other men of a philanthropic cast of mind conceived of the notion of planting on the southern border of South Carolina a colony of handy yeomen, newly rescued from debt, who would be capable of springing to arms from their plows when the necessities of empire called them. A charter was secured in 1732, Parliament supplied some funds, and well-meaning philanthropists rushed to offer donations. A first contingent of carefully recruited unfortunates—few of them were in fact debtors—arrived at the

2. Main, 66.

south bank of the Savannah in 1733, and were soon followed by others, both English and German. By 1744, about 2,500 Protestants had been lured to Georgia to take part in the experiment.

Experiment it was in every sense, carefully regulated by Oglethorpe and the other Trustees in London for the first eighteen years of its existence. The poor settlers were not expected to have the capacity to govern themselves or to realize without supervision the ideal that glimmered in the minds of their benefactors. Georgia was planned rather on the scheme of a military fief, whose people must always be ready to shoulder arms. Lands were therefore granted in tail-male—that is, when a male heir was lacking, the land would revert to the Trustees. Female heirs would be otherwise compensated, but each plot of land was to be in the hands of a potential soldier. Moreover, each plot was to be small— fifty acres was estimated to be the amount a man could cultivate without servants— though those settlers who emigrated at their own expense bringing menservants with them could receive as much as five hundred acres. Rum was forbidden—a ban much at odds with the habits and the economy of an American colony—and, even more troublesome, so was slavery. The ban on slavery was not humanitarian but military and prudential in conception. If slaves were permitted, a society of large planters would quickly develop, as South Carolina's had. Such a society, far from breeding numbers of fighting yeomen, would foster a few plantation-bound whites and a menacingly large number of blacks. Precariously perched on the border, such a Georgia would be extremely vulnerable in wartime to foreign provocation of slave insurrections—a fear which haunted the South Carolinians. The last thing the empire-minded Oglethorpe and his associates wanted was to spend their efforts and the funds entrusted to them on the establishment of another South Carolina with its peculiar vulnerabilities.[3]

Almost from the beginning, however, the idealistic imperatives of the Trustees were at odds with the aims of the colonists who had to carry them out. The Georgia settlers engaged in the formidable heavy labor incident to the first settling of a colony knew that just across the Savannah in South Carolina there were planters living in comparative idleness while the work was done by blacks. Because of the law prohibiting rum, they could not economically trade with the West Indies, their most obvious outlet, and hence could not sell their most readily available commercial product, lumber. To make matters worse, some bold South Carolinian planters moved southward into Georgia with their slaves and began to establish the plantation regime that was forbidden to Georgians, their illegality winked at by sympathetic officials. All this was quite a provocation to a people situated directly on the border in a position of maximum exposure. In fact, when war did begin between England and Spain, Georgia began to break up; some planters fled to South Carolina, and a pacifistic colony of Moravians left for North Carolina and Pennsylvania. In the course of the war Oglethorpe, transmuted again from philanthropist and administrator to commander, failed to capture Saint Augustine from the Spaniards, but he did manage to save the new colony from Spanish conquest in 1742.

By the early 1740's the colony was rife with discontent, and gradually, under continual pressure from the inhabitants, the Trustees gave up the essential features of their

3. Herbert L. Osgood, *American Colonies in the Eighteenth Century* (1924), III, 61–6.

experiment. In 1740 freeholders were permitted to rent their lands to tenants and the maximum landholding was raised from 500 to 2,000 acres. In 1741 the tail-male proviso was abandoned in favor of general inheritance. The effort at prohibiting rum, already being widely violated, was abandoned in practice the next year, and in law the year after that. The ban on slavery remained, and a few high-minded Georgians hoped to keep it. But one of them, Martin Bolsius, the antislavery pastor to the Salzburgers who had settled at Ebenezer, found that his Georgia neighbors "all from the highest to the lowest vote for Negroes and look upon me as a stone in their way toward which they direct all their spite and they will, I suppose, not rest until they have removed it one way or another." [4] Reluctantly, and after prolonged resistance, the Trustees gave way on this, the last of their venturesome negations, and in the summer of 1750 the antislavery law was repealed. Georgia, despite its relatively equalitarian beginnings, was now a true Southern colony, and when its real growth began in the 1750's and 1760's it became a planter society, less noted, to be sure, for its aristocracy than South Carolina but well on its way toward increasing inequalities that seemed to come in the course of the economic development of the colonies.

7

In histories of American society the influence of the frontier has often been heavily overestimated. Yet in the colonial period, when there was so much frontier and so little society, the leverage of the frontier was at its greatest, and

4. Gipson, II, 175.

it cannot be minimized. For those who were willing to face the hardships and hazards of the backcountry, an escape from landless poverty into proprietary comfort on cheap land was a tempting prospect. On the frontier a substantial and vital portion of the white population regularly edged its way upward into the middle class. An enormous movement of frontier expansion went on in the two decades before the Revolution, varying from place to place in intensity and in its effects on the more settled parts of society.

It was not in the Northern Colonies that the most striking frontier advances were made between 1740 and the 1760's. New England had sprouted westward with great rapidity during the forty years that followed the Peace of Utrecht, but by mid-century had come to a pause. By 1750, when war with the French seemed imminent, Rhode Island and Connecticut were filled to their western borders, and, except for some tracts in its northwest corner, Massachusetts also. Settlement in thin lines had reached southeast Vermont and southern New Hampshire, and had stretched up along the Maine coast beyond the forty-fourth parallel.[5] The need for further expansion to accommodate her growing rural population was great, but New England had vivid memories of fierce wars and Indian massacres, and the next episode of expansion began, at first slowly and then with increasing momentum, only after the fall of Quebec in 1759.

In New York and Pennsylvania, frontier advances in the 1750's were relatively modest. The further settlement of New York was opposed by the Albany fur traders, who had no desire to see a tide of settlers drive off the animals

5. Mathews, *passim;* see esp. the map of New England settlement in 1754, facing 98.

or the Indians who trapped them. But a greater barrier
was New York's ungenerous land policy, forbidding as it
was to new settlers who knew land could be acquired on
easier terms to the south. The Pennsylvania frontier too
was approaching a moment of temporary saturation. Settlements had already reached and passed the Susquehanna
River. They were now approaching the point where a
string of English forts had been set up as a barrier to
French and Indian encroachments, a dangerous area fated
to be an early cockpit of a stupendous imperial struggle.
It made little sense to push westward into this no-man's-
land when land to the south was known to be safer and
cheaper. By the 1740's the great flow from the North to
the Southern hinterland was already under way.

The deepest penetration of the interior took place in the
Southern backcountry where the fall line had been reached
as early as the 1660's and where movement into the
Shenandoah Valley had begun in the second decade of
the eighteenth century. The Southern backcountry, taking
its several parts together, was a large area varying in width
from as little as 20 to as much as 160 miles and running in
length about 600 miles from the northern boundary of
Maryland to the Savannah River. In 1730 still the province
of the Indian and an occasional white fur trader or hunter,
by the time of the Revolution this enormous region had
an estimated population of a quarter of a million; and in
every Southern colony but Georgia the people of the
backcountry had come to constitute an important part of
the whole population.[6]

In the middle of the century, when the entire Virginia
and Carolina Piedmont was still in private hands, land

6. Bridenbaugh, *Myths and Realities*, 120–1.

speculators began to look hopefully to the Great Valley of the interior, where the Palatines, Scotch-Irish, and other immigrant peoples were streaming southward from Pennsylvania, following the heavily traveled Great Wagon Road, an enlarged Indian trail which carried them toward cheaper land. As they moved into the Southern backcountry, they were sometimes joined by settlers of English stock coming westward from the Piedmont or the tidewater areas. As the settlers moved on, the Germans hugging the Shenandoah River Valley and settling on good soils, the Scotch-Irish venturing farther westward toward the forbiddingly steep barrier of the Alleghenies, they drove before them the hunters and fur traders and the rapidly thinning ranks of deer, beaver, and bear. The forest world provided good subsistence, and on the whole the early frontier settlers, though crudely housed, ate heartily and cheaply, deer and bear meat supplementing their corn and vegetables. To the English and Scotch-Irish settlers the trees in this thickly forested area were like enemies; as their predecessors farther eastward had done, they solved the exasperating task of clearing the land by simply girdling the trees, shutting off the sap, and choking them to death, so that they could be pushed over. The Germans, more mindful of sound farming practice, carefully and laboriously cut them down and rooted out the stumps.

Two pictures of the frontier have come down from early travelers and observers, one portraying a deterioration of life to almost barbaric conditions, the other picturing a largely self-sufficient benign pastoral scene. Both are true, since the state of life in any part of the backcountry depended upon the duration of its settlement, the ethnic background of the frontier people, and their farm-

ing practices. A visitor to the wilderness settlements of
the Scotch-Irish in the deep interior of North Carolina
found them living in a primitive state: "The clothes of the
people consist of deerskins, their food of johnnycakes,
deer and bear meat. A kind of white people are found here
who live like savages. Hunting is their chief occupation."[7]
Yet accounts of the German farmers of the Shenandoah
portray a life of measured comfort and an enviable regime
of pastoral order and plenty.

Both pictures, though not untrue, are misleading. Barbarization was limited mainly to the fringe of the frontier;
and the pastoral democracy of the self-sufficing honest
yeoman, which did indeed sometimes exist, was only a
transitional stage in the development of a commercial
society.[8] Most frontier families came, to be sure, in relative poverty: a few horses or a yoke of oxen, a few cows
and hogs, some poultry—such would be the property of
the more substantial among them; and there were many
single men who came with little more than the essential
ax and rifle. But all looked forward to the day when they
could shift from subsistence farming and turn at least a
modest profit from the cash-crop production that was
emerging in their region. The ideal of the simple yeoman
living close to nature, applying himself with loving care to
the soil, and supplying virtually all his modest needs with
his own labor and that of his family was an ideal first of
the educated elite who read pastoral poetry and later of
agrarian ideologues and politicians who wanted to claim a
moral superiority for the farmer. It was never an ideal of

7. Quoted in Ray Allen Billington, *Westward Expansion: A History of
the American Frontier* (1949), 93.
8. See Robert L. Meriwether on the backcountry, in *The Expansion of
South Carolina, 1729–1765* (1940), chapter 13.

the yeoman farmers themselves. They might pride themselves on being able to meet the demands of self-sufficiency, but they were in haste to get out of their original lean-tos and log cabins into comfortable frame houses which they might hope to furnish with a respectable share of the world's comforts such as they had seen in Europe, Pennsylvania, or the tidewater country. Carl Bridenbaugh, in a penetrating brief account of the Southern backcountry, finds "a backwoods existence that was constantly becoming rural in imitation of or in extension of Pennsylvania and of the Chesapeake and Carolina societies." [9] In large portions of the Southern backcountry the preconditions for a quick transition from subsistence farming to the commercial farm or small plantation were widely available. Some slaves, numbering perhaps one-twelfth of the frontier population, were brought in. The rivers provided a ready means for sending the agricultural surplus to market, and in some parts of the Southern interior, outlets to the seacoast by roads, bridges, and ferries were developed in the third quarter of the century.[1]

It would be a mistake to assume that the Southern frontier produced a thoroughly egalitarian society. A great deal of the land passed through the hands of speculators before it passed to common farmers and small planters, and the inequalities brought to the frontier by the settlers themselves tended to be perpetuated or increased. It has been estimated [2] that, counting slaves and whites together, about one-third of the Southern frontiersmen were landless workers, though not all of them were poor and though the prospects of a young man with a family to set up a farm of

9. Bridenbaugh, *Myths and Realities*, 195.
1. Ibid., 144–7; *cf.* Merrens, 144–5.
2. Main, 49.

his own were extraordinarily good.[3] At one extreme, on the Northern Neck of Virginia where the Fairfax grant had put five million acres into a single hand, planters bought large tracts of land to be rented to tenants or worked by slaves. Far more representative of the frontier was Lunenberg County, Virginia, which was just emerging from the frontier phase in the early 1760's. The richest 10 per cent of the men held about 40 per cent of the land. Such a distribution, characteristic of the more democratic portions of the Southern frontier, was low for the South but would have been high in the North. Landless whites were about a third of the population in Lunenberg County, but less than twenty years later about four out of five of these appear to have secured land there or elsewhere.[4] In North Carolina's large interior, where fewer opportunities for commercialization existed than in other parts of the Southern frontier, a broad distribution of land rather similar to that of the Northern Colonies was common.[5]

Settlers were not long upon the ground before they were followed by gentleman farmers and planters with slaves, small merchants and artisans, lawyers and preachers, and above all by those commanding adventurers who, with one foot in politics and one in land speculation, everywhere appear and reappear in the history of the frontier. Soon, around the county courthouse, the mill, the village store, the ferry landing, the crossings of main roads, and other places of necessary resort, there formed a string of inland towns and villages running from Frederick and Hagerstown, Maryland, to Winchester and Staunton in Virginia, to Salem, Hillsboro, and Charlotte in North

3. Ibid.; on mobility in the frontier South, 168–80.
4. Ibid., 170–3.
5. Ibid., 48–9, 53–4, 66.

Carolina, and ending with Camden and Augusta in South Carolina and Georgia. Out of the ranks of the better-established husbandmen and planters, the outstanding ministers, the more charismatic speculators and adventurers, there arose a gentry which, much in the manner of their counterparts to the east, sought and won the deference and the votes of the common farmers. With great rapidity between the 1740's and the eve of the Revolution, the pattern of eastern society, though visibly modified, was reproduced in surprisingly faithful detail in the west.

CHAPTER VI

✿

The
State of the
Churches

1

Perhaps the most striking fact about the organized religious life of the colonials in the eighteenth century is the large number of people who were left out of it. Whether they had lost their faith before migrating or had been torn loose from church life in the business of moving, or whether they resented the authority of the dutiful ministers or the loose ways of the less dutiful, or were lost through the inability of the churches to establish viable church-community life in the open spaces and diffused settlements of America, surprisingly large numbers in the English continental colonies enjoyed little or none of the amenities and comforts of a religious community, and many seemed not to be trying very hard to get them. America has always liked to dwell upon those who came to win religious liberty or to realize some other religious ideal. But the extraordinary number who were content to live either without organized religion or with only a weak or a token relation to it suggests that the majority of white colonials may have come for very mundane reasons—not to reach the glories of the other world but to relieve the hardships of this.

Even in New England, the best churched section of the colonies, where town life was cohesive and church attendance was compulsory, the requirements of the churches for membership had been loosened since 1662. Yet it is likely that not more than one person in seven was a church member. Southward the position of the churches was weaker. In the Middle Colonies, many groups of German and Scotch-Irish immigrants had come without ministers, and were slow to form churches. Compelled by no establishment, living among many sects, they felt free to belong to any church or none. Probably less than one in fifteen was a church member there, and farther south where many merely professed Anglicanism, the number was still less.[1]

This huge body of religious indifferents facilitated the advance of toleration. Christian theorists of persecution have always held that toleration was bred by indifference. The presence of large numbers of those who did not care to join the churches was a constant deadweight upon those who did care enough not only to join but to compel others to do so. Hector St. John de Crèvecoeur, after observing the sects of the Middle Colonies and the feeble religious instruction of the children, thought this a world of waning zeal. In the mixture of the sects "religious indifference is imperceptibly disseminated from one end of the continent to the other. . . . Persecution, religious pride, the love of contradiction, are the food of what the world commonly calls religion. These motives have ceased here; zeal in Europe is confined; here it evaporates in the great

1. W. W. Sweet, "The American Colonial Environment and Religious Liberty," *Church History*, 4 (1935), 52–4.

distance it has to travel; there it is a grain of powder in-
closed, here it burns away in the open air, and consumes
without effect." [2]

Still, the communities of the devout were the active
atoms in the large, inert mass of the indifferent. In religion
as in politics, the organized churches had more influence
than numbers, and their creeds and quarrels command our
attention. Aside from theology, there were two sets of issues that constantly troubled the political and religious
life of the colonies: first, what rights dissenters might
enjoy under established churches; second, those questions of religious style and conviction which racked major
denominations during the Great Awakening.

All the great European states, and each of the major
denominations, hoped to set up establishments linking
church and state in a unified system of power. But in the
English colonies on the continent, the few establishments
that had ever been strong had been seriously impaired.
On the whole—and the exceptions were hotly contested—
the basic right of open public worship had been won by
the main dissenting groups. But the energies of protest
grew with success, and discontent was only made keener
by concessions. From the 1740's to the Revolution, those
colonies that had not yet granted the rights of dissenters
faced constant agitation for freedom from taxes to support
the establishment; freedom from civil discrimination (inability to hold office or vote) on account of one's faith; freedom of preaching; and the extension of all these rights to
all religions. The campaign for full religious rights toppled
establishments everywhere outside New England during
the Revolution, and ended in the American system of
separation of church and state.

2. Hector St. John de Crèvecoeur, *Letters from an American Farmer*
(1782; edn. 1957), 47; *cf.* 44–7.

As one looks at the churches in the middle and later decades of the eighteenth century, one realizes not only how heavily the Anglicans were outnumbered by what one of them called a "swarm of sectaries" [3] but also how the two established churches, the Anglican and the Puritan, though themselves growing rapidly, were being outstripped by other denominations. The numbers of parishioners are uncertain, but relative growths may be very roughly compared by looking at the number of churches in 1740 in the colonies as a whole: Congregationalist, 423; Anglican, 246; Presbyterian, 160; Baptist, 96; Lutheran, 95; Dutch Reformed, 78; German Reformed, 51. The Quakers, harder to number with precision, had about the same number of churches as the Baptists or the Lutherans. Aside from these denominations there were others: a sprinkling of Catholics, with well over a score of churches, mostly in Pennsylvania and Maryland; a number of pietistic sectarians—Mennonites, Schwenkfelders, Dunkers, Seventh-Day Adventists, and the like; as well as tiny groups of Jews in New York, Newport, Philadelphia, Savannah, and Charles Town. (At the first census in 1790 only 1,243 Jews were enumerated, or less than one-twentieth of 1 per cent of the population.) [4]

As the population mounted rapidly, the religious denominations appear on the whole to have grown more slowly. Still, each of them grew impressively, and a few explosively. Relatively, the two establishments were falling behind. Between 1740 and 1780 the number of Congregationalist churches had grown by more than 75 per cent, the Anglican by more than 60 per cent. But the two Reformed churches, German and Dutch, starting from a

3. Thomas Barton in 1764, as quoted in E. S. Gaustad, *Religious Issues in American History* (1968), 23.
4. On numbers and location of churches, see E. S. Gaustad, *Historical Atlas of Religion in America* (1962), *passim.*

much smaller base, had grown 290 per cent, the Presbyterians almost 310 per cent, the Baptists over 470 per cent.
The Quakers too were prospering, though not gaining in
relative numbers. By the end of the century there are estimated to have been over 200 meetinghouses and from
50,000 to 60,000 Friends.

Two of the most constant notes in eighteenth-century
commentaries on religion are the complaints of Anglicans
about the sea of sectarian dissenters in which they are im-
mersed and the bemused remarks of observers on the multi-
farious character of American religion. Before the end of
the previous century Governor Dongan, in a comprehen-
sive report on New York, had said of its religion: "New
York has first a Chaplain belonging to the Fort of the
Church of England; secondly a Dutch Calvinist; thirdly a
French Calvinist; fourthly a Dutch Lutheran. Here be not
many of the Church of England; a few Roman Catholics;
abundance of Quakers preachers men and women especially; Singing Quakers; Ranting Quakers; Sabbatarians;
Anti-Sabbatarians; some Anabaptists; some Independents;
some Jews; in short of all sorts of opinions there are some,
and the most part, of none at all." [5] This observation on
the plurality of religions was echoed a half century later
by Gottlieb Mittelberger, as well as by observers like
Peter Kalm and Crèvecoeur.[6]

Eighteenth-century America was happy terrain for sects
such as the Quakers and the Baptists stemming from the
left wing of Puritanism. By the end of the century there
were almost as many Friends in the colonies as in England.

---

5. E. T. Corwin and Hugh Hastings, eds., *Ecclesiastical Records, State
of New York* (1901), II, 879–80.
6. See, e.g., Gottlieb Mittelberger, *Journey to Pennsylvania* (edn. 1960),
ed. and trans. by Oscar Handlin and John Clive, 41.

The Quakers, with their belief in the direct relation of the individual to God and their bare minimum of church structure, bore testimony to the power of zeal. They seemed to survive and for a time to flourish by the sheer apostolic intensity of their witness. By flooding Massachusetts with more martyr fanatics than it had the heart to execute and by a skillful appeal to Charles II they had been successful, even before the Anglicans, in denting the persecutory powers of the Bay Colony. As their martyrdom came to an end, some of them settled in Massachusetts, and more in the freedom of Rhode Island. Their earliest center of concentrated strength, however, was North Carolina, where during the last quarter of the seventeenth century they appear to have been the only organized religious body, and where they were capable for a long time afterward of rallying dissenters against the establishment. An early-eighteenth-century Anglican complained of them that they "have in a manner the sole management of the country in their hands." [7] By mid-century in North Carolina as elsewhere they were becoming well-to-do and respectable. In both Pennsylvania and the two Jerseys the Quakers were, of course, a colonizing power in their own right. The Pennsylvania Anglicans never ceased to resent them, and the colony's partisan politics came to be shaped by the struggle between Quakers and Anglicans and their respective allies. An Anglican cleric living in Chester lamented in 1712 that Quakerism "is generally preferred in Pennsylvania, and in no county of the province does the haughty tribe appear more rampant than where I reside." [8]

Yet it was in Pennsylvania above all that the Quakers enacted most impressively the transition from the primi-

7. Gaustad, *Historical Atlas of Religion in America*, 25.
8. Ibid., 25.

tive zeal of the Reformation sect to the staid, quietistic, essentially conservative church. On both sides of the Atlantic the Quakers were recognized as good traders even before the end of the seventeenth century. Quaker personal discipline was good for the business regimen; Quaker asceticism fed capital accumulation; and the Quakers' reputation for scrupulous honesty brought them business. An observer of the post-Revolutionary era noted "the order which the Quakers are accustomed from childhood to apply to the distribution of their tasks, their thoughts, and every moment of their lives. They carry this spirit of order everywhere. It economizes time, activity, and money." [9] Wealth, social acceptance, and steady habits brought them from aggressive, proselytizing zeal into a quiet and relatively passive personal cultivation of the spirit. During the Great Awakening of the 1740's, Quakerism, now a century old, could contemplate with condescension or disapproval the antics of the newest generation of revivalists. The Quakers had gone through it all long ago, and the spiritual descendants of the inspired maniacs who had repeatedly invaded Massachusetts at the risk of their lives in the 1650's now balked at the emotional excesses and enthusiastic disorders they saw in other revivalist groups. Whittier wrote long after:

> *The Quaker kept the way of his own,*
> *A non-conductor among the wires,*
> *With coat of asbestos proof to fires.*
> *And quite unable to mend his pace*
> *To catch the falling manna of grace,*
> *He hugged the closer his little store*
> *Of faith, and silently prayed for more.*

9. F. B. Tolles, in *Quakers and the Atlantic Culture* (1960), 64, quoting Brissot de Warville.

The rise of the Baptists from a small sect in 1700 to one of the leading denominations at the time of the Revolution is one of the touchstones of the American temperament. The Baptists, who did not represent a single unified tendency in thought and were not all united in a single church fellowship, were an offshoot of English Puritanism and Continental reform. Baptists tended to appear wherever reformers, in their search for the spirit of primitive Christianity, concluded that there was no scriptural warrant for infant baptism. A stress on adult conversion and baptism was usually accompanied by austerity, asceticism, an intense aversion to elaborate forms of church organization, by a spirit at once folkish, democratic, and anti-intellectual. Baptists would accept no church-state relation, needed no formally educated ministry. Theological commitment might vary: early Baptists often leaned toward the easygoing Arminian approach to salvation, but Calvinism grew strong among Baptists in the eighteenth century, especially after the Great Awakening. The main centers of Baptist strength were Rhode Island, New Jersey, Pennsylvania, and North Carolina. The Baptists grew fastest on the frontier. Their growth, notably strong after 1720, became explosive after 1760. They seemed to thrive on antagonism: their remarkable progress in Virginia in the 1750's and 1760's took place in the teeth of serious oppression. But their role in the struggle for religious liberty just before and during the Revolutionary era was decisive.

2

An amiable legend has it that toleration was won by religious idealists like Roger Williams and William Penn and their followers, whose humane arguments gradually came to prevail. Much credit in fact must be given to such men, and perhaps even more to brave sectarians like the early Baptist and Quaker martyrs. Yet in large measure the growth of toleration and religious liberty were gifts of circumstance. In America (outside New England where establishments lasted longest) there simply was no majority religion. Hence one basic prerequisite of a firm, enforceable religious establishment was missing. America was not persuaded into toleration in response to some general campaign. On this count it stumbled into virtue. But if toleration was no one's plan, it still had to be someone's work. The work of two quite different types of men can be discerned in its development: the minority sectarians, who knew persecution from painful experience, who argued the case against oppression with heartfelt sincerity, and endured much punishment for opposing establishments; and the secularists, loosely speaking—men who in pursuit of national power, profits, stability, prosperity, or other worldy ends put mundane considerations before the propagation and enforcement of doctrine. The first argued for freedom of conscience largely on religious, the second largely on political, grounds.

Religious liberty came about when society was no longer susceptible to being pulled entirely in one direction. America was always a competitive forum for religious groups. But quite as important, it was always a competitive arena in which the religious impulse had to battle with other intense and countervailing impulses. The political and military orders of society competed with the clergy. Commercial profit, national unity, and imperial power competed with the goals of faith. In an age of commercial expansion the profit motive quietly undermined the desire to impose a creed; in an age of imperial rivalry the passion for national unity and strength overruled the passion to persecute. Lord Keynes may have exaggerated when he said that men are rarely so innocently engaged as when they are merely making money; but when one compares the pecuniary motive with the fierce persecutory tyranny of religious fanatics, one begins to see his point. It was the two foremost trading nations, England and Holland, that led the way toward toleration in the Western world. It was English proprietors, hungry for revenue and hence for settlers, who opened the colonial gates to members of all faiths and enticed them into living at peace with one another. It was proprietary governments, commercial and imperial ambitions, that made the colonies into a hive for so many Protestant sects that, as Perry Miller once put it, "no power on earth could whip them into a system of uniformity." [1]

A regime of toleration had not been planned or decreed by any European power for the New World. The universal goal of churchmen and monarchs had been to transplant the European church-state system whole. The Spanish and the French had succeeded: in Spanish America the church-state association was even tighter than in Spain; and by the time of Richelieu the French government was carefully excluding foreigners and Protestants from its colonies. In the English colonies too a church-state system, either of the Anglican or the Puritan variety, was planted everywhere from the American continent to the West Indies. But the English, and the Dutch in their colonies, were disposed to push aside uniformity of faith in favor of power, profits, and internal unity. In 1660, to be sure, only two of the English mainland colonies—Maryland and

---

1. Perry Miller, "The Contribution of the Protestant Churches to Religious Liberty in Colonial America," *Church History*, 4 (1935), 62.

Rhode Island, which together contained hardly a tenth of the colonial population—were not living under a tight church-state system. Yet by the end of Charles II's reign in 1685, when religious compulsion still reigned in New France and New Spain, it was dying in the English colonies. By the beginning of the eighteenth century even the Puritans had been forced to make important concessions to toleration. By mid-century the colonies were astir with the ideas that finally led to the complete separation of church and state, and the struggle for religious liberty was developing political attitudes and aptitudes among some Americans that boded ill for imperial control.

However, what men could see during the early eighteenth century was the immediate advantage of toleration to empire. As a way of attracting immigrants and earning profits from land and trade, of developing strong and viable colonies, the English system of competitive pluralism in religion proved decisively superior to the French and Spanish church-state systems. The English, while accepting the church-state system in theory, had attracted settlers by welcoming dissenters of all kinds from all nations; and while the European populations of the French and Spanish colonies remained small, the English developed in the continental colonies a substantial nation of rugged farmers and enterprising planters and merchants. The English had on their side more than sea power and commercial ingenuity: an inviting system of religious accommodation, a realization that unity could best be forged by placating the *individual* as to his mode of worship and by uniting several religions behind the state in return for considerable freedom for all of them.

Since toleration in America was a seventeenth-century English inheritance, we must look backward to trace it.

Despite strong popular passions and sporadic bursts of prejudice and compulsion, in the four decades following the Restoration, at a vital moment in American settlement, a note of increasing skepticism and relaxation among sophisticated men, a rising political pragmatism and intermittent coolings of religious animosities, laid a basis for gentler religious policies. "When I was a child," John Aubrey remembered, "and so before the civil wars, the fashion was for old women and maids to tell fabulous stories, night-times, of spirits and of walking ghosts, etc. . . . When the wars came, and with them liberty of conscience and liberty of inquisition, the phantoms vanished. Now children fear no such things." [2] It was true: the last English witchcraft case, for example, occurred in 1712. But before that the change in the English mental world had been manifest in the genial mockery of a man like Charles II, who, when an astrologer proffered his services, took him to Newmarket and asked him to pick winners. One can indeed plot the widely different yet convergent sources of Anglo-American toleration by looking at two points on its political spectrum in the persons of Charles II, the exemplar of pragmatic court politics, and William Penn, who strikingly combined the high idealism of Quaker dissent with the calculating motives of the English proprietors.

Charles II was no doubt an improbable instrument for the furtherance of toleration in the raw, ascetic Protestant world that was emerging across the sea. His personal religious preference was Catholic, though religion itself did not hold the highest place among his tastes. Seasoned during his exile in Scotland on hardship and hypocrisy, some-

2. Christopher Hill, *The Century of Revolution, 1603–1714* (1961), 247.

what cynical, burdened by no excess of religious conviction, he had developed a tact that verged on insincerity;
yet this tact served to build a fairly broad-based Court
party, and to facilitate a certain measure of compromise
on religious issues which Charles sought out of an awareness that too much persecution might shake the state.
"The sad experience of twelve years," he said in his
thwarted Declaration of Indulgence, showed "that there
is very little fruit of all these forcible courses." For the
state itself he would kill, as he killed Sir Henry Vane, but
he had no lust to persecute, even though he occasionally
retreated or surrendered before those who did. "All appe-
tites are free," he once said, "and God will never damn a
man for allowing himself a little pleasure"—a cavalier
counterpart to William Penn's statement "I cannot think
that God will damn any man for the errors of his judgment." [3] Charles was much more a libertine than a liber-
tarian; but he was almost as intelligent as he was self-
indulgent, and he was afflicted by fits of open-mindedness
as well as rage. A candid voluptuary who left behind him a
gaggle of mistresses and fourteen acknowledged bastards,
he was also a candid opportunist with a series of abandoned ministers bobbing in his wake. Little disposed to
making long-range plans of state, on impulse open to experiment, he proved receptive to the "lively experiment"
in free conscience proposed to him by Roger Williams.
Hence there was an odd and fortunate, but not altogether
accidental, convergence between these two radically different men: a transient meeting of minds between the
seeker and the cynic. It was under Charles that Roger
Williams received the consolidated charter of Rhode

3. For Charles II, see J. P. Kenyon, *The Stuarts* (1958), 152; for Penn,
E. B. Greene, *Religion and the State* (1941), 57.

Island in 1663, with its categorical guarantee of freedom of conscience. It was again under Charles that the proprietaries of William Penn and of the profit-minded lords of the Carolinas were launched on such open terms that toleration became an irreversible commitment in their provinces. "The thing which is nearest the heart of the nation," Charles remarked in 1668, "is trade and all that belongs to it." [4] It was he who stopped the execution of Quakers in Massachusetts and who established the right of the Jews to reside and trade in England. At the end of his reign, there was still much left to be done for toleration in England and in the American colonies. But when he took the throne the church-state system in the English colonies was basically intact, and when he died the system had been cracked beyond repair.

At home the age of Charles II had seen its own excesses of intolerance—of Anglican persecutors, anti-Catholic mobs, and paranoid elaborations of Popish plots. But a prudent regard for considerations of state was gaining ground. Even the High Tory Anglican, Sir John Reresby, had come to see that "most men were now convinced that liberty of conscience was a thing of advantage to the nation." [5] And after the Glorious Revolution, it was this note —advantage to the nation—that was struck in the Toleration Act of 1689. Turning point though it was, this act contained no ringing appeal to broad principles of human liberty, but rather announced that freedom of conscience "may be an effectual means to unite their Majesties Protestant subjects in interest and affection." The Toleration Act was neither inclusive nor unlimited: it recognized the right of dissenters to practice their religion, but in licensed

4. Hill, 200.
5. Ibid., 246.

places of worship and under a suspicious public eye. Only Trinitarians were tolerated by the act, and all dissenters were placed under considerable disabilities: they had to pay taxes to the Church of England, they could be married only by its clergymen and buried only under its rites, and they were barred from holding office and from attending the universities. In America such limitations would be rather rapidly superseded.

There are times—however rare—when striking historical achievements are made by men of an excessive simplicity. Of such a simplicity William Penn, no more than Charles II, cannot be accused. Contemporaries charged him with duplicity, and historians have often seen in him a striking doubleness of character. A Quaker and a passionate idealist, he was also a Cavalier and a worldly courtier—indeed, a courtier and royal apologist at the court of a Papist king, James II. He had come by his doubleness legitimately, for his father, Admiral Sir William Penn, had been first a Roundhead and then a Royalist. Trying to wean young Penn from his inconvenient interest in unconventional religion, the admiral had sent him to France, where Penn developed a taste for gay dress, luxury, and an urbanity that went badly with the ascetic preferences of his sect. Penn also understood tact, a virtue foreign to many of the early Quaker proselytizers. Early converted to a sect noted for its antidoctrinal convictions and anti-intellectualism, he was widely read and displayed an active and penetrating mind, with a passion for elegance which flashes through the general dullness of his style in a number of apt and polished maxims. He pursued profits from his "holy experiment" in Pennsylvania almost as ardently as he pursued the Quaker interest and the principle of toleration. And in his several writings on toleration he appealed at once to the basic rights of conscience and to those worldly aspirations embodied in the Stuart monarchy and in the Restoration world's craving for property, stability, and prosperity. For him the high road of grand principle and the low road of practicality and prudence both led to toleration, and he could argue both cases equally well.

Converted to the Quaker faith at twenty-three, Penn found himself at twenty-four a prisoner in the Tower of London ("The Tower," he said, "is to me the worst argument in the world") for having preached illegally to a Quaker assemblage. During his subsequent imprisonment in Newgate he wrote the first of several appeals for liberty of conscience that he published in the 1670's and 1680's. His tract, *The Great Case of Liberty of Conscience* (1671), which was the most complete statement of the theory of toleration to be written under the later Stuarts, anticipated by more than fifteen years a substantial part of the case argued by Locke in his famous *Letter on Toleration.* At first Penn wrote simply as a Quaker, crying out with the familiar urgency of left-wing Protestants for liberty of conscience. Later he supplemented this appeal to human rights with a shrewd statement directed to practical considerations of state and to the desire for prosperity—a change reflected in the title of his essay of 1675, *England's Present Interest Discovered.*

Behind the Christian theory of persecution there had always been a terrifying logic: if one believed that one had beyond any doubt the essentials of a true and saving faith, and if one also believed that persecution could really force men to embrace this faith in full sincerity, then the torments suffered by heretics were a small price for them to

pay for an eternity of salvation. Religious liberty, the reformer Beza had said, required that everyone should be
left to go to hell in his own way. Nathaniel Ward of Ipswich, Massachusetts, put it sharply when he said that anyone who was willing to tolerate error either doubted his
own religion or was not sincere in it.[6]

As time went on, however, the number of doctrinal
points about which men were fully confident or which
were considered essential to salvation shrank, and, more
important still, experience with persecution showed that
external force did not bring about in its victims what
Locke called "the inward persuasion of the mind." Penn
was among those who repeatedly pointed out that force
could make hypocrites but not true Christians. Predesti-
narians might answer that they persecuted not to convert
but for the vindication and glory of God, but even this
cruel consistency was losing its persuasiveness. In the
seventeenth century God was being reborn in a benign
transfiguration, and many men were beginning to agree
with the dictum of Roger Williams that "forced worship
stinks in God's nostrils."[7] It was Penn's strategy to compare the situation of dissenters to that of the Protestants in
the Reformation, and to urge Protestants no longer to follow the inquisitorial Catholic example. He invoked a large
body of literature—"a whole cloud of famous witnesses,"
as he put it—to support his position. A forced faith, being
not genuine but hypocritical, was of no religious worth.
"Force never yet made a good Christian, or a good subject." Force actually subverts Christianity, since the king-

6. For Beza see Roland Bainton, "The Struggle for Religious Liberty,"
Church History, 10 (1941), 96; for Ward, Perry Miller, "The Contribution of the Protestant Churches," 57–8.

7. Anson Phelps Stokes, *Church and State in the United States*, I
(1950), 199.

dom of Christ is by nature spiritual and not carnal. A power over conscience, which presupposes infallibility, belongs only to God, and reverence requires that men refrain from assuming it. To punish dissenters is "to afflict men for not being what they can't be, unless they turn hypocrites." [8] By arguing that mental error should never be subjected to punishment, Penn was in effect arguing for the separation of church and state. His appeals for tolerance reflected the increasing desire of practical Englishmen—a desire which rings through Charles II's reluctantly withdrawn Declaration of Indulgence, the Toleration Act, and Locke's *Letter on Toleration*—to win, for once, a little peace and stability. Tolerance, Penn argued, was an asset rather than a danger to monarchy and to the unity of the realm, a source of strength to the economy and the state. "The interest of our English Governors is like to stand longer on the legs of the English people than of the English church." Dissenters must be thought of as taxpaying producers of wealth who were not to be ruined for their thoughts. Persecution would damage trade and check immigration. (The King had said virtually the same thing in 1672.) Shrewdly Penn added that ruinous persecution would increase the number of beggars and raise the poor rates—a telling point at a moment when parochial relief rolls were swollen and poor rates were already inconveniently high. [9]

In 1681 Penn received from Charles II, in payment of a debt owed to Penn's father, the province that became Pennsylvania; now he suddenly had a chance to realize the

8. W. W. Comfort, *William Penn 1644–1718* (1944), 121. For Penn's argument, see Comfort, chapter 3, and A. A. Seaton, *The Theory of Toleration under the Later Stuarts* (1911), 172–9.

9. William Penn, *The Select Works of William Penn in Five Volumes* (1783), III, 264.

old Quaker dream of a colony of refuge. Here, in an empire not much smaller than England itself, he could launch his "holy experiment," create an entire society in which Quakers and men of all other faiths would be free of religious compulsion, with a government more popular than most, with no official church and no persecution. Everything would be done right: the land would be honorably bought from the Indians and rented at an honorable and handsome profit to the thousands of immigrants Penn coaxed and advertised for; Christian principle and commercial gain would be united. Penn lived to be disappointed. In time he grew weary of political wrangles with his people, and the profits he expected were realized only after his death in 1718, enriching his children and not himself. But as a citadel of freedom—despite some enforced regression in 1696—Pennsylvania did stand. It showed all who were willing to see that a large commonwealth could embrace a variety of creeds and thrive. The fastest-growing province among the mainland colonies, a visible and undeniable center of wealth and solidarity, was triumphantly established on a foundation of religious liberty.

3

By the early eighteenth century the groundwork for toleration had thus been laid, though much remained to be done before full religious liberty could be achieved. It may be helpful here to consider the colonies under four headings. First, there were the old free colonies—that is, those which never had state churches: Rhode Island, Pennsylvania, Delaware, and New Jersey, the last three much influenced by Penn. Second were what might be called the vacant establishments—that is, colonies where the Angli-

can church was established in law but where there were
not enough Anglicans with morale enough to impose serious impediments for very long upon the free public worship of dissenters: New York, Maryland, the Carolinas,
and Georgia. In the free colonies and the vacant establishments considerably more than one-half of the colonial
population lived largely free of the threat of persecution.
Third on a rising scale of coercive power, Virginia stands
almost alone as an effective Anglican establishment. Despite the internal moral weakness of its church, the Virginia establishment was a force to be reckoned with—as
many a jailed Baptist preacher could testify—and even in
the Revolution was disestablished only after a severe
struggle. Fourth, the most powerful establishments were
the church-state systems of Puritan Massachusetts and
Connecticut, the only establishments which survived into
the nineteenth century.

Rhode Island, first and purest of the free colonies, was
promised in its second charter granted by Charles II in
1663 that "every person may at all times freely and fully
enjoy his own judgment and conscience in matters of religious concernments." There was to be no punishment or
even disqualification for religious views. The influence of
Rhode Island on her sister colonies may be a matter of dispute—she was the object of much malicious talk—but
she did at least show that complete religious freedom was
consistent with civil order.

Pennsylvania had no explicit provision for liberty of
conscience, but it opened office holding to all professing
Christians and promised to all believers in God freedom of
worship and freedom from taxes for the maintenance of
alien creeds. It required only observance of the Sabbath by
some form of public or private worship. In 1696 William

Penn was forced to accept the provisions of the Toleration Act, which were less tolerant than the prevailing practices in his province. In Pennsylvania there was no establishment to overthrow, and persecution for religious belief was never practiced. Delaware, part of Pennsylvania until 1702, enjoyed the same religious regime with even less pressure from the Crown. There is no record there of the molestation of individuals for their beliefs. New Jersey, despite the efforts of Anglicans to pretend that they had authority for an establishment, may be classified among the free colonies. Lords Berkeley and Carteret, given the Jerseys by James II, had tried to attract settlers by promising freedom of worship to all Protestants and soon drew more Puritans, Scotch Presbyterians, and Quakers than Anglicans. For a time West Jersey was owned by two prominent Quakers who put it under an unqualified regime of religious freedom. After 1702, when the two provinces were united, the extravagant and corrupt governor, Lord Cornbury, who was also an Anglican zealot, interpreted some ambiguous instructions as a mandate for creating an establishment, but neither the Crown nor the legislature ever erected one.

The vacant establishments make a motley category admittedly embracing a variety of conditions. These colonies had the legal form of establishment (whole or, as in the case of New York, partial) but attracted so many dissenters and had such small and feebly organized Anglican churches that limitation of dissenting worship either never existed or could not long be enforced. Among these colonies the religious history of Maryland is surely the fiercest, that of New York probably the most complex. The Baltimore family had never succeeded in making Maryland a satisfactory refuge for Catholics. From an early date the Puritan settlers outnumbered Catholics, and in 1652 they seized the government. Long and turbulent quarreling in the province culminated in 1692 with the institution of an Anglican establishment under which the Toleration Act was to apply—on terms far less generous than Lord Baltimore's Toleration Act of 1649. But the Puritan, Baptist, Presbyterian, Huguenot, and German Reformed settlers together constituted a substantial majority of the Maryland population, and although they could be compelled to contribute to the Established Church, it was politically impossible to interfere with their free worship. Even the Quakers won toleration in 1704, although Catholic worship remained private until a church was finally built in Baltimore in 1763—safely, although without benefit of legality.

The religious policies of New York, a polyglot settlement from earliest times, stemmed from the historical overlay of Dutch and English control. The Dutch had permitted private worship without benefit of ministers among practically all dissenters, and had granted the Congregational and Presbyterian dissenters special privileges of public worship and exempted them from supporting the established Dutch Reformed Church. An attempt by Peter Stuyvesant to introduce greater severity toward other denominations had been tartly rebuked by the Amsterdam directors of the Dutch West India Company, who shared the tolerant views prevalent in Holland and showed more interest in commerce than religion. When the English took over in 1664, they solved a ticklish problem in religious policy, not by abandoning the idea of an establishment but by pushing it back to the local level. The Dutch settlers were given full liberty of conscience, and no religious qualifications were set for officeholders. Each town would have a publicly supported church, but whose church it would be—Dutch or Congregational or Presbyterian—would depend upon the majority of the local inhabitants. Religious groups not adhering to varieties of the Reformed persuasion (that is, groups other than these three) were now granted the freedom of *public* worship which they had not had under the Dutch. After the Glorious Revolution there was some recession in religious freedom. Anglicanism was established without majority vote in the four lower counties of the state, and later the Anglicans under the leadership of the aggressive Lord Cornbury provoked a good deal of resistance among dissenters in these establishment counties. However, by about 1710 the Anglicans themselves had decided to let well enough alone, and subsequently they showed in New York the general spirit of tolerance then developing in the church at home. The governor also had to step carefully in religious matters because he was dependent on the Assembly for salaries and appropriations in a colony where Anglicans were outnumbered about fifteen to one. So, despite its partial establishment, the religious life of New York was largely ungoverned. "The body of the people," said the historian William Smith, Jr., in 1756, "are for equal, universal, toleration of protestants, and utterly averse to any kind of ecclesiastical establishment." [1]

In the South the establishments of North Carolina and Georgia had little reality. Probably in no colony was so large a part of its population unchurched as in North Carolina, and the nominal character of its early church establishment is clear: settlement of the colony began twenty years before the first Anglican minister was in-

1. Quoted in John Webb Pratt, *Religion, Politics, and Diversity: The Church–State Theme in New York History* (1967), 67.

stalled. Here as elsewhere the province was virtually turned over to a dissenting population by the proprietors' recruitment policies, and North Carolina was one of the least successful in later repairing this fundamental blow to Anglicanism. The first charter of Georgia in 1732 gave liberty of conscience to all but Papists, and the early settlers numbered a good many non-Anglicans, including a large colony of German Lutherans. In 1758, some years after the province became a royal colony, the Church of England was established, but it never flourished: as late as 1769 there were only two Anglican churches in the colony, and the disappearance of its establishment in the Revolution was hardly a matter of much moment.

Unlike its neighbors, South Carolina did evolve an Anglican establishment of some consequence. Proprietary enterprise and social idealism had at first united to promote a broad freedom which appealed to dissenting immigrants. Lord Ashley, later the first Earl of Shaftesbury, had drawn up with the help of John Locke the Fundamental Constitutions in terms of a liberality surpassing even William Penn's; public worship was allowed to all who acknowledged a God, including even "heathens, Jews, and other dissenters." Dissenters heavily populated the first settlements, but soon a considerable number of Anglican planters migrated from Barbados and demanded an establishment. The resulting struggle between dissenters and Anglicans was an important force in the factional politics of South Carolina until about 1712. In 1704 the Anglicans narrowly won a law barring dissenters from the Assembly, and soon thereafter established the Church of England. The dissenters, appealing to England, lost their case with the proprietors but succeeded with a subsequent appeal to the House of Lords and Queen Anne, and the obnoxious laws were disallowed. A new act, allowing dissenters to hold office, was soon passed, and in a few years, after the Assembly abolished parish taxes and gave financial responsibility for the Established Church to the provincial treasury instead, the dispute waned. The parish vestries of the Anglican church were the sole important agencies of local government in South Carolina during the colonial period; but the dissenters were quietly if illegally accommodated by being given the right of election to the vestries. As South Carolina prospered and became occupied with other problems, its leading men grew indifferent to religion, and religious issues died away.

4

The plight of the Anglican church in the colonies is one of the telltale signs of the inability of the English political order to reproduce itself effectively in the New World. Outnumbered in the colonies and outlobbied in England, even the strongest established Anglican church, that of Virginia, was never more than a pale imitation of the English church, while the other three Southern establishments ranged from the enfeebled to the skeletal. In New York, there was but a partial establishment in four counties, in New Jersey no legal establishment at all. In the other religiously free colonies Anglicans were weaker than dissenters. And under the Puritan establishments of New England they suffered the ignominy of being dissenters themselves, of pleading for and only slowly winning first their right to worship at all and then to worship without paying taxes to the Puritan ministry.

An establishment in a healthy condition is intimately linked, as was the Church of England, at home, to the power of the state. Its ranks supply a parallel hierarchy of authority, which both supports and is supported by the secular power. Through the state it has the power to compel; and though it may have the wisdom to indulge public worship by dissenting or alien groups, it characteristically retains the power to demand of them fiscal support. It commands the ready and willing allegiance of the majority of the population, for whom it is the inherited, the normal church; the agencies of education, charity, and welfare are in its hands; its local churches stand at the center of community life, and in the rhythms of daily existence it supplies the beat and tolls the bells. It is the core of the whole national system of values, spiritual, intellectual, and political, and it provides them with their distinctive texture. Such, with all allowance for the growing importance of nonconformists, was the Established Church in England in the eighteenth century, and such, with all due regard to their internal strains, were the Puritan churches of Massachusetts and Connecticut. And such, nowhere in the colonies, not even in Virginia, was American Anglicanism.

Since dissenters and adherents of alien creeds came more readily than Anglicans to the New World, they lacked the requisite numbers for successful establishment. Colonial Anglicanism was never able to mobilize behind itself the full authority of the state—neither in the provincial governments within the establishment colonies, where churchmen were often at odds with civil authorities, nor in the English state, where the Crown, the Prime Minister, and the Bishop of London (who had nominal authority and direction over the American church) found it politic to heed the sensibilities of colonial and English dissenters and their Whig allies. In England what seemed to matter most was tobacco, rice, indigo, and tranquillity, and not the spiritual condition of colonial Anglican communicants. Above all, in America the decisive link with church authority was cut. For there were no bishops on this side of the Atlantic, which meant not only that spiritual confirmation of parishioners and consecration of churches could not take place but also that potential ministers could only be ordained by making a lengthy and hazardous transoceanic trip. Without bishops or a proper system of ecclesiastical courts, the internal discipline of the American church was always haphazard and ineffectual. Hence an Anglican establishment in an American colony is not by any means the same thing as the Establishment in England.

Another weakness was the low average caliber of Anglican clergymen and the high degree of authority claimed and exercised by Anglican laymen. Paradoxically, Anglican clergymen in America were least distinguished where the Church was established and most distinguished where it existed in dissent or in free competition with other denominations. In the Middle Colonies and in New England, Anglican clergymen worked in relatively compact communities, under the watchful and often hostile eyes of other groups, and undertook with some hardihood the task of proselytism, and there the church mobilized a considerable number of native colonials of energy and dedication. But in the tobacco colonies the plantation economy scattered parishioners and added an exhausting and sometimes hazardous stint of travel to other clerical duties. The arduous tasks and small salaries, the crude conditions of life that prevailed in so much of the South, made assignment to its churches unattractive and demoralizing. Few natives became clergymen, so that ministers had to be sent to the Southern colonies, and they usually were men without influence or preferment in the English Church, men who could expect no more than the most undesirable curacies at home. Exiled into a society that offered them few pleasures and fewer prospects, and subjected there to little fear of ecclesiastical discipline, more than a few Southern clergymen lapsed into drink or lechery. From the very beginning the true power in the Southern Churches had been held by the influential laymen of the vestries, who kept control by the simple device, illegal in England, of hiring the minister on a temporary basis, usually for one year. Having done their bit to make the Southern ministry a thing of little appeal, the planters received from England a reluctant or inferior breed of minister, and then made matters worse by citing the poor caliber of their clergymen to justify the low salaries and limited powers of the ministerial office. Their own expectations were indeed low: at one point Virginia parishes were hiring many of their ministers not through the ecclesiastical patronage of the Bishop of London, but upon the recommendation of the London merchants with whom they traded.

After the turn of the century a sustained effort was made to remedy the poor state of colonial Anglicanism by the Society for the Propagation of the Gospel, founded in 1701. The S.P.G. provided missionaries, and undertook to strengthen the ministry by supplementing ministerial salaries. But its operations were more successful in New England, and especially in Connecticut, than in the South. Townspeople excluded from the New England churches by the membership requirements of the Puritan system drifted back toward Anglicanism in gratifying numbers, and during the Great Awakening there were fresh accessions when persons of all classes who were offended by the excesses of enthusiastic religion embraced Anglicanism as a serene and orderly alternative.

But in the South efforts to improve the Anglican Church came to relatively little, and on the whole it lost ground to the dissenters. By the third quarter of the century every major dissenting group was proselytizing its faith—sometimes under grave disabilities, as in the case of the Virginia Baptists—in the Anglican-established colonies. The English Church, hardly able to fill the ministries of settled parishes with creditable men, had little energy for propagating religion on the frontier. Its potential parishioners most often slid away into a churchless life, but many joined dissenting groups. In Georgia at mid-century only two parishes were regularly supplied with ministers; in South Carolina membership of the Church vestries was actually shared with leading dissenters as part of a program of religious and social accommodation; in North Carolina the Anglicans were heavily outnumbered by Quakers, and made hardly any inroads into the progressive anarchy and barbarization of frontier life. And in Virginia and Maryland the clergy were beginning to be hotly embroiled with the vestries over salaries that were keyed to the fluctuating value of tobacco.

5

The Puritan churches of New England suffered from major strains internal to their own religious system and from pressures brought to bear upon their establishment by dissenting groups, notably the Quakers, the Anglicans, and the Baptists. By the end of the seventeenth century in Massachusetts and by 1705 in Connecticut the Puritan leaders had been forced, partly through pressure dissidents put on increasingly receptive provincial legislatures and partly through warnings from England, to grant the right of open public worship to these three main dissenting bodies. The powerful and relentless Quaker lobby in London had been chiefly responsible for breaking resistance to toleration in Massachusetts, and members of the Anglican and Baptist churches were quick to benefit from the Quaker achievement. In Connecticut it was the Anglicans who constituted the avant-garde in the campaign for toleration. A second phase of change came in the 1720's and 1730's when both colonies succumbed to further agitation by granting to the major dissenting groups partial but effective exemption from the liability to be taxed to support the established churches.

The basic internal problem of the Puritan churches of New England stemmed from the long, slow, tormenting transition from being sects into being churches in which they had been engaged since the days of the seventeenth-century migrations. Organized at first for rebellion and purification, once they had taken their own domain and set up their own establishments they suffered from the demands of institutional life and the responsibilities of government and control. Founded on hardship and discipline, they developed toward prosperity and materialism. Harried out of England as victims of persecution, they themselves became persecutors who harried out Quakers, or, worse, put them to death, who suppressed Anglicans and Baptists, until they were forced to relent by pressure from London. Committed to an intense but volatile combination of rationality and pietism, they found their rationality veering toward a perilous rationalism and their pietism toward enthusiastic extremes. Devoted to the sectarian ideal that the visible church should be, as far as possible, identical with the invisible church of God's true saints, they succumbed at length to the reality that the visible church is a social institution and the invisible church an eschatological fantasm whose true constituents only the most arrogant Puritan could claim with certainty to be able to identify. When one considers the odds against their whole vision, what is impressive is not that the pristine Puritan way finally faded but that it survived so long and left so lasting an imprint upon the New England mind and character.

If one holds firmly in mind the gulf that separates a sect from a church, many of the twistings and turnings of the Puritan polity and Puritan thought become intelligible—the quest for new and firmer forms of organization that carried New Englanders even further away from the primitive vision of Congregationalism, adopting Presbyterian forms as they moved southward from Massachusetts into Connecticut and the Middle Colonies; the gradual abandonment in practice of the ideal of union between visible and invisible churches; the compromises of the Halfway Covenant; the increasing sense of community failure that is manifest in the jeremiads of the clergy; and the ultimate retreat before Arminianism and Unitarianism. One also understands better the impulse of enthusiasts and visionaries to reverse the religious decline, to revert to the piety of their fathers, to restore the old ideal of church polity, and to check the drift away from Calvinism.

One of the distinguishing features of sects is that membership in their churches is not quietly inherited or externally compelled but individually and warmly embraced. Each generation, every person, is expected to undergo the experience of conversion and discovery. The spirit of religion is not gently preserved but constantly reborn. The Puritans, for example, required of potential members a narration and confession of religious experience acceptable to the old members and the minister.

There was, however, as Baptist apostates insisted from time to time, a disturbing inconsistency between the Puritan ideal of a converted membership and the Puritan practice of baptizing the children of members, infants who of course could not have undergone conversion. As the first generation of Puritan immigrants died, parents began to present children for baptism even though they themselves had not yet been able to report any conversion experience. Now the church was faced with a terrible dilemma: if it denied baptism on the ground that parents were not yet church members, ever larger numbers of children would be unbaptized; but if it granted baptism, which was a privilege of membership, to children of the unconverted, it would be breaking with its central ideal of keeping the visible and the invisible churches as nearly identical with each other as was humanly possible. In the Halfway Covenant of 1662 the Puritan leaders had arrived at a compromise: a person born and baptized in the church but not confessing his experience of faith could continue as a "halfway" member who could have his children baptized but who could not vote on church affairs or receive the Lord's Supper. But some leaders were dissatisfied with this compromise. After 1677, Solomon Stoddard, the powerful pastor of the Northampton congregation, began to practice open communion—that is, he admitted candidates to full church membership, Lord's Supper and all, without trying to search them for evidence of saving faith. Many churchmen, among them the Mathers, were shocked at this departure from Puritan ways, but Stoddard's example was followed widely in the Connecticut Valley and was taken up by the liberals of the Brattle Street Church in Boston. In effect, by breaking with the original Puritan conception of the church, Stoddard was giving the minister the power to admit members, and under the guise of a more open and "democratic" membership was actually enlarging the authority of the minister and thus moving closer to the Presbyterian system. Sharp as their differences in organization had once been, many Congregational clergymen and laymen now felt no horror at the tightly-knit Presbyterian or quasi-Presbyterian forms.

To understand this, it is necessary to see that the two great English-speaking, Calvinist-derived churches, the Congregational and Presbyterian, together constituted a kind of Puritan imperium which contained almost half the churches in the colonies; and that despite differences in church polity, their common Calvinist heritage and common struggles had forged them into a degree of intellectual and spiritual fellowship. For example, Francis Makemie, the great pioneer of American Presbyterianism, was welcomed by the Congregational leaders and engaged in a friendly intellectual correspondence with Increase Mather. In 1708, Connecticut's churches became united in consociations that were close to the Presbyterian form. In the Middle Colonies Presbyterian churches were supplied with ministers educated at Yale, and what happened at Congregationalist Yale, and even at Harvard, mattered to Presbyterians. A sermon delivered and printed in Boston might be read with eagerness in New York or New Brunswick. When young Jonathan Edwards was called to his first pastorate, he did not think it at all strange or unseemly that the call should come from a Presbyterian church in New York City. Led by the formidable Jonathan Dickinson, a group of New England-born or educated ministers serving Presbyterian churches in the Middle Colonies formed an important faction in their internal squabbles.

In England the differences between Congregationalists and Presbyterians, though not theological, had long prevented any union of dissenters. In the Congregational view, the Church of Christ had its real existence in individual congregations, and in these alone. The Church Universal was no more than the sum or aggregate of these atoms. Further, the real church was vested in the laity, whose earnest desire it was to assure that the visible church was, so far as possible, identical with the invisible church of God's true saints; to this end, candidates for membership were required to submit a profession of faith and religious experience to all the members, whose approval was requisite for admission. Ministers existed as such only in relation to the single congregation which called and ordained them; outside their own congregations they might preach by invitation and arrangement, but their clerical status lapsed when they broke their covenant with their congregation, and could be renewed only when they made a new covenant with another. For Presbyterians, on the other hand, the Church Universal was not the sum of its parts but a unified body. In individual congregations the essential power lay not with the whole body of members but with church elders, who alone examined and admitted new members, and who made no claim to do more than exercise the best human judgment as to who belonged among the elect. Presbyterian congregations were subordinated to church courts and presbyteries, and ministers were ordained once only in the Church Universal, ordination which was not dependent on a relation to any particular congregation.

By the end of the seventeenth century in England an effort to subordinate differences and achieve unity was considered desirable by members of both churches, but was not achieved easily or quickly. In America Congregationalism early began to show Presbyterian tendencies, which became strong outside Massachusetts. Even in Massachusetts ministers tended to look for ways of controlling the choice and ordination of new ministers, and as early as 1648 had begun to move toward Presbyterian views of the role of elders and of ordination. When Connecticut accepted the Saybrook Platform of 1708 its churches finally broke with the tradition whereby the separate parishes ran their own affairs and chose their own ministers by simple majority vote. The Saybrook system, instituted to strengthen clerical authority, set up county associations of established ministers, supplemented for some purposes by influential laymen, who approved the parish choices of new ministers and could expel those it judged to be not true to the faith and the practices set forth in the Platform and the ecclesiastical laws of Connecticut. The state was bound to uphold the decision of the associations, and to prevent any deposed minister from preaching and collecting his salary, whatever his contract with his town or parish. The Saybrook Platform was not approved or accepted by all congregations, and in time would become a major source of controversy.

South of Connecticut, where Puritans had no establishments and could not rely upon state legislatures, the systems of the New England churches were of no practical use. In the heterogeneous situation of the Middle Colonies, they had to compete with a variety of other sects and, in the years just after the opening of the eighteenth century when many Anglicans opened a strong drive for the supremacy of the English Church, to resist Anglican inroads. Hence Puritanism, as it moved out of New England and down into New York, Pennsylvania, the Jerseys, and beyond, tended to affiliate itself with

Presbyterianism to gain the strength and discipline its exposed situation required.

The Presbyterians had their own troubles, which led to seriously disruptive factionalism. Some of the same difficulties that plagued the Anglican church—scattered, small congregations, poor roads, poorly supported and inferior pastors—also beset the Presbyterians of the Middle Colonies. Presbyterianism there, to a considerable degree the outgrowth of Scotch-Irish immigration, reflected the character of the Ulster church, whose members often quarreled fiercely over doctrine but lacked piety and inner commitment. Ulster-born ministers were slow to grasp the necessities of the American environment; they failed to emulate the New Englanders in building a closely knit town-church life or to provide adequate schools. Poor congregations often had trouble finding good ministers, or any ministers at all, while the ministers might justifiably complain that they were underpaid and that their hard-drinking, somewhat secularized and materialistic congregations were given over to the scramble for success in the tempting American environment. Church discipline became lax. In 1720 a young Scotch-Irish pastor, Robert Cross, confessed to fornication in a synodical trial, and was punished only by suspension from his pulpit for four Sundays. Not only was he permitted to remain a member of the controlling synod, but he became not long afterward an important leader of the antirevival party within the church. Party factionalism added to the difficulties. The church split between the subscriptionists, who stressed the necessity of formal, creedal commitments and adherence to the Westminster Confession, and the scripturalists, led by Jonathan Dickinson, who argued that faith in the Bible rather than man-made systems of interpretation was the important thing for the purity of the church. The Dickinson group also had pietistic impulses: it urged careful examination of the religious experience of a ministerial candidate, in addition to an assessment of his religious belief. The doctrinal and ecclesiastical differences between the two groups were compounded by ethnic ones: the subscriptionists were largely Scots and Scotch-Irish and were regarded by their New England-derived colleagues as coarse, untutored, and undisciplined, a prejudice confirmed by the outcome of the Cross trial. Into this internal feud came yet another faction led by William and Gilbert Tennent, who were to be instrumental in reforming the church during and after the Great Awakening and in setting its future tone. But the Awakening itself, which for a time rent the entire Puritan imperium, was the first major intercolonial crisis of the mind and spirit, and it requires extended attention.

CHAPTER VII

The
Awakeners

1

As a moving force in colonial development, the series of religious upheavals known as the Great Awakening was comparable to the mid-century colonial wars. Indeed, the Great Awakening was in some ways even more fundamental: it created, as the wars did not, a popular intercolonial movement, the first to stir the people of several colonies on a matter of common emotional concern; it split several existing churches, heightened popular initiative in social and political life, and strengthened the forces that were making American culture distinct from that of England. But the American revivals were no isolated event. They were a counterpart of the changes that were stirring Western Christendom in the form of pietism on the Continent and Methodism in England. The first ripples in America were set in motion by immigrant pastors of the Scottish and Reformed churches, and the most heroic evangelist was George Whitefield, an English sojourner originally associated with the Wesleys.

We may regard these movements as a second and milder Reformation. The First Reformation had cracked the facade of Catholic unity by posing a competing scheme of salvation and alternative churches and by giving a sharp impulse both to individualism and nationalism. The Second Reformation came at a time of greater secularism, of relatively peaceful religious accommodation and waning persecution, but also of wider religious diversity and competition. Its essential effect was the internal reinvigoration of Protestantism through more popular styles of worship. It attracted men who were eager to explore the limits of the Protestant drive toward individualized piety and conviction. Before it was over it had tested the capacity of Protestant individualism to stay within the bounds set by professional clerical leadership and by stable church organization. In America it went far to define the dominant religious style.

One effect of the Great Awakening was to bring religion to many who had lost touch with it, to restore the terrors and consolations of Christianity to unchurched persons, especially in the South and on the frontier. But its main strength, and also its most controversial effect, were executed among those who already belonged to churches but were unhappy with their religion. Paradoxically, the revivals were a response both to the inner stagnation of the churches and to their amazing outward growth. The denominations hit hardest by the revivals were, like other churches and like the whole population, growing furiously; the instability that produced the Great Awakening was in some part a result of hectic expansion.

By the 1740's, it is now easy to see, the two major Protestant denominations, Congregationalism and Presbyterianism, were ripe for upheaval, vexed from without by the skepticism rising among the educated elite and from within by the visible lassitude of many communicants. They were torn by local quarrels between laymen and clerics, and troubled by the Arminian heresy on one side and revivalism on the other. The educated classes of the Western world had cooled on religion, leaving a vacuum in church leadership to be filled by men who longed for a return to the warm emotionalism of the first reformers. In England the attack on miracles and revelation, mounting since the seventeenth century, had produced a strain of rationalism that was notably strong within the Anglican church, and, worse still, had given rise to Deism, which needed no church at all. The end of the religious wars and extreme persecution, the rise of mercantile cosmopolitanism and a more affluent and luxurious life, had taken some of the terror out of existence and some of the spirit out of religion. Even in America, where not so long before men like the Mathers had seen the Protestant vanguard as leading a direct assault on Satan's wilderness bastion, the cooling of religion could be felt, and men, even clergymen, walked the streets of Boston who leaned unmistakably toward the Enlightenment heresies. A society that was beginning to produce deistical leaders like Benjamin Franklin, John Adams, and Thomas Jefferson was clearly loosening its religious stays, and the example of such men would soon affect the solid middle class, whose members wanted the best and latest of everything, including freedom of thought.

More important, many of those who did keep their church connections and held to their Christian belief were disillusioned or disappointed. In both England and America apathy and worldliness were noticeable.[1] Religion had become conventional and formal, and its enfeebled pulse was evident in a lack of interest in worship, a want of

1. Luke Tyerman, *The Life of the Rev. George Whitefield* (1876), I, 67 ff.

warm conviction. In the Northern Colonies the learned but frequently dull Congregational clergymen who read long, tedious doctrinal sermons from manuscripts to sodden and sometimes dozing congregations were felt to be supplying too much mind and doctrine, too much of works and not enough of faith, not enough heart and soul, not enough of the living word. The clerics themselves were, and had long been, quite aware of the religious diminuendo in New England, and had been moaning since the 1670's about religious and moral decline in those stylized sermons, the jeremiads, whose ritualized repetitions barely concealed the real problems with which they dealt.

There was, of course, as the Connecticut historian Benjamin Trumbull remembered almost a half century after the event, some successful preaching in the churches and a fair measure of peace and order. "Yet there was too generally a great decay as to the life and power of godliness. There was a general ease and security in sin," Trumbull thought. "The forms of religion were kept up but there appeared but little of the power of it. . . . The young people made the evenings after the Lord's Day and after lectures the times for their mirth and company keeping. Taverns were haunted, intemperance and other vices increased and the spirit of God appeared to be awfully withdrawn. It seems also that many of the clergy, instead of clearly and powerfully preaching the doctrines of original sin, of regeneration, justification by faith alone, and the other peculiar doctrines of the gospel, contented themselves with preaching 'a cold, unprincipled and lifeless morality.'" [2]

In Pennsylvania the Presbyterian awakener Samuel Blair found things little better. He admitted that there

2. Benjamin Trumbull, *Complete History of Connecticut* (1818), II, 135, 137.

were some sincerely religious people and a good many
who went regularly to church. But most seemed content
with mere attendance, which satisfied their consciences
"with a dead formality." People indulged in "worldly discourse on the Lord's day," and conducted themselves in
public with frivolity. "Religion, as it were, lay a-dying,
and ready to expire its last breath of life in this part of
the visible church." [3] New England pastors, growing
desperate, would even hope at times that a smallpox or
diphtheria epidemic or perhaps an earthquake would prod
the people into a revival. The Northern Congregational
churches, having already lost a good deal of their institutional self-confidence, welcomed the first efforts of the
awakeners with surprising warmth.

In the pietistic movements religious leadership was
soon to be assumed by those who saw that the shrinking
appeal of conventional worship to the intellect could be
more than made up by a strong appeal to the feelings.
"Our people," said Jonathan Edwards, "do not so much
need to have their heads stored as to have their hearts
touched." [4] It was men such as Edwards and George
Whitefield, drawn in the main from the educated strata
of the middle class on both sides of the Atlantic, men who
somehow had not yet been undone by cosmopolitanism
or luxury, or infected by a demoralizing enlightenment,
who seized upon the situation and came forward as
leaders of the new religion of the people. They brought a
breath of the first Reformation, an attack on the laxity and
decadence, the cold officialism of the churches; they were
also reminiscent of the Puritan sectaries, of a praying

3. Tyerman, I, 322.
4. Jonathan Edwards, "Some Thoughts concerning the Present Revival
of Religion in New England," in Alan Heimert and Perry Miller, eds.,
The Great Awakening (1967), 278.

army, stirring the devotional animus of the hardworking ascetic Protestant public against the easy style and relaxed ways of the aristocrat or the cosmopolitan intellectual.

It was within the Puritan imperium—that is, in the Congregational-Presbyterian world—that the Great Awakening became particularly controversial. There the widespread craving for a spiritual revival became interwoven with the internal difficulties of the churches, since both denominations, particularly the Congregationalists, were roiled by controversies between ministers and laymen. Now, just at a time when the ministerial profession might have been thought to need its greatest internal solidarity, it was split over issues of church polity, religious style, ministerial education, and basic questions of theological doctrine. The Great Awakening thus stemmed from and in turn exacerbated two crises: the crisis within the ministry and the crisis between the clergy and the laity.

One steady source of tension between clergy and laity was the struggle over ministerial salaries, an all but universal problem in the colonies, which afflicted Anglicans, Presbyterians, and Congregationalists in somewhat different ways. In a period of inflation, ministers complained that their salaries were inconsistent with the dignity of their office, and that their meager incomes drove them to a variety of other part-time occupations ranging from medicine to farming. Laymen often argued that their pastors spent too much time in farming, hunting, fishing, and even in land speculation.[5] They tried to keep salaries down, an impulse natural enough in an economy in which cash was scarce and in which tight-fisted farmers were

5. Clifford K. Shipton, "The New England Clergy in the 'Glacial Age,'" *Publications of the Colonial Society of Massachusetts, Transactions*, 32 (1933–7), 50–3 and *passim*.

trying to better their condition by using what money they had for improvements or speculation. Often the resistance to being taxed by the town for the minister's upkeep was coupled with an insistence on paying the minister partly in kind—a practice that might keep him generously over-supplied in edibles he did not want and undersupplied in other vital goods.

It is impossible to say how much this source of resentments and discontents contributed to the despair of some ministers, to their often-expressed hope for some new burst of piety that would reinvigorate the church, or how much it did to make laymen more ready to levy charges against their pastor—in one town that he was too dull and cold, in another that he was flirting with heresies, in another that he was too much taken up with new styles in preaching.[6] What is certain is that the salary question was affected by other kinds of quarrels in which the authority of the minister was constantly invoked and in which he was bound to displease leading personages or significant town factions.[7] The New Englanders in particular lived in a close and potentially abrasive familiarity with each other, and a host of animosities arising out of matters other than religion could easily be carried into the business of the town meeting or of the church—lawsuits, family feuds, personal dislikes, soured business dealings, any of the vexations that might arise among a people who were remarkable for their highly developed individuality, stubbornness, and self-righteousness.

Matters were made a great deal worse by the rapid growth and mobility that were characteristic of the early

6. *Cf.* ibid., 46–9.
7. For a summary of quarrels, see ibid., 50–1. On community conflicts, see O. E. Winslow, *Meetinghouse Hill* (1952), especially Book Three.

and middle eighteenth century—the movement westward, the occupation of fresh lands, the formation of new
towns, the sharp increase in many town populations.
These changes multiplied occasions for controversies,
since they increased the decisions that had to be made
about the disposition of lands, the formation or location
of new churches, and the choice of ministers. When we
consider ministerial authority, it is necessary to imagine
the situation of many towns, new and old, that had to
accept young ministers fresh out of Harvard or Yale; to
imagine communities in which much of the civil authority
was in the hands of men in their forties and fifties, but in
which the prime spiritual authority, and the traditional
office of moral exhortation, discipline, and scolding, was
supposed to rest in a man in his twenties. Moreover, one
must expect that some of these young ministers would
have been quaffing a bit too thirstily at the stream of
rationalist thought, and that they would have struck a
rather uncongenial note now and then before pews filled
by church members with an older and, as we would now
say, more fundamentalist disposition. Or quite the contrary might happen, if a solemn young minister, energized
by a recent college revival, would find himself trying to
excite a fresh outpouring of the spirit in a congregation
that was quite satisfied with the old ways. Or, perhaps
more characteristically, the church members and the
townspeople would themselves be of different minds on
the issues, and the towns would fall into fierce factional
disputes, with the minister allied with one group and
detested by the other.[8]

8. On the crisis in clerical authority in Connecticut, see Richard L.
Bushman, *From Puritan to Yankee* (1967), chapter x. On the settlement
of Massachusetts ministers in a period of expansion, see Susan M. Reed,
Church and State in Massachusetts, 1691–1740 (1914), chapter iv.

In addition to all this, the Puritan churches were sagging under the weight of their own history. While the Anglicans were bedeviled by the inability of their church to become an establishment, the Puritans were bedeviled by the inability of their sect to remain a sect. In fact the New England Puritans, even under Congregationalism, had had from the beginning a church consonant with their belief in religious compulsion, their union of church and state, their educated and formalized priesthood vested with a high degree of authority. Moreover, their tradition placed the power and moral appeal of the priesthood in the sanctity of the office, not in the peculiar qualities of any man. It was this tradition that the revivalists would most sharply challenge. Yet these churchly features were combined with some strong sectarian qualities, creating an inconsistent and unstable mixture of practice and theory. Above all, there was lay control and localism—the idea that the true church resided in the persons of its lay members and that decisions were to be made by individual congregations. Then there was the amazing notion, from which the Presbyterians were free, that church membership should be, as far as it was humanly possible to discern, identical with God's own elect. This last criterion opened up innumerable possibilities for controversies over church membership, and set in motion a train of arguments running from the Halfway Covenant of 1662 to Solomon Stoddard's open communion and finally to Edwards's reversion to a more rigorous principle of exclusion.

The Puritan order had still other inconsistencies: these resulted in a situation in which a New England town, responsible under the supervision of the legislature for its church, and indeed possessed through its town meeting

with some authority over the church, was filling with
persons who found it very difficult to become church
members, and hence to have access to those consolations
and hopes that were available to persons who had "owned
the covenant." Thus, as it entered the eighteenth century,
Puritanism had become an organizational puzzle at the
very time when it was in a state of moral self-questioning.
Everyone seemed to believe—the clergy kept endlessly
reminding the laity in the jeremiads—that New England
had undergone a religious and moral "declension" since
its honored early days. And in the midst of this concern,
ministers were being set against laymen, church members
against townspeople, and in Connecticut the old localism
was at odds with the Presbyterian tendencies favored by
the ministers and embodied in the Saybrook Platform.

2

Worst of all, the churches, Congregational and Presbyterian alike, were plagued by serious theological issues that
not only went to the heart of their faith but also had a
vital practical bearing on the prestige and authority of
the ministers. Puritan thinkers were haunted by the dilemma posed by the determinism that lay at the core of
Calvinist theology. To be brief about this, one must be
dogmatic. The Calvinist idea that the human soul is pre-
destined from birth either to salvation or damnation had
the great merit of being intellectually consistent with the
belief in God's omnipotence and omniscience. It was also
consistent with the image of God as the righteous, stern,
and punishing father dear to the hardier souls of the
sixteenth century, which was now giving way to the
image of the loving, merciful, and even somewhat reason-

able father. It had the psychological advantage also of
engendering much anxiety and self-searching, which was
good for personal discipline, but it had the immense
practical disadvantage of being wholly inconsistent with
the idea of the church as a saving agency or of efficacious
ministerial exhortation. If a man was damned or saved by
an all-knowing God's prevision of his spiritual future,
there was nothing he or anyone else could do to save him.
A church and a ministry could exhort men to behave in
ways likely to celebrate the glory of God, but they could
not exhort them to come and be saved. Puritan thinkers
were all too well aware of this difficulty, and long before
the Puritan fathers had moved a half step away from pure
Calvinism by taking up the federal or covenant theology.
But this theology, while it concealed the predestinarian
dilemma in elaborate folds of argumentation, and thus
enabled the ministers to go ahead more or less comfortably
with their task, did not really solve it. Calvinist theology
proved a rather unstable compound, constantly vulnerable
to a painful breach between the practical business of
salvation and the inherited belief in predestination.

Calvinism thus became exposed to a breed of liberal
theology known as Arminianism—and Arminianism became for good Puritans a curse word as full of resonance
as the word communism has become to modern Americans.
Jacobus Arminius of the University of Leiden, who died
in 1609, was among those in the Church of Holland who
balked at the central tenets of Calvinism. His theology
had been condemned at the Synod of Dort in 1618–9,
and his party had been hounded out of Holland, but his
ideas acquired much influence in the Church of England
just at the time of the first large Puritan emigrations to
America. Arminius's idea that man is not helpless in

achieving regeneration but that his will can be an effective force in his being saved was taken up by many Anglican theologians of a rationalist bent and became a basic source of liberal English theology. By the same token, it became identified by Puritans on both sides of the Atlantic with the dangers of Anglican prelacy.

How much Arminianism, strictly speaking, there actually was in New England at the time of the Awakening is uncertain. But everyone could remember the electrifying conversion to Anglicanism of Rector Timothy Cutler and three other Yale men in 1722, which was blamed on their reading in rationalist books; everyone knew that other such conversions had followed, and that Anglicanism in New England had since gained significantly; everyone was uncomfortably aware that in 1707 Harvard had been captured by liberals who, though they were not avowed Arminians, showed an excess of catholic tolerance and relaxation; and that Harvard was beginning to graduate ministers who pressed across the thin line that separated the covenant theology from Arminianism; everyone heard in 1735 of the celebrated case of Robert Breck (Harvard 1730), the newly elected pastor in Springfield, who was charged with Arminianism and whose ordination the Hampshire Association of ministers, joined by Jonathan Edwards among others, refused to confirm. It was still more disquieting that Breck was ultimately upheld by the General Court of Massachusetts, and that before the middle of the century Arminianism was openly espoused by respectable ministers.[9]

The term Arminianism was often loosely applied to

9. Conrad Wright, *The Beginnings of Unitarianism in America* (1955), chapters 1 and 2. On Harvard see Perry Miller, *The New England Mind: From Colony to Province* (1953), esp. chapter 27.

those who did not preach or defend it. But there were
always persons to whom Puritan religious anxiety, in all
its troublesome glory, became less and less acceptable,
and there were liberal ministers ready to accommodate
parishioners who wanted to believe that a righteous outward life and faithful churchgoing might really help to
save them. Outcries against Arminianism, though often
not technically correct, thus had a certain truth: the truth
that many New Englanders had ceased to believe in their
beliefs. Many persons associated this growing doctrinal
hollowness with the common religious laxity that was so
widely bewailed. Perhaps, it was thought, Arminianism
and laxity alike might be swept away by some new outpouring of the spirit. And so, when the outpouring actually came, each side among the ministers had its own
doctrinal bugbear: to the educated revivalists the main
enemy was Arminianism; to the liberal rationalist clergy
who opposed the revivals, it was the undisciplined religious style and the hysterical manifestations they stigmatized as "enthusiasm."

Enthusiasm: for all the clamor over Arminianism, what
was at issue in the Great Awakening was not so much
religious doctrine as religious style—with all that this
term implies concerning personal faith, church practice,
and public decorum and order. In eighteenth-century
polite literature enthusiasm was a term of disapproval,
applied alike to Methodists in England and revivalists in
America. Charles Chauncy, a leading Boston opponent
of the Great Awakening, defined enthusiasm as "an
imaginary, not a *real* inspiration" that would overtake one
"who has a conceit of himself as a person favoured with
the extraordinary presence of the *Deity*," and who "mis-
takes the workings of his own passions for divine com-

munications, and fancies himself immediately inspired by
the SPIRIT OF GOD, when all the while, he is under no other
influence than that of an over-heated imagination."[1]
Often it was revealed in a wildness of appearance, an
excess of energy and volubility in speaking, convulsions
and distortions, quakings and tremblings, freakish and
sometimes frenzied behavior, a fancy for bizarre ideas, a
repudiation of reason and learning, and a disposition to
be censorious and uncharitable.

To men like Chauncy, enthusiasm was a religious fail-
ing worse than coldness. Enthusiasm was a new name for
the old religious search for direct personal access to God
in a sudden moment of striking conversion, which would
then be followed—or so the devotee might hope—by a
life of saving faith. The enthusiast felt himself to be the
beneficiary of a direct outpouring of the spirit of God, a
visitation whose authenticity would be manifest in the
sheer intensity of his feeling and conviction. To all established creeds with professional ministries this kind of
religious subjectivism presented a sharp challenge. If the
grace of God descended in a sudden moment of inspiration, and if its authenticity was inwardly rather than out-
wardly established, the role of liturgical practice, of
rational theology, and of the knowledge of God's word
might become nothing as compared with ecstatic experience. If biblical and sacred knowledge were less useful
as aids to salvation than they had previously been imagined to be, the education of a minister of religion would
be far less important than his ability to generate the
ecstatic sense of conviction. But then, if the test of a
good pastor lay not in his formal qualifications, not in his

1. Charles Chauncy, "Enthusiasm Described and Caution'd Against,"
in Heimert and Miller, 231–3; on the general significance of enthusiasm,
see Ronald Knox, *Enthusiasm* (1950).

education and ordination, but in his warmth and conviction and the electrifying effect of his preaching, the structure and habits of existing churches might be entirely overthrown. It could always be said that some of the pastors (especially those whose preaching seemed dull and lifeless or whose lives were far from impeccable) were themselves unconverted, and that unconverted ministers would be worse than useless, would in fact be a peril to their flocks, since one could not receive conversion from a man not already converted.

Once such doubts could be raised, disturbing questions might follow. What lay enthusiast need have regard for the authority of a pastor he "knew" to be unconverted? What would stop ministers from setting upon each other and scrutinizing anew each other's spiritual authenticity? Where indeed was there any authority to establish the authenticity or the state of spiritual inspiration of the ministry? Enthusiasm—though in the end it was stopped far short of this in America—raised before some horrified minds the yawning gulf of anarchic religious individualism, the threat of the total fractionalization of the churches, and even of an ensuing social anarchy. Opponents of the Awakening tried to persuade their fellow ministers who were tempted by the signs of religious stirring that came with enthusiasm that it was false and therefore dangerous. But the awakeners themselves took on the task of reaping the spiritual outpouring of the holy spirit without letting the worst manifestations of enthusiasm run away with it.

3

The first signs of an American awakening came in the Middle Colonies as early as the 1720's when two immigrant pastors in New Jersey, William Tennent and Theodorus Jacobus Frelinghuysen, brought into the staid life of the Presbyterian and Dutch Reformed churches a strong breath of pietism. Frelinghuysen, the descendant of a Westphalian family that had gone over to the Reformed church in the seventeenth century, had been baptized by his father, a Reformed pastor. He was educated in the Gymnasium at Hamm, and then attended Lingen, the leading pietistic university in the Reformed church. Frelinghuysen had taken his first pastorate in East Friesland in 1717, and then for a short time had been co-rector of a Latin school. When asked by some of his acquaintances in the Reformed church, who hoped to spread the evangelical spirit in the New World, to accept a pastorate in "Rarethans," Frelinghuysen thought he was taking an assignment in Flanders or Brabant; when he discovered that he had agreed to go to the New World, he took it as a special call from God and kept his commitment.[2]

A sturdy, harsh, and often intemperate man, raised in an atmosphere of theological dispute, Frelinghuysen had a nose for controversy and a hardihood that promised a vigorous if not a tactful ministry. He arrived in America in the winter of 1720 at the age of twenty-seven, stopped long enough in New York to offend the senior pastors of the Reformed church, and then went on to Raritan, New Jersey, where he was the only pastor for miles around. He found himself ministering to Dutch farmers who had developed a solid materialistic culture, and who were much more enraptured by the opportunities of the New World than by the desire to live by the word of God. Before long Frelinghuysen was embroiled with his parishioners, who

2. James Tanis, *Dutch Calvinistic Pietism in the Middle Colonies: A Study in the Life and Theology of Theodorus Jacobus Frelinghuysen* (1967), supersedes other sources on its subject, which are often vague or inaccurate.

objected to his petty tyrannies, his disciplinary methods, and his excommunications. In 1734, after almost ten years of dissension during which the church was split between the critics and supporters of Frelinghuysen, the Classis of Amsterdam, under whose jurisdiction he was, finally prevailed upon him to make peace.

In the church records of Frelinghuysen's ministry there is more evidence of controversy than of successful revivals.[3] But he was a powerful, emotional preacher, whose sphere of influence was somewhat enlarged by many published sermons. Whatever his influence on laymen, he did excite other ministers, among them William Tennent, Sr., and his son Gilbert. It was the Tennents, and later, under their guidance, George Whitefield, who touted Frelinghuysen as a successful revivalist and considered themselves his followers. Just how intense a revival Frelinghuysen had been able to bring about is arguable, but there can be no doubt that Gilbert Tennent, who was nothing if not serious, took inspiration and encouragement from Frelinghuysen's ministry and borrowed something from the style of his sermons. On this count alone Frelinghuysen can be seen as an important figure in the revivals.

William Tennent, a native of Ireland and a graduate of Edinburgh, had come to America in 1716 during his early forties. Once a priest in the established Church of Ireland, Tennent had broken with it, presumably out of dissatisfaction with episcopal government and with the rise of Arminianism among the clergy. In 1718 he was admitted to the Presbyterian ministry by the Synod of Philadelphia, and after a few years of preaching near New York City, he

3. On the lack of evidence for a Frelinghuysen revival, see Herman Harmelinck III, "Another Look at Frelinghuysen and his 'Awakening,'" *Church History*, 37 (1968), 423–38.

went to Bucks County, Pennsylvania, as minister to two cooperating churches. There he made his central contribution to the awakenings as an educator. Tennent was convinced that the Presbyterian church could no longer permit itself to be dependent upon English and Irish clerics, who were infected with Arminian notions, and who were unresponsive to the difficult conditions of religious life in America, where Presbyterianism was losing large numbers of backsliding laymen. During the 1720's, when the Presbyterian church was splitting into an evangelical and a conservative party, Tennent and his sons, who demanded a conversion experience of potential ministers, became the most aggressive of the evangelists. In the absence of a suitable college, Tennent determined to train ministers of sound conviction as best he could. Having already given a sterling education to his son Gilbert, he opened a little school which by 1735 he was able to house in a twenty-foot-square log house at Neshaminy, Pennsylvania.

In his "Log College," as it was dubbed by scornful critics, Tennent led not only his three younger sons but also such leading evangelists as Samuel Blair and Samuel Finley through an intensive training in many subjects pertinent to divinity, including Latin, Greek, and Hebrew. But above all he conveyed to his pupils his own evangelical zeal, and in his long years of teaching he reared about a score of ministers who fanned out from the Log College at Neshaminy to ministries or similar informal educational enterprises elsewhere. Tennent never accepted an uneducated ministry, and as an awakener he became aware that some halfway house was needed between the unsatisfactory nurseries of clergymen in England and an illiterate evangelical ministry, which could

provide trained ministers without losing the full warmth
of the pietistic spirit. The example of the Log College led
to the founding of the College of New Jersey (Princeton)
in 1746, the year of William Tennent's death. Tennent,
having lived long enough to see the fruits of his work in
the revivals proliferating to the north and to the south, had
educated the corps of ministers whose pupils and converts
would set the pattern of American Presbyterianism even
into the nineteenth century.

4

In the mid-1730's the center of Awakening activities
moved for a time to the upper end of the Connecticut
Valley, where the vitalizing figure was Jonathan Edwards.
Edwards's place in the Great Awakening has been confused and exaggerated because he was by far the most
powerful mind connected with the revival and the sole
leader who could be called a writer of distinction. For
two hundred years America heard of him mainly as the
author of the Enfield sermon, "Sinners in the Hands of an
Angry God"—a piece hardly representative of his preaching—in which God holds man like a loathsome spider
over the fires of hell; and so Edwards has come down in
our legends as a typical fire-and-brimstone predecessor
of the evangelical tradition. In truth he differed in several
ways from the usual fiery evangelist; although he was indeed a revivalist and the most effective apologist for the
Great Awakening, he was neither its most typical nor its
most influential preacher.

Edwards was born in 1703 in a parsonage in East Wind-
sor, Connecticut. His father, to whom he was exceptionally close, was a rural minister of good family ante-

cedents, and his mother was the daughter of the Reverend
Solomon Stoddard, a towering figure in church politics.
At thirteen Edwards was sent to Yale College, then a
young institution struggling to find a permanent home.
At Wethersfield, Connecticut, where the college faction
with whom he allied himself was studying, this highly
disciplined, studious, withdrawn young man first read
Locke and Newton and started himself upon a career of
philosophical inquiry. He had barely finished a brief
period of postgraduate study when the College, and indeed all of New England, was scandalized by the an-
nouncement of Yale's rector, Timothy Cutler, two of its
tutors, and four neighboring ministers that they had embraced Episcopacy and were going over to Anglicanism.
In 1722, when Edwards went to New York City to take his
first pastorate, no one could fail to be aware that Calvinism was menaced by Arminian tendencies, and that between religious lassitude on one side and heresy on the
other the churches and colleges were in trouble.

In 1727 Edwards was called from New York to succeed
his grandfather, Solomon Stoddard, in the church at
Northampton, Massachusetts, which Stoddard had made
the central ministry of western New England. In the
same year he married Sarah Pierrepont, daughter of one
of Yale's founders and granddaughter of Thomas Hooker,
leader of the 1630 emigration to Connecticut and founder
of Hartford. So married and connected in the interrelated
and tightly knit small-town ruling caste of the Connecticut Valley, Edwards stood at the pinnacle of its social and
religious world, and might easily have turned into an
ecclesiastical autocrat like his maternal grandfather. Instead he persisted in being a pious frontier intellectual,
and in this role cast his lot with the reformers, made

enemies among his tribe of cousins, and found a secure niche in history.

In 1731, when signs of doctrinal factionalism were flashing through the New England churches, Edwards accepted an invitation to preach in Boston which he took as an occasion to fling into the teeth of the Boston liberals a sermon, "God Glorified in Man's Dependence," setting forth an older and purer Calvinist doctrine of grace than the Boston congregations were accustomed to hear. In emphasizing God's arbitrary grace and man's utter dependence, Edwards was asserting a position that even the least congenial Boston ministers would not have been willing to deny but with which they were beginning to feel uncomfortable. Henceforth Edwards preached with growing confidence and assertion, reinterpreting the older theology in the light of ideas taken from Locke and Newton. What must have seemed proof of the validity of his efforts came in a few more years. His grandfather had succeeded on five occasions in prodding local revivals, the last of them when Edwards was fifteen and old enough to take notice. Now, in the year 1734–5, Edwards reaped his own harvest of souls. It began rather suddenly, even casually. A young man and a young woman died unexpectedly, and Edwards seized upon their deaths to quicken the religious interest of the young of the town. Months later a young woman of easy ways underwent a surprising conversion, and now somehow the dam burst. Northampton seemed to fling itself into a revival, until a height was reached at which Edwards believed "scarcely a single person in the whole town was left unconcerned about the great things of the eternal world." By the spring of 1735 the revival hit its peak, affecting towns all up and down the Connecticut Valley. But then Joseph Hawley,

Edwards's uncle and a pillar of the community, became despondent over the state of his soul and slit his throat. His suicide was followed by others, and the fervor cooled. The next major New England revival was not to come until the visit of George Whitefield in 1740.

In the early and middle 1740's, when enthusiastic manifestations came under fire from the rationalist clergy, Edwards became the most subtle and formidable defender of the Great Awakening. There is reason to think that Edwards himself regarded preachers like Whitefield as somewhat too enthusiastic, but on balance he stood firmly with the revivalists. He conceded that some of the excessive emotional manifestations of religion were tinctured with pathology, not least with an excess of spiritual pride, and he agreed that an effort should be made where possible to restrain some of the overheated manifestations of the revival. He also concluded, at least by 1742, that the revivalist habit of censuring and questioning the spiritual condition of uncongenial ministers was a dangerous thing, contrary to scripture, and spiritually presumptuous.[4] He urged other revivalists to leave to Christ the prerogative of judging the spiritual condition of other men. But on several counts he roundly defended the revivals. He suggested that the anti-revival ministers leave off trying to diagnose the psychopathology of the revivals and return to their true business. If congregations wept and shrieked and moaned, one ought to take such behavior, he thought, as an evidence of an underlying reality; as with a new language, one had to try to learn the meaning of such things. The excesses of the revivals, Edwards argued, were temporary, an overreaction to the

4. Edwards, "Some Thoughts concerning the Present Revival of Religion in New England," 282-5.

previous dullness of religion. No one, after all, had gone permanently out of his mind from the religious excitement, and in many cases those most affected were persons "in the heat of youth" whom one must expect to be vulnerable to extreme modes of statement. In so many cases there were unmistakable evidences of a "real change of heart," in so many the floods of tears had been attended by "a great appearance of contrition and humiliation," that there was every reason to see the revivals not only as a work of God, but as a central and decisive episode in the whole Christian drama of salvation.[5] He portrayed America, and especially New England, as the site of God's most important and climactic work, the redemption foretold in scripture. This work, already begun in New England and manifest in its revivals, "if it should go on and prevail, would make New England a kind of heaven on earth."[6]

Repeatedly Edwards made elaborate, though balanced, arguments for the place of emotion in religious life— welcoming the appearance of just that which had been most missing in recent New England Puritanism. Religious emotion, he argued, did not exclude the understanding, since the two were complementary rather than opposed; but there could be no true religion without a profound stirring of the affections. The affections conveyed light to the understanding, and preachers who appealed in searching terms to the emotional life of their parishioners were therefore on entirely sound ground. Edwards himself did not shrink from making just such appeals. After a visit from Whitefield, which gave him a chance to see the

5. Jonathan Edwards, "The Distinguishing Marks of a Work of the Spirit," in Heimert and Miller, 205–11.
6. Edwards, "Some Thoughts . . ." 274.

great awakener at work, Edwards himself returned vigorously to his old evangelical warmth, and it was during this phase of his life that he delivered his famous Enfield sermon. With its vivid portrayal of the horrors of infinite damnation, this remarkable work holds a signal place in religious literature. (One thinks, oddly enough, of the priest's sermon in James Joyce's *Portrait of the Artist as a Young Man* as a comparable effort at terror.)

"I think," Edwards once said, "it is a reasonable thing to endeavor to fright persons away from hell."[7] The purpose of "Sinners in the Hands of an Angry God" was to do just this, to bring his listeners to a vivid sense of eternal punishment and to impress them with the necessity of immediate contrition, since death might strike at any moment. A sermon such as a sadist might have trembled to deliver, it was presented by Edwards in a posture of transfiguration, his gaze firmly fixed on the bell rope that led upward to the steeple. The people of Enfield were urged to consider the torment of burning like a livid coal not for an instant or a day but for "millions of millions of ages," at the end of which they would know that their torment was no nearer to an end than ever before, and that they would "never, never be delivered." "The sovereign pleasure of God, for the present, stays his rough wind: otherwise it would come with fury, and your destruction would come like a whirlwind, and you would be like the chaff of the summer threshing floor." "God will crush you under his feet without mercy; he will crush out your blood and make it fly, and it shall be sprinkled on his garments, so as to stain all his raiment. . . . And when you shall be in this state of fright, the glori-

7. Jonathan Edwards, *The Works of President Edwards* (1829), III, 578.

ous inhabitants of heaven shall go forth and look on the awful spectacle, . . . and when they have seen it they will fall down and adore that great power and majesty." At the end the pastor puts his case simply: "There is reason to think that there are many in this congregation now hearing this discourse, that will actually be the subjects of this very misery to all eternity. . . . And it would be no wonder if some persons, that now sit here in some seats of this meeting-house in health, and quiet and secure, should be there before tomorrow morning." [8] (Edwards might have had good reason to think so: it was only a half-dozen years since one of his earlier discourses had pushed Joseph Hawley toward his eternal fate.) "A most awakening sermon," said one who heard it, "and before sermon was done there was great moaning and crying through the whole house—What shall I do to be saved—oh I am going to Hell—oh what shall I do for Christ, etc. etc. So that the minister was obliged to desist —the shrieks and cries were piercing and amazing. . . ." [9]

After the new burst of revivals, Edwards passed the zenith of his influence as a preacher, though he was still to write his powerful apologies for the awakenings and his major theological works. Among his own people in Northampton he had made enemies. When some of the young were reported to be relishing a book of advice to midwives, he took it upon himself to intervene, identified the culprits by name, and thus offended many of the most upright families in town. His final difficulties with his congregation came over an old issue of church organization. Convinced of the rightness of the pristine Puritan

8. Jonathan Edwards, "Sinners in the Hands of an Angry God," *Works*, VII, 163–77.

9. Ola E. Winslow, *Jonathan Edwards* (1940), 192.

ambition to make the visible church as much identical as possible with the invisible church of saints, he repudiated Solomon Stoddard's practice of admitting almost all applicants to church membership. Now once more, before anyone in Edwards's church could be accepted for membership, he must unburden himself of a full profession of faith and religious experience. In 1748 the first applicant under this revised ruling refused to conform to Edwards's standard. In 1750 a council of neighboring churches convoked to decide on that issue voted that Edwards should go. He took a dignified formal leave of his congregation that year. For a time he preached at Stockbridge, Massachusetts, both to a small white congregation and to the Indians. It was in this period that he wrote his works on the *Freedom of the Will* and on *Original Sin.* In 1757 he was called to assume the presidency of the College of New Jersey (Princeton), a position that promised great influence but for which he perhaps rightly wondered whether he had the proper temperament. He accepted the invitation, but shortly after reaching Princeton he was inoculated against smallpox, took the inoculation badly, and died before he could take up his duties. At the end he was puzzled by the irrationality of it all—that God should have called him to this role and then left him no time to fill it.

Edwards, with his literal faith in the sufficiency of scripture as a guide both to history and to the scheme of salvation, his opposition to the advancing rationalism of his age, his belief, as he put it, in "the insufficiency of reason as a substitute for revelation," his desire to go back beyond New England's compromises toward a stronger and sterner Calvinism, his total faith in the tangible reality of hell, his defense of the usefulness of the hellfire sermon, has seemed to many historians a two-century throwback to the primitive spirit of the early reformers. This view of him is confirmed by his attempt, however impolitic and feeble, to return to the early sectarian scheme of church membership. Yet ever since the late Perry Miller wrote his imaginative critical study of Edwards in 1949, the chief debate over Edwards has centered around the question of his "modernity." In the cycles of time there are bound to be moments when almost any thinker of power and subtlety will be found to have a new relevance, and Miller's view of Edwards was forged in a decade of neo-orthodoxy and existentialist thought which demanded the reconsideration of such a figure. A thinker like Edwards, with his keen sense of human limitation, is always likely to seem to some of us profounder and in many ways more rewarding than, say, such a genial and externalized mind as Benjamin Franklin's. He is modern, then, in the sense that he appeals to some of our contemporary pre-occupations. And there is one other sense, internal to the New England tradition and Puritan intellectual history, in which Edwards was unmistakably striking out for something modern. The first Puritan way of thought, which had been shaped by post-medieval scholasticism and its intellectual method, the elaborate "technologia" inherited from the sixteenth century, had become hopelessly antiquated. Edwards, responsive as he was to Locke and Newton, tried to put the Calvinist tradition into a new, more empirical setting, and to make Puritan psychology consistent with Lockean sensationalism, and the Puritan sense of cause and effect consonant with the Newtonian world view.

Here it might be more useful and more accurate to think of Edwards not as being precisely modern but rather as trying to be up-to-date. He was using the most advanced intellectual instruments he could find to devise a more certain means of going backward. In the eighteenth century, with the first tendrils of an American Enlightenment growing in his vicinity, he was using seventeenth-century philosophy and physics to restore a sixteenth-century sense of conviction. If we are to define Edwards as distinctively modern, we must then think of such antithetical eighteenth-century minds as Hume and Gibbon, Diderot and Voltaire, Franklin and Jefferson, as being somehow reactionary or retrogressive. There are modernities and modernities, and the earnest efforts of Edwards to make Lockean philosophy out of the spiritual writings of New England villagers is thinly related to most of the modernities we know. The hell that was preached at Enfield was surely not fashioned out of the same fires as the hell that burns in modernist literature.

5

It was not Edwards the native but George Whitefield the transatlantic sojourner who was the heart and soul of the American Awakening. Where Edwards rocked his own little corner of the world, Whitefield shook the religious sensibility of the seaboard as a dog shakes a rag, and when he was finished the religious life of America was permanently changed. Mid-eighteenth-century Americans were to think of two fellow Englishmen as being truly great: Pitt, whose task was to beat France, and Whitefield, whose task was to beat the Devil. As preachers it is doubtful that even such sterling nineteenth-century Americans as Charles Grandison Finney and Dwight L. Moody matched Whitefield, and none of the later plat-

form clowns of the evangelical tradition, such as Billy
Sunday, would bear comparison. It was as a preacher, not
a thinker, that Whitefield excelled, but excel he did beyond the measure of anything England or America had
known, possibly beyond the measure of anything known
in Christendom since Peter the Hermit. Alexander Pope
thought him a "braying ass" and there must have been
scores of clerics in England and the colonies who wished
at times that he had never been born, but there were
none who could deny his power. The most famous tribute
to Whitefield was paid by the actor David Garrick, who
said Whitefield could make audiences weep or tremble
merely by pronouncing Mesopotamia, and it was Garrick
too who even more persuasively remarked: "I would give
a hundred guineas if I could only say 'O!' like Mr. Whitefield."

Comely in his younger days, despite a distinct squint
that led Horace Walpole to say that he had one eye on
earth and one on heaven, lively in his movements, holding
a Bible aloft in his hand, and raising his ringing voice to
reach huge crowds in open fields, Whitefield could use
an audience as an instrument. "He has a clear and musical
voice," said an observer of one of his sermons in New
York, "and a wonderful command of it. He uses gesture,
but with great propriety. Every accent of his voice, every
motion of his body speaks; and both are natural and un-
affected. If his delivery be the product of art, it is certainly the perfection of it, for it is entirely concealed." [1]
When he spoke to the colliers of Bristol, straight out of
the mines, their blackened faces were striped by little
white rivulets of tears. One American crowd that show-

1. Tyerman, I, 329–30.

ered him with gifts of food for his Georgia orphanage so
moved him that he wrote: "Indeed I could almost say
they would pluck out their own eyes and give me." "A
wonderful power was in the room," he wrote of one of his
efforts before a group of young women at Philadelphia,
"and with one accord they began to cry out and weep
most bitterly for the space of half an hour. They seemed
to be under the strongest convictions. . . . Their cries
might be heard a great way off. . . . Five of them seemed
affected as those that are in fits . . . and at midnight I was
desired to come to one who was in strong agonies of body
and mind." [2] "Most of the people were drowned in tears,"
he reported of another of his sermons in the country
nearby, "the word was sharper than a two-edged sword.
The bitter cries and groans were enough to pierce the
hardest heart. Some of the people were as pale as death;
others were wringing their hands; others lying on the
ground; others sinking into the arms of their friends; and
most lifting their eyes to heaven, and crying to God for
mercy. They seemed like persons awakened by the last
trump, and coming out of their graves to judgment." [3]

Whitefield reached the sophisticated as well as the
simple. At a sermon delivered under the auspices of Lady
Huntingdon, the friend and patron of the Methodists
whom he served as chaplain, Lord Chesterfield became so
wholly absorbed in Whitefield's dramatic account of a
blind man, moving and tottering on the brink of a precipice like an endangered soul, that he jumped up at last,
exclaiming, "By heavens, he's gone!" Benjamin Franklin,

---

2. George Whitefield, *Journals* (edn. 1960), 361, 421.
3. Ibid., 423. On Whitefield's sermons, see James Downey, *The Eighteenth Century Pulpit* (1969), chapter 6.

who took warmly to Whitefield, reported coming to one
of his appeals for the orphans of Georgia resolved not to
give a thing because he disapproved of the location of the
orphanage. "I had in my pocket, a handful of copper
money, three or four silver dollars, and five pistoles in
gold. As he proceeded I began to soften, and concluded
to give the copper. Another stroke of his oratory determined me to give the silver; and he finished so admirably
that I emptied my pocket wholly into the collector's dish,
gold and all." Skeptical at first of stories of Whitefield's
having preached in the fields to crowds of thirty thousand
and more, Franklin moved backward down Market Street
in Philadelphia from the point at which Whitefield was
holding forth until the preacher's voice began to be in-
distinct, then, characteristically, measured the radius, calculated the area filled with auditors, counting two feet
per person, and computed "that he [Whitefield] might
well be heard by more than thirty thousand." "The multitudes of all sects and denominations that attended his
sermons were enormous," Franklin remembered, "and it
was a matter of speculation to me, who was one of the
number, to observe the extraordinary influence of his
oratory on his hearers, and how they admired and respected him, notwithstanding his common abuse of them,
by assuring them that they were naturally *half beasts and
half devils*. It was wonderful to see the change soon made
in the manners of our inhabitants. From being thought-
less or indifferent about religion, it seemed as if all the
world were growing religious, so that one could not walk
through the town in an evening without hearing psalms
sung in different families of every street." The Reverend
Thomas Prince said of Whitefield's visit to Boston that

the town had "never seen anything like it before, except at the time of the general earthquake." [4]

George Whitefield was born in Gloucester on December 16, 1714, at the Bell Inn, a tavern kept by his parents. Both their families had good connections, and the White-fields came of the solid middle class. But his father died when he was two years old, and at twelve his mother's declining fortunes took him out of school to work at the inn washing mops, cleaning rooms, and drawing beer, and for a long time it must have seemed that his formal education was at an end. As it happened, his mother learned almost by accident that it might be possible for him to go to Oxford and support himself as a servitor, so in 1732 he matriculated at Pembroke College (hard on the heels of Samuel Johnson, who would later judge his work to be on balance a good thing, despite the "famili-arity and noise" of his sermons). There Whitefield fell in with the Methodists, began to live by their demanding rules, and formed a close friendship with John and Charles Wesley, which, however, did not long survive their doc-trinal break over Calvinism and Whitefield's arrogant remonstrances.

Shortly after Easter, 1735, Whitefield had a poignant conversion, which led him to leave behind himself all the habits of what he considered a rascally youth, including what he candidly advertised as his "abominable secret sin." [5] Soon he was regularly visiting the sick, comforting

4. Benjamin Franklin, *The Works of Benjamin Franklin*, ed. by J. Sparks (1844), I, 138, 136, 140.
5. Whitefield, *Journals*, 42.

prisoners, and preaching with all his heart the doctrine of justification by faith alone, which he considered to be "the good old faith of the Church of England." In 1736 at twenty-one, a few weeks before taking his Oxford B.A., he was ordained a deacon in the English church. "The boy parson," he was called by some, but the powers of a man were evident as soon as he began preaching. Even now he was beginning to take an overweening, though quite understandable, pride in his extraordinary popularity. He rarely failed to count the house, and as his triumphs continued he developed a colossal conceit, but a conceit wrapped in such an opaque integument of Christian humility that it was all but invisible, preeminently so to himself. Yet it was a token of great earnestness in one who had taken on so magnificently and so quickly in his calling that he chose to offer himself as a missionary in Georgia.

Early in May 1738, after a stormy crossing, Whitefield, not yet twenty-four, arrived in Georgia, a new colony thinly peopled by some of Oglethorpe's released prisoners and a few other motley bands of colonists, all perched on the edge of wild swamps fringed by Spaniards and Indians. John Wesley, no less, who had been there for some time, had failed in his mission, and had given up preaching to "this careless people." But Whitefield saw something that Wesley had missed, the need of new and more open ways, of an ecumenical approach, of a cordial view of dissenters—an openness of heart and a plainness of manner that may have proved his early days in the pub to have been a better rearing for the American task than Wesley's youth in his parents' severe parsonage. "America," Whitefield concluded after his first brief experience, "in my opinion is an excellent school to learn Christ in," [6] and for himself he was right.

It was part of his discipline to be always at work on a humanitarian project, and even before his conversion he had disciplined himself to stop eating fruit and give the savings to the poor. In Georgia Whitefield's first project was an orphanage. The German pietists at Halle had founded a famous orphanage and the idea was first suggested to him by Charles Wesley, but it perhaps appealed to the demi-orphan that young Whitefield was. At Bethesda, about a dozen roadless miles from Savannah, a place where children could presumably be sheltered from the bad examples of town life, he soon built an orphanage large enough to accommodate about forty. There is something puzzling, even a little comical, about settling on a large orphan house as the first charitable need of a small rural colony, which might have been expected, even if it could do little else for its poor, to care informally and decently for its orphaned young. There were not, in fact, very many helpless orphans in Georgia, and Whitefield was soon up to his neck in difficulties over the imperial arrogance with which he reached out to appropriate a pair of young orphans who were doing perfectly well for themselves outside institutional walls. But orphans could always be supplied: there were Spaniards and Indians lurking in the bush eager to manufacture some, and on his fifth visit to America in 1754 Whitefield finally supplied the orphans himself, by importing twenty-two destitute children from England.

Whitefield's second and most successful trip of 1739–41 began in Philadelphia, then continued slowly southward

6. Ibid., 165.

by land to Savannah where he took time to establish and dedicate his orphanage, back north by sloop to Philadelphia, New York, and New Jersey, again to Savannah, now by ship, and to Charles Town, once more by ship to Newport, thence to Boston and at a leisurely pace through all of eastern New England, New Jersey, Pennsylvania, and to the South a final time before his departure in January 1741. Everywhere he preached, and everywhere there were the crowds, the professions and conversions, the cries and sobbings, the revivification of the religious community that seem to have struck him as more imposing even than his work in England. "God shews me that America must be my place for action," he concluded.[7]

Of course Whitefield met other leading awakeners: first he was singled out at Philadelphia by the embattled Tennent, who needed his help against the conservative Presbyterians, and later he visited Tennent at Neshaminy, where Tennent received him with the utmost cordiality. The Log College, he thought, resembled the "school of the old prophets." He also met Gilbert Tennent, who later professed, after watching Whitefield's labors in New York, "a willingness in my heart to die with you, or to die for you." After his magnificent success in Boston in the autumn of 1740, where he gave his heart to the revivalists and alarmed their opponents, Whitefield journeyed out to Northampton, met Jonathan Edwards, and reinflamed the revival that Edwards had kindled some years before. He preached, of course, to Edwards's congregation, reminded them of their former revivals, and "both minister and people wept much."[8] He was presented to Sarah Pierrepont Edwards, who thought his voice was "perfect music"

7. Tyerman, I, 419.
8. Whitefield, *Journals*, 354, 476.

and whose benign presence set him to praying that he might find such a wife for himself.

If we ask, What did Whitefield preach? we must be prepared to find little that was distinctive in the content, especially the doctrinal content, of his sermons. He was remarkably ecumenical. He worked with the evangelical Presbyterians, he was cordial to Moravians and Baptists, he was accepted by many New England Congregationalists, and yet he never left the Anglican church. "Don't tell me," he would say, "you are a Baptist, an Independent, a Presbyterian, a dissenter, tell me you are a Christian, that is all I want." [9] His basic appeal was to the Bible. His basic strategy was to pose before his listeners on one side a living Christ and on the other a burning hell. He attacked the notion that an orderly decent life without "a saving, experimental knowledge of Jesus Christ" would save a man, and he scourged many of the established clergy on both sides of the Atlantic for suggesting it. Man was justified by faith, and chosen by God. By the time he returned for his second American visit, now ordained to the priesthood in the English church, he professed himself a Calvinist, though Stuart C. Henry, a recent biographer, observes that "he professed Calvinism, lived by an Arminian faith, and preached them both." [1] He was bitterly disappointed when John Wesley published a sermon on "Free Grace" embracing Arminian views, but as he confessed to Wesley: "Alas, I never read anything that Calvin wrote," and he seemed as little troubled by some of the inconsistencies of his own theology as he was by the muddled character of his metaphors. The venerable Harvard tutor Henry Flynt, who thought Whitefield was on balance a

9. Stuart C. Henry, George Whitefield, Wayfaring Witness (1957), 152.
1. Ibid., 106, 113.

force for good, still considered him disorganized in argument and "not much acquainted with books—which makes me wonder at his positive and dogmatical way of expressing himself in some things."[2] Whitefield's learning was indeed thin, and sometimes his understanding was surprisingly limited: he thought the veil of the temple was a "curtain that parted the two places where the Jews and Gentiles worshipped."[3] He inveighed against worldly amusements but warned that eschewing them would not bring grace. He preached that God's election firmly decided men's eternal fate but called on them, as evangelists will, to exert themselves to reach a saving faith.

Throughout his life Whitefield showed little concern for the requirements either of consistent doctrine or of institutions. It was his main concern to produce the orgiastic conversions and the repentant tears that he knew so well how to evoke, then to move on and leave others to cope with the social or institutional consequences. A priest in the Anglican church, assigned to a living at Savannah, he rarely appeared in his parish. Unlike Wesley, he organized nothing aside from his orphanage (which soon after his death became a school and not long after that burned down). He wrote a brilliant and moving condemnation of the treatment of slaves in Georgia and Carolina, but soon discovered that his orphanage could not be managed without slave labor, then drew the same conclusions about the colony of Georgia as a whole, decided that plantations in hot-weather colonies required Negro labor, bought slaves himself, and became instrumental in removing both the prohibition on slavery and the prohibition on rum with which that visionary colony had been launched. The re-

2. Winslow, *Edwards*, 185.
3. Henry, 98.

quirements of ecclesiastical organization did not interest him. He was a free-floating evangelist, the greatest of a long line, and if he worked nowhere in particular and left nothing tangible beyond his strangely conceived and ill-fated orphanage, he could answer that he had worked everywhere in general, and that he had given everything that was in him. He evangelized in Scotland on fourteen preaching tours, made strenuous trips to North America seven times, preached—his admirers have calculated—eighteen thousand sermons, and reached more souls than anyone before him in the history of Christendom. It seemed appropriate that he should have died in America, which he had so shrewdly seen as a theater ideally de-signed for his kind of drama. In September 1770 he gave one of his moving two-hour sermons at Newburyport, paused on the stairway to his bedroom for a last exhorta-tion to some late visitors, and died the next morning, felled by a violent fit of asthma. "My sun has arisen," he had said the previous day, "and by aid from heaven has given light to many. It is now about to set." [4]

6

Gilbert Tennent, the Presbyterian awakener, was the only native preacher of the revivals whom one might dare to compare with his friend Whitefield. The most influential of native American revivalists, and for a brief moment the most terrible scourge of their opponents, he settled in the end upon the middle ground of the Great Awakening: he began with a bang but he ended with a whimper.

4. Quoted by Canon Hay Aitkin, "An Appreciation of George White-field and His Journals," in *Whitefield's Journals*, ed. by William Wale (1905), 11.

The eldest of the four sons of William Tennent, Gilbert was tutored by his father to a considerable level of competence in humanities and the ancient languages, and in 1725, when he was licensed by the Presbytery of Philadelphia, his learning was recognized by Yale with an honorary M.A. Tennent began his ministry in New Castle, Delaware, then moved to New Brunswick, New Jersey, where he was much taken by the effectiveness of Frelinghuysen's ministry and by the godliness of Frelinghuysen's congregation—both of which he contrasted with the dispiriting results of his own early efforts. But in time Tennent himself, heartened by Frelinghuysen's success, seems to have taken fire, and by 1729—five years before Edwards's conversions in Northampton and eleven years before Whitefield turned America upside down—he was beginning to effect a revival among congregations scattered between New Brunswick and Staten Island. Tennent was disturbed by what he called the "presumptuous security" of his parishioners, who imagined that because they were orthodox in belief, faithful in their church life, and uprightly moral, they therefore had a saving faith. Tennent took it upon himself to force them to examine their hearts, to realize that they were not truly Christian, and to drive them out of every soothing refuge. Once they had experienced the anguish of realizing that they were *not* Christians, the joy of becoming Christians might be opened to them. His was stern preaching that often brought men and women to tears, groans, and even to hysterics, but it was effective.

The Tennent men were under heavy fire from their enemies when George Whitefield arrived at Philadelphia in the fall of 1739 and William Tennent sought him out, no doubt with the thought of reinforcing the revival that

had been begun by the Log College men. At this time
Whitefield probably got some hints as to the mode of
address most suitable to his American audiences from
Gilbert Tennent, more than ten years his senior. After his
stunning successes in England, Whitefield needed lessons
in preaching from no one, but listening to Tennent at
work in the meetinghouse in Elizabethtown, he was impressed. Never before, he wrote, had he heard such a
"searching sermon." "He has learned experimentally to
dissect the heart of natural man. Hypocrites must either
soon be converted or enraged at his preaching. He is a
son of thunder and does not fear the faces of men." [5] It is
likely too that the Calvinism Whitefield soon began to
embrace was strengthened in him by his conversations
with the Tennents. At any rate, he prevailed upon Gilbert
Tennent to follow him in making an evangelizing tour of
New England, and Tennent too labored there with remarkable results from mid-December 1740 to the following March.

Intelligent, passionate, yet rather coarse, Tennent appears as a prototype of a kind of man later more familiar
in American business and politics than in the ministry, a
scorner of polish and gentility, a rebel who would bluntly
come straight to the point. In terms familiar to modern
criticism of American letters, he was a redskin in full cry
against the palefaces, and there must have been genteel
reformers who had hoped for a revival but would rather
not have had it if ministers such as he were its necessary
agents. An activist and a leader by temperament, he was
also vulnerable to depressing convictions of failure, which
at the beginning and again at the end had a vital effect on

5. Whitefield, *Journals*, 347–8.

his decisions. Contemporaries differed on the manner of his preaching. Some stigmatized him as a shouter, a thumper, and a pounder who terrified his audiences into convulsionary manifestations. Timothy Cutler, a prejudiced Episcopal witness, called him "a monster! impudent and noisy," who dinned into his hearers "that they were *damned! damned! damned!* This charmed them; and in the most dreadful winter I ever saw, people wallowed in snow, night and day, for the benefit of his beastly brayings; and many ended their days under these fatigues. . . ." At any rate, for all the hardships of the New England winter, which he confessed troubled him, Tennent reported at the end "surprizing and manifold successes." [6]

Tennent returned, no doubt somewhat puffed up by his successes, to an extremely roiled and controversial situation in the Presbyterian church. The battle between the revivalists and their foes had now come to a head, and there was a sharp dispute between them over the ministry of a vacant church in Nottingham, New Jersey. There Tennent delivered a sermon that posed the issue all too sharply and soon led to an open schism in the Presbyterian church. This celebrated discourse, "The Dangers of an Unconverted Ministry," which when reprinted in Boston caused as much of a sensation in New England as it did in the Philadelphia Synod, was cited again and again for its lack of charity and tact, but its substance was even more important than its manner. For in it Tennent, with unmistakable clarity, raised the charge, so common among enthusiasts in all ages, that one cannot be led to grace through the agency of an unconverted minister, and, still more important, he asked what the practical implications

6. Edwin S. Gaustad, *The Great Awakening in New England* (1957), 33–4.

were for parishioners who concluded that their ministers were dull and presumably unregenerate. Tennent was criticizing something more than the style of the opposing ministers: he was not simply saying that they preached dull sermons, but that they preached dull sermons because they were unregenerate. At least, said Tennent, "we only assert this, that success by unconverted ministers preaching is very improbable, and very seldom happens, so far as we can gather." [7]

The religious world echoed with shock over Tennent's characterizations of the "ungodly ministers" whom he likened to the Pharisees of old. They were caterpillars who labored to devour every green thing, bigots about human inventions in religious matters, plastered hypocrites, "fooling builders" who strengthened men's carnal security with their soft discourses, dead dogs that can't bark, stone-blind and stone-dead hireling murderous hypocrites, blind leaders of the blind, dead drones—an arresting catalog of invective against his Christian brethren. And Tennent's reasoning went as far as his rhetoric: by mistake men might put into the ministry preachers who were not truly converted, not sent by God. Scripture, reason, and experience all argued that men of this kind, so careless of their own souls, would be ill equipped to care for the souls of others: a man who had not learned the art himself would hardly be able to teach others to swim. Those who were ministered to by such men were to be pitied—what was more, they were to be helped. It would do some good to stock the church with a faithful ministry by encouraging private seminaries (like the Log College) to make up for

7. Leonard J. Trinterud, *The Forming of an American Tradition, A Re-examination of Colonial Presbyterianism* (1949), 91.

the corrupted state of the public academies. But more important: if the ministry were indeed as bad as Tennent and others had found it, it would be lawful for parishioners to "go from them to hear godly persons"—and indeed as natural to do so "as for birds to fly to warmer climates to shun the winter cold." It was utterly sinful "to bind men to a particular minister, against their judgment and inclinations, when they are more edified elsewhere." Indeed, it was a violation of Christian liberty and—this was most provocative—it would be "a yoke worse than that of *Rome* itself." Hence, Tennent took it upon himself to advise "those who live under the ministry of dead men, whether they have got the form of religion or not to repair to the living, where they may be edified." [8] Here with a vengeance was the extreme of Protestantism: laymen, perhaps with the guidance of the rebel clergy, might judge of the converted or unconverted state of their ministers, and if they found them lacking should feel themselves privileged, in fact should feel themselves obliged on peril of their souls, to seek a better ministry elsewhere. The door was now wide open to itinerancy, to uninvited preaching, and to separation from recognized religious bodies. What use, then, Tennent's critics might ask, are presbyteries, consociations, synods, ordination, and church laws? The issue had been put in such strong terms that even Tennent, who was by no means the ecclesiastical anarchist his sermon may have suggested, soon found it necessary to recede from some of its implications.

The depth of the struggle in the Presbyterian church

8. Gilbert Tennent, "One Danger of an Unconverted Ministry," in Heimert and Miller, 72–99.

began to be painfully clear in June 1741, when the Tennent party was read out of the Synod of Philadelphia and
what had been one church now became two, the Old Side
and the New Side (Tennent) Presbyterians. But everywhere Tennent himself could see a rising impatience
among laymen with due form and order in the churches,
and a tendency toward subjectivism and factionalism.
There were also new converts to be considered, drawn to
the church by the revivals but largely unfamiliar with
Presbyterian ways, and it seemed improbable that their
loyalty could be kept by an organization rent by internal
bickering. Already some were beginning to drift off to the
Baptists. Finally, two menacing developments put Tennent
through a period of dejection and reconsideration: the
challenge of the Moravians, and the news of the wild
doings of James Davenport, a Congregationalist but a
friend of the Presbyterian revivalists, during his Connecticut tour of the summer of 1742. The Moravian leader,
Count Nikolaus Ludwig von Zinzendorf, arrived for a
year of intensive preaching in November 1741, and during
his extensive itinerations in Pennsylvania and New Jersey,
Gilbert Tennent had a talk with him and became alarmed
at the Moravians' tendency toward antinomianism and
separatism and at their universalist notions of salvation.
Some Old Side leaders were already arguing that the
Moravians were only realizing some of the logical implications of the New Side doctrines.

Tennent now went into headlong retreat. Taking up his
pen against the Moravians, he shrank from the unre-
strained individualism that had been touched off by the
revivalists, pronounced it a shame that while Moravians
and other Pietists and enthusiasts were beginning to unite,
ministers of sound religion should still be "divided and

quarreling," [9] and now made it clear that he thought it a bad thing to level charges of unregeneracy against upright ministers. The chastened Tennent also wrote to an influential friend in the Presbyterian ministry that he too had mismanaged things and had shown an "excessive heat of temper." [1] He also took care to repudiate in detail the extreme views of James Davenport and to say how much they had vexed him.

For Tennent, as for many others, the active phase of the awakenings was now over. Feeling that his usefulness in New Brunswick had come to an end, he took up a pastorate in Philadelphia in 1743, using (over the protests of the Moravians) the tabernacle that had been built there not long before for Whitefield's followers. The next year he preached a sermon significantly entitled "The Necessity of Studying to be Quiet and Doing our own Business," and he withdrew from polemics and controversies. As time went on, his dress and pulpit manner became more restrained, his style more reserved and literary. He played a leading part in trying to reconcile the Presbyterian factions, although the Old Side men long resisted. In 1749, in a notably conciliatory sermon, he broached once again the possibility of Presbyterian union. It was "cruel and censorious," he now thought, to condemn the spiritual state "of those we know not," and he warned feelingly against "*back-biting, slandering, wrath, malignity*." [2] In his passionate ministry he had strayed a long way, and had come to the brink of a precipice. Gazing into the abyss, what he had seen, in effect, was the alarming image of James Davenport.

9. Tanis, 85.
1. Trinterud, 115.
2. Gilbert Tennent, "Irenicum Ecclesiasticum," in Heimert and Miller, 367–75.

7

James Davenport was God's gift to the conservatives. In his antics all the dangers in the revivals became so evident that other revivalists were gravely disturbed. Davenport came to the ministry under the best of auspices, being the son of a pious pastor in Stamford, the great-grandson of the venerated founder of New Haven, and the youngest graduate of the Yale College class of 1732. In 1738, at twenty-two, he took a pastorate at Southold on Long Island. Suddenly taken by revivals in a neighboring parish and inspired by news of Whitefield's successes, Davenport began his berserk career as a witness: he summoned his flock, harangued them unceasingly for twenty-four hours, and then collapsed. He fired himself up by traveling briefly with Whitefield from New York to Philadelphia on his 1740 tour, and by the summer of the next year he had completely taken flight as an evangelist and was making quite a stir in Connecticut. He launched himself upon New London in July, where he left a good portion of his listeners in hysteria and went off singing through the streets. He visited various other churches in the vicinity, preaching in the fields when meetinghouses were not opened to him, denouncing local ministers as unconverted whenever the spirit moved him to do so, and invading their studies on occasion to question them about their spiritual condition. Finally in Stratford he ran afoul of the new Connecticut law of 1742 passed to curb itinerant preaching, was hauled into court ("Strike them, Lord, strike them!" he called out when the sheriff laid hands on him to stop a harangue at the courtroom door), and although he got no providential help, he almost succeeded

in inciting a mob to riot against the magistrates. Forty
militiamen were called up to prevent disorder.[3]

The Assembly, which conducted Davenport's trial,
showed great common sense: it found that he was "under
the influence of enthusiastical impressions and impulses,
and thereby disturbed in the rational faculties of his mind,
and therefore to be pitied and compassionated, and not to
be treated as otherwise he might be," [4] and ordered him deported to his own congregation forthwith. Between a file of
musketeers large enough to overwhelm his supporters, he
was marched to a vessel and put on board. Perhaps some
members of the Assembly were encouraged to arrive at their
decision by some of Davenport's classmates who remembered he had had a breakdown in college. Beset by obscure
physical ailments (among other things, it was sometimes
hard for him to walk without assistance) that aggravated his
mental state, Davenport was, at the very least, what we
would now call a neurotic, and the Connecticut Assembly
had humanely chosen to deal with him as a clinical case.
It was only a matter of weeks, however, before Davenport
was in Boston and once again under censure by the
ministers for attacking one of their colleagues, acting on
random impulses, singing in the streets, and holding public
meetings. With church doors closed to him, he took to the
open fields—after all, Whitefield had set a venerated
example here—and on occasion recruited crowds that
would follow him through the streets, Davenport rending
his garments, his followers singing at the top of their
voices. Boston was at last outraged. "Were you to see him
in his most violent agitations," said one observer, "you

3. On Davenport, C. C. Goen, *Revivalism and Separatism in New
England, 1740–1800* (1962), 20–7.
4. Ibid., 23.

would be apt to think that he was a madman just broke
from his chains." His followers, charging down the street
and singing and howling at his heels, said the Boston
Evening Post, looked "more like a company of bacchanal-
ians after a mad frolic than sober Christians who had been
worshipping God." [5] Davenport was arrested, found once
again "*non compos mentis*, and therefore . . . *not guilty*,"
and once again deported.

At a last debauch in New London in March 1743,
Davenport's physical ailments and psychic aberrations
were at their pitch, and he induced his followers to burn
their wigs, jewelry, and fine clothes and religious books
by allegedly unsound writers. It made a macabre and
melancholy scene as Davenport's zealots marched around
the bonfire intoning curses on the authors of the works
they were throwing into the flames. Davenport, however,
was finished. As he exhausted his body, he seems somehow
to have discharged his spiritual rage. After returning
home, where a council of ministers had removed him for
neglecting his parish responsibilities, he began to seek
advice from ministers he trusted as to how to put himself
right, and in 1744 he published a confessional pamphlet
in which he allowed that his ventures, particularly the
last gaudy New London episode, had been carried out
"under the powerful influence of the false Spirit." He
joined the New Side Presbyterians, and closed his career
as a quietly settled preacher in New Jersey. In his brief
moment of public ecstasy he had made of himself a
caricature, a kind of walking cartoon illustrating the evils
of enthusiasm as they were portrayed by the anti-revival-

5. John C. Miller, "Religion, Finance, and Democracy in Massachusetts," *New England Quarterly*, 6 (1933), 34–5.

ists, and even, on occasion, feared by many revivalists themselves.

8

The awakenings moved southward from New England and the Middle Colonies, and long after the revivals had passed their peak in New England they were still shaking Virginia and North Carolina; South Carolina alone seems to have felt no lasting effects. In New England and the Middle Colonies the revivals had flourished among dissatisfied members of existing churches. In the South they redeemed larger numbers of people who had no churches at all. And there the revivalists had to come to terms with the Anglican establishment.

In Virginia the first important signs of popular interest came when Whitefield passed through in 1739. The first notable changes occurred in 1742–3 when the Reverend William Robinson, a Log College "graduate," was sent out by the New Side New Brunswick Presbytery to visit Presbyterian settlements in western Virginia and North Carolina. Robinson's successes were striking and others came, including the younger William Tennent, Jr., Samuel Blair, and, once again, Whitefield on his trip of 1745.

But the large figure in the Virginia revivals, whose work led to the building of a strong Presbyterian church in eastern and central Virginia, was Samuel Davies, a Pennsylvanian.[6] Academically and intellectually Davies was a grandchild of the Log College. Born in 1723, he had been educated in a school at Fagg's Manor (New Londonderry),

6. On Davies and his work, see W. M. Gewehr, *The Great Awakening in Virginia, 1740–1790* (1930).

Pennsylvania, run by Samuel Blair, one of William Tennent's most promising pupils. In 1747 young Davies was ordained as an evangelist by the New Side Presbytery of New Castle, and despite precarious health began work in Maryland and Virginia, finally settling in Virginia in 1748. At this time there was neither a single organized Presbyterian church in the older parts of Virginia nor another Presbyterian pastor within two hundred miles of Davies's church in Hanover County. But the ground had been prepared for him: the Anglican church was ineffective there and many of its members demoralized; there were large numbers of Scotch-Irish immigrants and unchurched people to work with. In 1751, he reported that "religion has been, and in most parts of the colony, still is, in a very low state. A surprising negligence appears in attending on public worship; and an equally surprising levity and unconcernedness in those that attend. Family religion is a rarity, and a solemn solicitude about eternal things is still a greater." [7]

As evidence of the pathetic yearning for religion, Davies cited a group in his congregation who some years before had been brought to religious consciousness by Whitefield and others, and yet who were so lacking in religious instruction that when called up by the court to account for their absence from the worship of the established church and asked to declare to what denomination they belonged, they found that they had no ready way of identifying themselves. Then, remembering at length that Luther was "a noted reformer" and that they had reckoned his doctrines agreeable, they decided to declare themselves

7. Heimert and Miller, 377.

Lutherans, and so remained until William Robinson came along to gather them into the Presbyterian fold.

Like some of his predecessors, Davies and his contemporary New Side evangelists were harassed by members of the Anglican establishment, but after a long, hard struggle for toleration their freedom to preach and proselytize was upheld by the authorities in England, and Davies went on from one organizing triumph to another. The people, it seems, were ripe for evangelism and responded eagerly when they were exposed to it. A man of considerable eloquence (he appears to have been the model for the oratorical style of young Patrick Henry, who in his teens often listened to his preaching), Davies established Presbyterianism so firmly in eastern and central Virginia that by the late 1750's he had probably become the most celebrated of American Presbyterians. During the Seven Years' War he turned his oratory to the imperial cause and urged Virginians on against the French as he had formerly urged them on to reject sin. After Braddock's defeat, he called upon his followers "in the name of Jesus, the Captain of your salvation, . . . to enlist in the spiritual warfare." A man who would shrink from his duty now would expose himself "to the heavy curse of God both in this and the eternal world." [8]

Not long after the death of Jonathan Edwards, Davies received a call to the presidency of the College of New Jersey, but presidents of Princeton were running in poor luck, and he was there less than two years before he died early in 1761. The revivals, however, went on, echoing outward into western Virginia among the rapidly growing

8. Trinterud, 134.

Scotch-Irish settlements, and southward into North Carolina. The later phases of the Southern revivals, which brought into action first the Baptists in the 1760's and then Methodist reformers in the 1770's and after, are closely linked to the development of religious liberty and then to the politics of the Federalist era.

CHAPTER VIII

The
Awakening and
the Churches

1

THE flames fanned by Whitefield, the Tennents, Edwards, and their numerous cohorts spread very wide, burned very intensely, came to a sudden peak in the early 1740's, and then almost as suddenly died away. Whitefield must have felt the differences between his triumphal trip to the Northern Colonies and his return to New England in 1744–5, when some pulpits that had been cordially opened to him were now firmly closed, and some old friends candidly warned him that he was now widely discounted as a troublemaker and a fomenter of separation.[1] In the intervening time a great deal of ink had been spilled, a great many angry words uttered, and the Great Awakening in New England and the Middle Colonies had cooled. James Davenport had repented, Gilbert Tennent had recanted, and ministers in the Presbyterian and Congregational churches were giving sober thought to the consequences of their divisions and separations. The Great Awakening was exciting, and it brought many new faces

1. George Whitefield, *Journals* (edn. 1960), 528 ff.

into the churches, but it was also divisive, and for a brief moment it appeared that piety might become a menace to order.

There are several ways in which one may look at the revivals. One may consider them important primarily for the intellectual and doctrinal disputes they aroused, or for their effects upon the churches and the communities, or for the means they offered of extending and deepening human faith. But one can hardly fail to see in them what happens when a hitherto unified elite such as the Congregational ministry cracks and splits, falls into disharmony, and then finds that its authority is threatened by its loss of unity. Here one must look both at the effects upon the elite itself, and at the way in which the disruption of the elite affected the people who lived under its authority. Up to the time of the revivals—and, it must be said, afterward as well—the ministers of the two leading Calvinist-derived churches had enormous intellectual, moral, and political prestige. Their authority rested upon the presence among the people of a unified faith and among the ministry of a unified theology and supposedly settled practices of church organization. Among these practices were the solid education of the clergy and their regular ordination; firm covenants between clergy and congregations defining their relationships; the ability of the clergy (whether under the presbyteries and synods of the Presbyterian church or the consociations and more informal meetings of the Congregational ministers) to agree upon matters of church policy; certain habits of mutual deference and accord among the clergy. It was a system in which the minister of each congregation held a virtual monopoly of attention and authority within his own congregation insofar as he was to be its pastor (a few of the larger churches had two) and in which his people would be exposed to other ministers only upon his invitation and with his consent.

Before the Awakening, then, the clergy stood strong, as members of a profession which recognized standards and had a spirit of solidarity. Laymen, though active and quite capable of expressing themselves about the governance of the churches, were basically deferential, respectful of the minister's role as such. And even where they were critical of the failings of a particular minister, they would rarely attack any significant portion of the ministry as a whole. In the Great Awakening some ministers and laymen began to be uneasy about the way in which many ministers were performing, hence doubtful about the efficacy of the churches in bringing people to grace. One group of ministers, which soon constituted a new dissenting branch of the elite, struck out against existing ways not so much because of doctrinal differences as religious style and the lack of energy with which they felt religion was conducted. In the pursuit of reform, they split many of the churches. Of course they won new converts and stirred up a new spirit among many old adherents. But at the same time, by dividing the ministry they gave the laymen more choice and initiative in religious matters than laymen were accustomed to have, and more than most clerics thought it good for them to have. Laymen were now faced with deciding which faction to join, and, in those towns where separations actually took place, deciding which of two churches to worship at. Religious consciousness was intensified—this was the first and primary aim of the Great Awakening—but also the sense of the religious self was quickened, and, following that, the sense of possibility for individual choice in civic action. The Great Awakening shook people as well as churches. It drove deeper into the grain of American life the principle of lay choice and lay decision and in this sense it was a quintessential expression of Protestantism.

Some of the issues in the awakenings were, of course, doctrinal: both sides might subscribe to the covenant theology, but each was emphasizing different views of the way to grace. Repeatedly the revivalists emphasized justification by faith and the experience of conversion, discounting the efficacy of good works and an upright life. Repeatedly the conservatives charged them with enthusiasm and antinomianism. But beyond the doctrinal issues were issues of practice that threatened the life of the churches and the harmony of the communities: itinerancy and uninvited preaching; censorious accusations against the spiritual state of the regular clergy; the use of lay exhorters to supplement the work of regular ministers; and the tendency of the churches to divide, of congregations to separate and go their different ways in an atmosphere of charge and countercharge, anger and resentment.

Up to now, ministers had spoken from pulpits other than their own only upon invitation from the resident minister, and on condition that their own parishioners were properly taken care of during their absence. Now the itinerants, sometimes neglecting their own flocks and without invitation, were invading the precincts of other preachers near and far. The fresh competition from spellbinding sermonizers was a thing deeply resented, perhaps especially by pastors whose fare had grown dull and uninteresting. "The old divinity, which has stood the test above seventeen hundred years," complained one New Hampshire minister, "is become stale and unsavory to many wanton palates; and nothing will please them but new preachers, new doctrines, new methods of speech, tone, and gesture." "Pedlars in divinity," [2] one contemporary called these itinerants. Settled ministers of Old Light persuasion were often disposed to see the itinerants as wandering minstrels, superficial religious entertainers, strong on noise and spectacular effects, weak on learning and sound understanding of the gospel, appealing most to the least intellectually stable of their parishioners. Often an obnoxious pressure was brought to bear upon the incumbent minister: when an itinerant came to town, if the minister did not "request" him to speak, he might preach without the incumbent's consent, and might touch off a serious breach in the congregation.

The itinerants, moreover, came not with peace but a sword. They were agitators who lived on differences and on stirring up animosities. Most galling of all to the settled ministry was the itinerants' habit of calling ministers who stayed aloof from the revivals unconverted, carnal spirits, warning that those who endured the ministry of such men would be deprived of grace. Whitefield had spoken all too freely of the demands of many of the ministers ("How can dead men beget living children?" he had asked), and Tennent had compiled a scandalous summa of their alleged failings in his sermons on "The Dangers of an Unconverted Ministry." Some awakeners, notably James Davenport, went beyond Whitefield and Tennent in that they did not confine themselves to speaking of the problem in general terms but named individual ministers who they were sure were unregenerate. It was precisely this lack of charity, this arrogation of assurance, that persuaded some wavering ministers that a work of revival with such consequences could not be a good work.

2. Edwin S. Gaustad, *The Great Awakening in New England* (1957), 71–2.

2

In retrospect it is clear that the Great Awakening fell considerably short of revolutionizing the churches; its innovative force was contained, even though not altogether resisted. But at its peak it seemed like a brush fire; where it would stop no one could predict. It cut across the line between town and country, between the seaboard cities and the frontier. Perhaps most important, it cut across class lines. As a movement restricted to the poor and powerless, it might have been more limited. But however strong its appeal to people of lower station, it took much of its driving force from its ability to reach the solid middle classes of the villages and even some of the well-to-do in the seaboard towns. A Connecticut Anglican clergyman, Ebenezer Pemberton, observed that the conversions shook men "of all orders and degrees, or all ages and characters," and Jonathan Edwards was pleased to find, even in Northampton, that among those who humbled themselves before the Lord were "some that are wealthy, and of a fashionable, gay education; some great beaus and fine ladies." In Boston the senior pastor, Benjamin Colman, saw many converts "among the rich and polite of our sons and daughters." Repeatedly the solid citizens of the interior towns, heads of old reputable families and holders of substantial lands and honorable offices, put their signatures to the pleas and manifestos of the Separates, or, like the once famous Elisha Paine of Canterbury, Connecticut, launched upon careers of itinerancy and controversy.[3]

3. For Edwards, and other evidences, see Richard L. Bushman, *From Puritan to Yankee* (1967), 185; for Colman, Gaustad, 52; *cf.* C. C. Goen, *Revivalism and Separatism in New England, 1740–1800* (1962), 188–91; William G. McLoughlin, *Isaac Backus and the American Pietistic Tradition* (1967), 22.

For a time the Awakening threatened—or promised, depending upon one's point of view—to become a mass movement. "Multitudes," the Reverend Ezra Stiles remembered almost twenty years later, "were seriously, soberly, and solemnly out of their wits." [4] The leading awakeners quickly became celebrities, objects of caricature and imitation: a Bostonian advertised in 1742 for the return of a runaway slave who was distinguished by his ability "to mimic some of the strangers that have of late been preaching among us." [5]

Village pietists and amateur theologians had a field day. Dr. Andrew Hamilton of Maryland, on his celebrated trip through the Northern and Middle Colonies in 1744, was distracted at Wrentham, Massachusetts, by a landlady whose prayers he could hear through the thin walls of her house for an hour after going to bed: "She abounded with tautologies and groaned very much in spirit, praying again and again for the *fullness of grace* and the blessing of regeneration and new birth." At Saybrook, Connecticut, delayed by a storm that held up his ferry, Hamilton dined with a local worthy who had disapproved of Whitefield's conduct there; but "after dinner there came in a rabble of clowns, who fell to disputing upon points of divinity as learnedly as if they had been professed theologues. 'Tis strange to see how this humour prevails, even among the lower class of the people here. They will talk so pointedly about justification, sanctification, adoption, regeneration, repentance, free grace, reprobation, original sin, and a thousand other such pretty chimerical knickknacks, as if they had done nothing but study divinity all their lifetime, and perused all the lumber of the scholastic divines,

4. Gaustad, 103.
5. Ibid., 128.

and yet the fellows look as much, or rather more like clowns, than the very riffraff of our Maryland planters." [6]

Enthusiasm without discipline: this became the besetting fear of the conservatives, particularly after some revivalists began to commission lay exhorters. This new kind of creature, the exhorter, wrote one hostile New England pamphleteer, "is of both sexes, but generally of the male, and young. Its distinguished qualities are ignorance, impudence, zeal. Numbers of these exhorters are amongst the people here. They go from town to town, creep into houses, lead captive silly women, and then the men. Such of them as have good voices do great execution; they move their hearers, make them cry, faint, swoon, fall into convulsions." [7]

Could such cadres of the revivalist vanguard be controlled? At times it seemed doubtful when raw village enthusiasts, whose zeal was as great as their education was slight, grew bored with their own towns and took off on unsupervised forays, developing their own techniques of invasion and disruption, and stimulating local malcontents or enthusiasts to follow their lead. Without invitation or warning one might descend upon a meetinghouse while service was being held, take up a post at a corner, and begin to harangue the congregation. If the minister intervened, the exhorter might denounce him as unregenerate, and often he would find sympathizers in the audience to support him. At one meeting in Ipswich a man rose and cried out "Come to Christ" incessantly for a half hour while an old woman denounced lawyers from the rear of the congregation and a third devotee preached ardently from the balcony.[8]

---

6. Andrew Hamilton, *Itinerarium*, ed. by A. B. Hart (1903), 181, 200.
7. Gaustad, 72.
8. Ola E. Winslow, *Jonathan Edwards* (1940), 196–7; *cf.* Goen, 200–2.

The standard apology for the exhorters was that they really did no preaching and performed no other ministerial functions. But the difference between their exhorting and the preaching of ministers, barring certain features perhaps of noise and ignorance, was hard for anyone to see. And the practice of setting up cadres of non-ministers who might ultimately compete with the ministry was too dangerous to be endured very long. In the end the fear generated by the exhorters boomeranged and reawakened many of the revivalists themselves to a sense of their professionalism and their desire for order. Edwards never approved of itinerants, Tennent became convinced by early 1742 that sending out laymen to preach and exhort, even if they were indeed real converts, would be "of dreadful consequence to the churches' peace and soundness in principle . . . introduc[ing] the grossest errors and the greatest anarchy and confusion."[9] Using lay exhorters was one of the sins to which James Davenport confessed after he came to his senses, and Andrew Croswell of Groton, one of the most belligerent of the revivalist itinerants, who admitted having been the first in New England to commission exhorters, concluded sadly that "the tendency of their ways is to drive learning from the world, and to sow it thick with the dreadful errors of Anabaptism, Quakerism and Antinominianism."[1]

3

Under the pressure of religious excitements, the revivals became divisive in several ways: in some communities they widened the breach between laymen and ministers; in many they split the laymen themselves into two fac-

9. Gaustad, 72.
1. Ibid., 73.

tions, splits which often became permanent when the disaffected brethren became Separates or drifted off to the Baptists. And finally, in the Presbyterian fold, with its tight system of church organization, the schism that followed the expulsion of the Tennent faction bitterly divided the whole sect for seventeen years.

In the spring of 1741 the conservative Presbyterian group apparently came to the meeting of the Synod of Philadelphia with the intention of forcing the Tennent group into submission or schism, and since the Tennents' New England allies were absent, the antirevivalists had the majority. The Tennent faction was charged with heresy and anarchy, intrusion into other congregations, and rash judging of their ministerial colleagues, with false views of the call to the ministry and of the assurance of salvation. They were told to make a full confession of subscription to doctrines adopted by an earlier synod, on pain of losing the right to vote in this and future synods. After some fruitless discussion, the revival group was disowned and rejected, and the Presbyterian church was now broken formally, as it had long been spiritually. Four years later the New Side Synod of New York was formed out of the Presbyteries of New Brunswick and Londonderry, which had been set up by the Tennents, and the Presbytery of New York, which was dominated by New England men. In the uncomfortable period that followed, most of the advantages lay with the revivalists: not only did they have more zeal and discipline, but thanks largely to the efforts of the elder Tennent, a more learned and capable body of men. And although in 1743 they made the aggressive decision to invade Old Side precincts by authorizing Gilbert Tennent to set up a pastorate in Philadelphia and by sending Samuel Finley, another Log Cabin graduate,

to Connecticut (from whence he was soon expelled), in the
long run they proved to be the more conciliatory of the
two factions: it was their overtures that at length brought
about reunion in 1758. In the meantime, the New Side
flourished and the Old Side languished, with the consequence that the reunited church which emerged after
1758 for a long time drew the greater part of its vitality
and spirit from the New Side men.

Strongly committed as it was to a formal structure of
congregations, presbyteries, and synods, the Presbyterian
church came apart in large chunks. In the relatively de-
centralized Congregational regime of New England, the
separations tended to be fought out on the local level,
town by town. Actually, only a minority of the towns were
sharply divided, but in those places where unbridgeable
differences led to permanent separation, the hostilities
touched off tended to cut deep into the texture of community life, leaving permanent scars. Congregationalism
was haunted by a special problem of community organization. The church existed for the town as well as for the
church members, and nonmembers not only attended the
church but were taxed to pay the salary of its minister. In
the town meetings, the town as a whole had something to
say about the person of the minister and his remuneration,
and the double lines of authority opened up possibilities
for a sharp factional division among members and nonmembers—the whole body of townspeople—over either
the minister and his practices or the criteria of church
membership. A permanent break might occur when the
majority of church members were of one conviction and
the majority of townspeople of another.

Discontent with ministerial authority began to be articulate and philosophical. During the 1730's Roger Wolcott,

a leading figure in Connecticut who became governor in
1750, wrote a privately circulated tract against the Saybrook Platform. "Understand us not," he explained in this
document, "that we speak against clergymen as such, but
it is not safe to trust the whole power of order in their
hands." [2] The discipline imposed by the Saybrook Platform
turned out not to be foolproof against dissatisfied congregations. Laymen always had the power of retaliation in
their control over ministerial salaries, an especially telling
form of control when rapid inflation brought frequent
cries for raises, and one which also put pastors under a
constant pressure to please. As the issues were fought out,
the ministers became storm centers for many a troubling
community controversy, since an appeal to the moral
authority of the clergy was constantly being made by one
side or the other. A clash of political ambitions, a personal
or family feud, an economic grievance, became a church
issue the minute it was carried to the meetinghouse door
and hence a possible source of a local schism. Personal
controversies, Thomas Clap declared after he had been a
minister for some years, "usually end in a quarrel and
contention in the church . . . which unavoidably centers
upon the minister at last." "It is very distressing to the
minister," he added, "to have the parties come to him,
expressing a censorious and uncharitable spirit, and exclaiming against one another. . . . I believe there are but
few instances, where people are generally uneasy with
their ministers, but it originally sprung from such jealousy,
or party spirit among themselves." [3]

This leads us to another important aspect of New
England life which made the agitations of the Great

2. Bushman, 154.
3. Ibid., 162.

Awakening there, despite the deep wellsprings of religious emotion it released, especially frightening. New England communities were not prepared to cope effectively with collective dissent. The goal of the New England town was ethnic and religious homogeneity, conformity, and consensus.[4] It had efficient ways of driving out strangers and disciplining and humbling individual deviants within its own fold. But it had not yet worked out any satisfactory processes by which to cope with any factional dissent strong enough to strike a sharp cleavage through the whole town, no machinery of compromise for keeping a town morally and spiritually intact. Conflict of such magnitude could be solved in only one way—by separation. But no one could fail to see that separation was a defeat for all concerned, since it tore into the texture of the unitary Christian community and marked the triumph of pride and animosity over love and charity. Moreover, it pointed the way toward a dangerous political fractionalization of the Puritan world. And in this danger, quite aside from the fears that haunted the clergy, one finds another reason why the revival enthusiasts had to be contained, and why after two years the passion for the new outpouring of the spirit faded so fast: it was not only the authority of the clergy that was threatened but the unity of the New England town itself. Much as New Englanders might feel the need for religious revivification, they were not yet ready to be launched into the unknown world of religious and political pluralism.

And here one must reckon with the formidable quality of the Puritan character under stress or in the heat of con-

4. This point is emphasized, probably overemphasized, for the Massachusetts towns by Michael Zuckerman, *Peaceable Kingdoms* (1970). For somewhat different views see the works by Grant, Bushman, and Lockridge already cited.

troversy. Many New England villagers were not long removed from forefathers who had been among the most
crusty and venturesome of English dissenters. These
"fierce and wrathful people," as one Hartford pastor called
them,[5] were often flinty and suspicious in their dealings
with their neighbors. The boundary line between towns
or between farms, the location of the church, the choice
of the minister, the style of worship, the manner of singing
during service, a business misunderstanding, a well-
remembered insult—any of these might touch off feuds
and wrangles among villagers whose vocabulary was full
of the well-worn phrases of Christian love. Hardy in suffering, they could be cranky in dispute. Rebekah Hawley,
one of the daughters of Solomon Stoddard, was making
cheese when word was brought to her that her husband,
Joseph, driven to despondency by Edwards's preachings,
had cut his throat and died, and it was reported that "she
did not leave the buttery until she had finished turning
the cheeses."[6] A Connecticut layman, cut out of the same
durable cloth, grew angry over what he judged to be the
doctrinal deviations of his minister. At length he took his
ax to the meetinghouse, chopped out the entire pew in
which he and his family had worshipped since the church
was built, and took it home to his attic. The pew became
the symbolic center for other dissenting members, who
soon formed a new church of their own.[7]

Some of the hard qualities of the sectaries who had
fought for Cromwell seem to have come to the surface
again in their descendants during the Great Awakening.

5. Bushman, 160; on village disputes see also Charles Grant, *Democracy in the Connecticut Frontier Town of Kent* (1961), and Ellen D.
Larned, *History of Windham County, Connecticut*, I (1874).
6. Perry Miller, *Jonathan Edwards* (1949), 103.
7. O. E. Winslow, *Meetinghouse Hill* (1952), 237.

But the revival also had its touching moments. The presence of alternate modes of worship in those towns which had been riven by separation put some church members through moments of great anguish; many separated only after a new and second conversion in which the lives and ways of their fellows, close and intimate neighbors, suddenly seemed to them hollow, superficial, and corrupt. Even some years after the greatest excitements had passed, one Hannah Cory of Sturbridge, Massachusetts, asked to explain along with other separators why she broke her covenant and left her brothers and sisters in Christ, testified: "One time as I was coming to the lecture the words came to me in Cor., Come out from amongst them, and then these words in Amos, Can two walk together except they be agreed, so I went to the meeting house, and when I came in there was nobody and as I sat there these words came to me, my house is a house of prayer but ye have made it a den of thieves, then suddenly fear came over me so I got up and went out and walked over to the burying place and I thought I had rather lie down among the graves than go into the meeting house, but when I saw Mr. Rice [the minister] coming I went in but it seemed to be a dark place, ministers deacon and people looked strangely as if they were all going blindfold to destruction, and though my body was there, my soul was with the Separates, praising God as soon as I was dismissed at the meeting house I went to Brother Nevil's where my soul was sweetly refreshed, the Lord alone be praised for it was He alone who brought me out and not any creature. ..." [8]

At great emotional cost and considerable financial

8. Ibid., 232; *cf.* Goen, 101–3.

strain, many small towns were soon supporting two churches instead of one. One modern historian of the New England Awakening has found, apart from a few separations initiated by Old Light believers and over thirty temporary separations which did not lead to permanent new churches, a significant number of long-lasting or permanent cleavages: almost 100 Separate New Light churches organized and 149 Separate or New Light Baptist churches, as well as two score other breaches of organization in the New England colonies and their adjacent offshoots on Long Island and in New York.[9] To such community quarrels and schisms no responsible pastor, revivalist or Old Light, could afford to be indifferent. It was not surprising that formidable opposition to the work of the revival was quick to assert itself, or that many who had originally looked upon the Awakening with favor came to think of it as not being a work of God. Moreover, it soon became clear that, particularly in Connecticut, Congregationalism was beginning to lose adherents in two different directions. Quiet souls, distressed by the inability of the churches to keep a spirit of Christian fellowship, drifted toward Anglicanism, embracing the church, as the Anglican Reverend Samuel Johnson put it, "as their only ark of safety." [1] At the other end of the religious spectrum, many ardent souls influenced by New Light doctrines concluded that belief in a church of true saints logically required adult and not infant baptism, and drifted off to the Baptists, under whose aegis they could also avoid church taxes.[2]

---

9. Goen, 307–27, esp. 327.
1. Bushman, 166, 222–3.
2. Goen, 206–7, 272–95; cf. McLoughlin, *Isaac Backus* . . ., chapters 1 and 2.

4

The colleges could hardly be insulated from the struggle. None of the colonial colleges had been conceived as a theological seminary, each being intended to produce civil leaders as well as future clerics; still, the task of raising pious ministers was regarded as central by churchmen. In any factional struggle within or between the churches, it would be a decisive advantage to control a college and to put one's own stamp upon the young ministers that emerged from it. The pietists also hoped to check the growing tendency of colleges to become centers for the gay young bloods of the colonies, whose antics were sure to make a college atmosphere unsuitable for fledgling ministers. Hence the colleges could not help but be involved in the controversies set off by the Great Awakening.

It has long been one of the clichés of American historical writing that the Great Awakening was a major force in the development of American higher education. Yet its main effects on education were felt very tardily and indirectly. Four colonial colleges, the College of New Jersey (Princeton), the College of Rhode Island (Brown), Queens (Rutgers), and Dartmouth, were indeed founded under the influence and patronage of pietistic groups, but the last three were founded in a distinctly different intellectual environment, a quarter of a century and more after the Great Awakening in New England and the Middle Colonies had passed its peak; and one of them, Queens, was long a negligible institution. Some of the impetus behind the new educational foundations must be charged simply to the growth of population and the difficulties of transportation—the College of New Jersey, when it began instruction in 1747, was the only college between New Haven and Williamsburg. Moreover, by the time the College of Rhode Island (Brown) and Dartmouth were founded in the 1760's, the American colonies had moved into a new and more tolerant era, somewhat softened by rationalism, secularism, and compromise. Some denominations had already begun to learn that sectarian exclusivity would not work. King's College (Columbia) and the College of Philadelphia (University of Pennsylvania) had already been dedicated to general civic purposes and placed under interdenominational control. The College of Rhode Island boldly took a stand for a liberal education useful for the secular purposes of society, welcomed "youth of all religious denominations" to attend, and opened its faculty to "all denominations of Protestants." By the beginning of the Revolutionary era, the American colleges incorporated the spirit of the Enlightenment as well as the spirit of pietism.

The expansion of colonial higher education is attributable as much or more to the growth of the colonies and to their increasing wealth and sophistication as it is to the pietistic urge, with the significant exception of the College of New Jersey, the only college to be founded immediately in the wake of the revivals and as a consequence of the Presbyterian split. In 1746, the year the College of New Jersey won its first charter, William Tennent, who for some years had been too feeble to carry on as heroically as he once had done, died at seventy-three. Although his pupils, Samuel Finley and Samuel Blair, were doing their best to carry on in his tradition, the educational needs of New Side Presbyterianism were becoming acute. The very successes of its ministry in propagating the faith had

created a demand for more ministers. New Side men—
especially those from New England who were almost all
Yale graduates—were increasingly sensitive to the Old
Side charges of irregular and insufficient education, and
were increasingly aware that they needed a proper college
with a corps of instructors, an adequate library, and scientific apparatus. Yale seemed hopeless as a source of
sound evangelical ministers, since its young president,
Thomas Clap, was becoming notorious for his arbitrary
expulsion of undergraduates sympathetic to the revivals.
At length the New England men in the New Side faction,
led by Jonathan Dickinson, who was trusted by both the
New Englanders and the Tennent group, took the initiative in seeking a charter for a college in New Jersey. The
first charter was secured in the face of much resistance
from Anglicans; and later, in 1748, the sympathetic Calvinist governor, Jonathan Belcher, persuaded the sponsors
to take out a second charter which strategically broad-
ened the political base of the trustees by including a significant number of laymen and a broader spectrum of the
ministry. From its beginning even the founders of Princeton moved away from narrow sectarianism: they announced their intention was not merely to educate ministers but to train "men that will be useful in other learned
professions—ornaments of the State as well as the
Church." They also promised to keep their doors open to
undergraduates of "every religious denomination" without prejudice, and to accord them equal liberties and
advantages. For all its pietistic origins, Princeton thus
moved a full step away from the notions of men like
Thomas Clap who wanted to make colleges restrictive
sectarian agencies. However, it was not until the regime
of President John Witherspoon, which began in 1766, that

both major factions in the Presbyterian church were
equally satisfied with the college.

During and after the revivals Harvard and Yale remained centers of Old Light strength, and therefore were
regarded with disapproval by the awakeners. Edwards
looked upon the New England colleges as spoiled divinity
schools, altogether too indulgent to "vice and idleness,"
and condemned them as places where "one cannot send
a child . . . without great danger of his being infected as
to his morals." What troubled him most was that the
presidents and tutors did not often sit and converse individually with their pupils about the state of their souls;
and this indeed was the basic pietist complaint. It was
Whitefield, however, with his gift for impulsive insolence,
who stirred up a real controversy. In 1740 he was received
pleasantly when he spoke at Harvard and Yale. But in his
journals, parts of which he published from time to time,
he made biting remarks about his hosts. Harvard, he said,
was "not far superior to our Universities in piety"—a
severe gibe to those who knew the current state of Oxford
and Cambridge. Discipline was at a low ebb at Harvard,
he complained, and bad books by latitudinarian theologians were preferred to works by evangelical writers. Of
Yale he said: "I hear of no remarkable concern amongst
them regarding religion." And in a final entry he remarked
of both colleges: "I believe it may be said their light is
now become darkness—darkness that may be felt—and
is complained of by the most godly ministers. I pray God
these fountains may be purified and send forth pure
streams to water the city of our God." [3]

When Whitefield returned in 1744 the colleges had had

3. Whitefield, *Journals*, 462, 480; Luke Tyerman, *The Life of the Rev.
George Whitefield* (1876), II, 132.

ample time to smolder over his words. The Harvard faculty, in a tart pamphlet, denounced him for his lack of charity, censoriousness, and slander, and refuted his charges circumstantially, one by one. In a rather hypocritical and quasi-apologetic reply, Whitefield neither defended his charges nor retracted them, and his pretensions were then once more elaborately demolished by Harvard's divinity professor, Edward Wigglesworth. The Yale faculty too issued a brief counterblast which echoed Harvard's, and all three manifestos only added to a shower of hostile pamphlets that greeted the evangelist in New England.[4] In later years, he regretted his charges and made a charitable peace with members of both institutions.

Harvard and Yale, each in its own way, confirmed the fears of the awakeners. Harvard made no effort to exclude undergraduates of New Light persuasion nor to stir up sectarian controversy, but during the quarter century after the Great Awakening, Edward Wigglesworth, a man of rather broad views, raised a generation of ministers with Arminian sympathies who paved the way for the Unitarian conquest of Harvard. Yale was more troubled. Thomas Clap, newly installed as rector in 1740, regarded colleges strictly as schools for the rearing of ministers,[5] and after a disturbing visit by Gilbert Tennent in 1741 firmly closed his mind against the New Lights. Henceforth he was quick to crush all enthusiastic tendencies at Yale, not hesitating at the most arbitrary and provocative expulsions of undergraduates. For many years he was a leading force in the heady church controversies of Con-

4. For the pamphlets, see Richard Hofstadter and Wilson Smith, *American Higher Education; A Documentary History*, I (1961), 62–74, and for the pamphlet wars, Tyerman, II, 120–42.

5. Hofstadter and Smith, I, 111–17; *cf.* Louis Tucker, *Puritan Protagonist* (1962).

necticut, and the effect of his long term of office was to keep Yale at the center of them. Much later, when the factional struggle had considerably changed its character, Clap switched allegiances, but clung rigidly to his determination that Yale should reflect his own theological preferences. All in all, pietism did not succeed, nor indeed except in the case of Clap did it try very hard, to make the new colleges narrow sectarian instruments, nor did the revivalists create colleges that were antipathetic to the new interest in science, the new concern for secular knowledge, or the new receptivity to denominational compromise in education.

5

The Great Awakening did not, as the conservatives feared it would, altogether revolutionize American religion or destroy the professional standards of the clergy in those denominations in which high standards had previously prevailed. It did, however, affect what America was to become by intensifying what it already was: in religion the most Protestant of Protestant cultures, and in morals the most middle-class country of the emergent bourgeois world. It brought back an impulse akin to that of the Reformation, reintroducing vivid emotion—terror and joy —into religious experience, and restoring a vivid sense of the condition of man as suspended between eternal salvation and eternal punishment. It reclaimed many people for religion who had lost contact with the churches, and revitalized the interest of many more who had lagged. It put the evangelical impulse, as opposed to churchly formalities, at the very heart of American religious and intellectual experience. The ecstasy of conversion, the sense

of a personal, felt relationship with God, was to over-
shadow both the formal learning and religious understanding provided by the earlier clergy, and the churches' sac-
ramental aids to salvation. Long afterward Emerson in
his Divinity School Address would put in his own way the
age-old enthusiast's conviction, that the saving word can
come only from the regenerate teacher: "The spirit only
can teach. Not any profane man, nor any sensual, nor any
liar, nor any slave can teach, but only he can give who
has; he only can create, who is. The man on whom the
soul descends, through whom the soul speaks, alone can
teach."

When the essence of religion lies in that which is experienced and felt, the central criterion of personal merit is
to be found in the heart, not the head. Although the
Puritan-derived churches, with their strong traditions of
learning, were not themselves prepared to break sharply
with their past, the Awakening, by unleashing the evangelical strain and strengthening the revival meeting as a
religious technique, was to lay the foundation for that
anti-intellectualism which has been so characteristic of the
American mind. In the short run, the more extreme revivalists may have lost the day; but in the longer run, as
successive revivals refreshed the evangelical strain, ·it
would always be possible for those who were sure of their
religious feelings to discredit those who put their basic
reliance on intellect.

To many people the Awakening, by presenting a choice
between religious styles, church affiliations, and pastors,
heightened the sense that people, as individuals, had the
power to act and decide, that it was their preferences that
counted in the religious world. America had always had
the capacity to call forth the active powers of the common

man. Now there would be a wider popular activism, as people were stirred by religious conflict, and by countless community dramas of schism and separation. Americans, moreover, were given an issue that affected them across the boundaries of the several colonies, a set of causes and controversies that reminded them, especially from the Virginia Presbyterian domain northward through New England, of their common religious culture and common concerns. Finally, by fragmenting the established Puritan-derived religious bodies in New England and the Middle Colonies, the Great Awakening intensified the pluralistic religious structure, the multiple religious allegiances of the populace, and forced them to face the problem of accommodating a variety of persuasions. Here one is impressed by the unforeseen and unintended consequences of human behavior: the Great Awakening began with rebellion and criticism, and quickened into embittered controversies and schisms; it ended by establishing more firmly than ever the plurality of forces that made increased toleration, and finally full religious liberty, the most amenable solution for civic life.

Some historians, finding in the Great Awakening the seeds of the American Revolution, have drawn, so to speak, a straight line from George Whitefield to George Washington. If their case is made to rest too narrowly upon doctrinal continuity, it can easily be overstated. There were several paths to the Revolution: the liberal theologians and the orthodox, the Puritan, the Anglican, and the Baptist, the religious man and the secular man, each found his own. Since social position, economic interest, personal temperament, and the accident of geography also affected men's attitudes toward resistance to England, it is artificial, even in considering New England, to put too much weight on religious affiliations or creeds. But it is true that only a small liberal elite could experience the moral and emotional meaning of the conflict with England in purely secular terms. Many Americans who took part in the Revolution did so *as Christians* for whom it was intellectually necessary that the Revolution appear as an incident in some providential scheme; their moral energies could best be enlisted through the familiar Protestant methods of self-examination, self-accusation, discipline, and purgation.[6]

The Great Awakening enlarged considerably those spiritual qualities that set the Americans off from the dominant classes in the mother country: their ascetic rigor, their middle-class morality, their Puritan sense of duty, their disposition to identify the events of history with the designs of Providence. The American colonies, even those which were officially Anglican, had become a concentrated repository of the Protestant ethic. The Revolution came the more readily because England and America had become quite different societies, the first still the sphere of a worldly aristocracy and a worldly establishment, the second a center of ascetic Protestantism and middle-class morality. As the century went on, Americans increasingly regarded England as abandoned to corrupt morals and as losing its liberties, and came to think of their own soil as the providentially chosen home for the future both of Christian morals and the liberties of Englishmen.

6. Perry Miller, "From the Covenant to the Revival," in J. W. Smith and A. Leland Jamison, eds., *Religion in American Life* (1961), I, 322–68.

INDEX

A NOTE ON THE TYPE

THE TEXT *of this book is set in Caledonia, a Linotype face designed by W. A. Dwiggins, the man responsible for so much that is good in contemporary book design and typography. Caledonia belongs to the family of printing types called "modern face" by printers—a term used to mark the change in style of type-letters that occurred about 1800. Caledonia borders on the general design of Scotch Modern but is more freely drawn than that letter.*

This book was composed, printed, and bound by The Haddon Craftsmen, Inc., Scranton, Pa.

The typography and binding designs are based on originals by
W. A. DWIGGINS